Banks on the Brink

This innovative analysis answers a complex question of tremendous economic and political importance: Why are some countries vulnerable to banking crises, while others are resilient? In *Banks on the Brink*, Copelovitch and Singer focus on the political decisions that shape the structure of financial markets and the international economic forces that make some countries especially vulnerable to financial instability. They highlight the effects of two variables in combination: foreign capital inflows and the relative prominence of securities markets versus commercial banking in the domestic financial system. Foreign capital is the fuel for banks' potentially dangerous behavior, whereas banks are more likely to take on excessive risks when operating in a financial system with large securities markets. The book analyzes data from the 1970s through the early twenty-first century for most of the world's developed economies and provides historical case studies of two key countries – Canada and Germany – which explore how political decisions in the nineteenth and early-twentieth centuries continue to affect their financial stability today. The analyses in this book have crucial policy implications for identifying potential regulations and policies that can work to protect banking systems against future crises.

Mark Copelovitch is a Professor of Political Science and Public Affairs at the University of Wisconsin–Madison. He is the author of *The International Monetary Fund in the Global Economy: Banks, Bonds, and Bailouts.*

David A. Singer is a Professor of Political Science at the Massachusetts Institute of Technology. He is the author of *Regulating Capital: Setting Standards for the International Financial System.*

POLITICAL ECONOMY OF INSTITUTIONS AND DECISIONS

Series Editors
Jeffry Frieden, *Harvard University*
John Patty, *Emory University*
Elizabeth Maggie Penn, *Emory University*

Founding Editors
James E. Alt, *Harvard University*
Douglass C. North, *Washington University of St. Louis*

Other Books in the Series

Alberto Alesina and Howard Rosenthal, *Partisan Politics, Divided Government, and the Economy*
Lee J. Alston, Thrainn Eggertsson, and Douglass C. North, eds., *Empirical Studies in Institutional Change*
Lee J. Alston and Joseph P. Ferrie, *Southern Paternalism and the Rise of the American Welfare State: Economics, Politics, and Institutions, 1865–1965*
James E. Alt and Kenneth Shepsle, eds., *Perspectives on Positive Political Economy*
Josephine T. Andrews, *When Majorities Fail: The Russian Parliament, 1990–1993*
Jeffrey S. Banks and Eric A. Hanushek, eds., *Modern Political Economy: Old Topics, New Directions*
Yoram Barzel, *Economic Analysis of Property Rights (2nd edition)*
Yoram Barzel, *A Theory of the State: Economic Rights, Legal Rights, and the Scope of the State*
Robert Bates, *Beyond the Miracle of the Market: The Political Economy of Agrarian Development in Kenya*
Jenna Bednar, *The Robust Federation: Principles of Design*
Charles M. Cameron, *Veto Bargaining: Presidents and the Politics of Negative Power*
Kelly H. Chang, *Appointing Central Bankers: The Politics of Monetary Policy in the United States and the European Monetary Union*
Tom S. Clark, *The Supreme Court: An Analytical History of Constitutional Decision Making*
Peter Cowhey and Mathew McCubbins, eds., *Structure and Policy in Japan and the United States: An Institutionalist Approach*
Gary W. Cox, *The Efficient Secret: The Cabinet and the Development of Political Parties in Victorian England*
Gary W. Cox, *Making Votes Count: Strategic Coordination in the World's Electoral System*

(*Continued after the Index*)

Banks on the Brink

Global Capital, Securities Markets, and the Political Roots of Financial Crises

MARK COPELOVITCH
University of Wisconsin–Madison

DAVID A. SINGER
Massachusetts Institute of Technology

CAMBRIDGE
UNIVERSITY PRESS

CAMBRIDGE
UNIVERSITY PRESS

University Printing House, Cambridge CB2 8BS, United Kingdom

One Liberty Plaza, 20th Floor, New York, NY 10006, USA

477 Williamstown Road, Port Melbourne, VIC 3207, Australia

314–321, 3rd Floor, Plot 3, Splendor Forum, Jasola District Centre, New Delhi – 110025, India

79 Anson Road, #06-04/06, Singapore 079906

Cambridge University Press is part of the University of Cambridge.

It furthers the University's mission by disseminating knowledge in the pursuit of education, learning, and research at the highest international levels of excellence.

www.cambridge.org
Information on this title: www.cambridge.org/9781108489881
DOI: 10.1017/9781108779630

First published 2020

Printed in the United Kingdom by TJ International Ltd., Padstow, Cornwall

A catalogue record for this publication is available from the British Library.

Library of Congress Cataloging-in-Publication Data
Names: Copelovitch, Mark S., 1975- author. | Singer, David Andrew, author. | Cambridge University Press.
Title: Banks on the brink : global capital, securities markets, and the political roots of financial crises / Mark Copelovitch, University of Wisconsin, Madison, David Singer, Massachusetts Institute of Technology.
Other titles: Political economy of institutions and decisions.
Description: New York : Cambridge University Press, 2019. | Series: Political economy of institutions and decisions | Includes bibliographical references and index.
Identifiers: LCCN 2019044103 | ISBN 9781108489881 (Hardback) | ISBN 9781108747714 (eBook)
Subjects: LCSH: Bank failures--Case studies. | Banks and banking--Case studies. | Financial services--Case studies.
Classification: LCC HG1521 .C66 2019 | DDC 332.1--dc23
LC record available at https://lccn.loc.gov/2019044103

ISBN 978-1-108-48988-1 Hardback

For Beth, Micah, and Dafna;
and for Steve

Contents

Figures

Tables

Preface

Banks on the Brink explains why some countries are more prone to systemic bank failures than others. We focus on the political decisions that shape the structure of financial markets and the international economic forces that make some countries especially vulnerable to financial instability. We highlight the effects of two variables in combination: foreign capital inflows and financial market structure – specifically, the relative prominence of securities markets versus commercial banking in the domestic financial system. Foreign capital is the fuel for banks' potentially dangerous behavior, whereas banks are more likely to take on excessive risks when operating in a financial system with large securities markets.

The study of banking necessarily leads to a focus on politics, but not in the way that many observers might imagine. Bankers themselves have political preferences and may express them publicly, and some banks lobby for favorable public policies and donate to political campaigns and political action committees. But at a deeper level, banks are embedded in financial markets, which themselves reflect an accumulation of government choices. Banks today operate in an environment shaped by these choices, some of which make banks more resilient, others of which make them more prone to crisis.

Our research design combines statistical analysis with comparative historical case studies. We assemble and analyze data from the 1970s through the early twenty-first century for most of the world's developed economies, and we compile detailed historical narratives of two countries – Canada and Germany – to explore how countries embarked, often inadvertently, on divergent financial development paths in the nineteenth and early twentieth centuries. The long-term effects of their early political decisions are still manifest today in the structure of their respective financial systems. Our quantitative empirical analyses include macro-level investigations of the correlates of banking crises across developed countries as well as micro-level studies of banks' risk taking.

The concluding chapter addresses policy responses to bank instability. Perhaps surprisingly, our findings suggest that Glass-Steagall regulations, which separate commercial and investment banking would *not* address the underlying reasons for banks' excessive risk taking. We also argue against capital controls. Instead, we suggest that regulators should focus their efforts on tightening bank capital requirements, especially in financial systems with prominent or growing securities markets. We also discuss the pros and cons of combining bank regulatory agencies, securities regulators, and central banks.

Acknowledgments

This book is the culmination of two decades of bickering between old friends. Our friendship and research collaboration began in graduate school in the early 2000s, with a shared interest in the politics of international money and finance. During our years in the Government Department at Harvard, and in the years that have followed, we spent many hours standing at a chalkboard or sitting at a bar, arguing over the politics of capital mobility, central banks, and the secret to financial stability. For a long time, we made little progress in spite of those spirited brainstorming sessions, but we solidified a lasting friendship that has endured the stresses of academic life and a thousand miles of physical separation. Today, we still bark at each other like an old married couple (our respective spouses are endlessly amused), arguing over the same set of topics, questions, and shared interests. Fortunately, though it has taken many years, our ideas have gelled into this book.

We have many people to thank. Together, we thank Jeff Frieden, whose graduate seminar nearly twenty years ago spurred many of our early research ideas and whose ongoing guidance and support has meant a great deal to both of us throughout our careers. Without Jeff's mentorship, both of us would surely have taken very different paths, and this book almost certainly would not exist. We are deeply in his debt.

We also thank a number of colleagues who have influenced our thinking and supported us personally and professionally, including Gabriel Aguilera, Axel Dreher, Julia Gray, Alexandra Guisinger, Mark Hallerberg, Soo Yeon Kim, Mareike Kleine, David Leblang, Lisa Martin, Layna Mosley, Tom Pepinsky, Stephanie Rickard, Stefanie Walter, and Rachel Wellhausen. For comments and suggestions specific to this book project, we also thank Puspa Amri, Jeff Chwieroth, Christopher Gandrud, Lucy Goodhart, Shane Martin, Mark Manger, Allie Myren, Guillermo Rosas, Peter Rosendorff, David Rueda, Thomas Sattler, David Stasavage, and Paul Tucker. We thank audiences at the Free University of Berlin, the London School of Economics, the Munk School of Global Affairs at the University of Toronto, the Norwegian Institute in Rome, Stanford University, University of Zurich, Washington University in St. Louis, and Yale University.

For excellent research assistance, we thank our students at MIT and Wisconsin, including Michael Freedman, Nicholas Intscher, Michael Pearson, Jason Poulos, Briitta van Staalduinen, Alyse Samoray, William Wallo, Andreas Wiedemann, and Soong Kit Wong. Their many hours of digging into historical sources, new research, media reports, and financial data were essential to completing the book, and we are very grateful for their help. We are also grateful to our undergraduate and graduate students at MIT and UW–Madison, whose curiosity, engagement, and tough questions have pushed us to sharpen our own thinking about international political economy in general – and financial crises in particular – over the years.

Copelovitch thanks his current and former colleagues at Wisconsin in political science and the La Follette School of Public Affairs, especially John Ahlquist, Rikhil Bhavnani, Menzie Chinn, John Coleman, Helen Kinsella, Lisa Martin, Greg Nemet, Jon Pevehouse, Nadav Shelef, Jessica Weeks, Susan Yackee, and John Zumbrunnen. I am particularly grateful to Nils Ringe, Elizabeth Covington, and the European Studies centers at UW–Madison, as well as the Graduate School, the La Follette School, and the Vilas Associates Trust, for generously supporting my research during the writing of this book. I also thank the Hertie School of Governance in Berlin for hosting me for as a visiting scholar in 2013–14. Hertie was an intellectually rich and exciting place to spend the year, and much of the research for this book project began during my time in Berlin. In particular, I thank Mark Hallerberg for his gracious hospitality and insights into German finance and politics, as well as Henrik Enderlein, Mark Kayser, and Dayna Sadow for their help, feedback, and collegiality during my stay. I also thank Michael Kaeding and the Department of Political Science at the University of Duisburg-Essen for hosting me as a visiting scholar in January 2016. A substantial portion of this book delves into German history, politics, and finance, and these opportunities to visit Germany were an essential part of the project. Finally, on a personal note, I would like to thank the many friends who politely asked about this book over years of meals and drinks together, and who patiently endured my surely too-detailed responses. I'm especially grateful to the Beth Israel Center cycling club, the Door County contingent, and my bandmates in the Lost Wax Process (Andy Kydd, Michael O'Russa, and Jon Pevehouse) for helping me to maintain the balance.

Singer thanks his colleagues at MIT, including Adam Berinsky, Andrea Campbell, Devin Caughey, Taylor Fravel, Danny Hidalgo, In Song Kim, Chap Lawson, Evan Lieberman, Maria DiMauro, Rich Nielsen, Melissa Nobles, David Randall, Janine Sazinsky, Charles Stewart, Lily Tsai, and Teppei Yamamoto. I also thank Rick Locke for personal and professional support during the critical early stages of this project. Finally, I thank the Singapore University of Technology and Design, which provided a comfortable workplace for me during the summer of 2015.

Together, we thank Claire Conceison, a theater professor at MIT, who, upon hearing a summary of the book, quickly dispensed with our former title and came up with *Banks on the Brink*. We also thank Robert Dreesen at Cambridge University Press and three anonymous reviewers.

Last and most importantly, we thank our families who are everything that truly matters and the ones to whom we are most deeply in debt. All financial crises (and book projects) involve substantial costs and distributional consequences, and Steve, Beth, Micah, and Dafna have borne the lion's share of these as we have spent the last decade traveling to present our research and attend numerous conferences on the Great Recession, the Eurozone crisis, and the politics of international finance. We are eternally grateful for their love, patience, and support, and we dedicate this book to them with love and gratitude.

1

The Politics and Economics of Financial Instability

There is an old joke in the banking industry, told and retold at cocktail parties and conferences, about the "3-6-3 plan." It goes something like this: bankers should pay depositors a 3 percent interest rate, issue loans at 6 percent, and head to the golf course by 3 o'clock. The joke now comes with a whiff of nostalgia for the old days of banking, in which financial intermediation was viewed as a relatively boring industry that provided simple financing for customers and predictable middle-class careers for bankers.

But even in its simplest form, banking has always been an endeavor fraught with danger. A bank's managers, hidden behind marble façades and mahogany desks, can extend loans to risky borrowers, thereby jeopardizing the stability of the bank if the borrowers fail to repay. As memorable scenes from the films *It's a Wonderful Life* and *Mary Poppins* remind us, trust in a bank can evaporate quickly, and nervous depositors can withdraw their funds en masse and cause a bank to collapse. One bank failure can lead to the next, causing disruption to the entire financial system. In fact, the annals of US history include more than a dozen named "panics" all resulting from bank failures. One particular crisis, known as the Panic of 1907, was so severe that the US Congress created a new central bank, the Federal Reserve, to try to prevent future crises.[1] And in the last decade, the Great Recession – in which multibillion-dollar financial institutions like Lehman Brothers, Bear Stearns, and AIG

[1] On the panic of 1907, see Friedman and Schwartz 1971, 156–68. On the founding of the Federal Reserve, see Broz 1997; Grossman 2010, 243–5; White 1983, chap. 2; Wood 2005, 158–66.

either collapsed or required emergency bailouts – taught us that banking systems remain vulnerable even as they become more sophisticated and global in scale.[2] Clearly, there is something precarious about the process of banking, whether it is the simple 3-6-3 variety of the old days or the more complex modern-day variety.

It is an unfortunate feature of modern societies that bank failures happen regularly. When banks collapse, entire economies can be thrown into disarray.[3] Banks are the critical link between savers and borrowers and the drivers of economic activity.[4] When banks collapse, credit becomes scarce and the process of mobilizing a society's savings grinds to a halt. In the wake of a banking crisis, businesses that previously relied on banks for their day-to-day working capital must cut back on their operations, shrink their balance sheets, and possibly reduce their workforces. Similarly, individuals must hold off on purchasing homes, automobiles, and other consumable goods. In the aggregate economy, consumption and investment plummet, the real estate market collapses, unemployment rises, and currencies crash as international investors run for the exits.[5] Political leaders may also face dire consequences if the public blames them for lax supervision or negligence.[6]

No country is immune from the devastation of a banking crisis. In the 1990s alone, countries including Finland, Indonesia, Japan, South Korea, Sweden, and Thailand all experienced severe crises. In the 1980s, the casualties included Argentina, Chile, Mexico, and Norway, among many others. In all of these cases, the consequences to the broader national economy were severe, sometimes enduring for many years.

[2] See Woll 2014.

[3] See Barth, Caprio, and Levine 2008, 2.

[4] Grossman 2010, chap. 1.

[5] Reinhart and Rogoff 2009b, 145–6.

[6] See Ahlquist, Copelovitch, and Walter forthcoming; Chwieroth and Walter 2015a, 2019; Crespo-Tenorio, Jensen, and Rosas 2014; Funke, Schularick, and Trebesch 2016; Genovese, Schneider, and Wassmann 2016; Hernández and Kriesi 2016; Hobolt and de Vries 2015; Pepinsky 2012; Rosas 2006, 2009; Trebbi, Mian, and Sufi 2012; Walter 2013. On the connection between protest and transparency, see Hollyer, Rosendorff, and Vreeland 2015. On the political consequences of the Eurozone crisis, see, e.g., Accornero and Pinto 2015; Alt, Lassen, and Wehner 2014; Armingeon and Guthmann 2014; Bechtel, Hainmueller, and Margalit 2014; Bellucci 2014; Bulmer 2014; de Vries 2018; Dinas and Rori 2013; Fernandez-Albertos and Kuo 2016; Hobolt and de Vries 2016; Hobolt and Wratil 2015; Howarth and Quaglia 2014; Katsanidou and Otjes 2016; Matthijs and Blyth 2015; Matthijs and McNamara 2015; Schneider 2019; Walter 2016.

Every region of the world has at least one identifiable "lost decade" of economic stagnation associated with a banking crisis.[7]

Why do banking crises occur? Existing political science research on the causes of crises is limited, as scholars have focused overwhelmingly on the political consequences of and policy responses to crises.[8] Our goal in this book is to focus a political lens on the question of causes, while maintaining a close eye on the economic drivers of financial instability.

We begin with a simple observation: banks collapse because their customers lose confidence in them. Even in the old-fashioned 3-6-3 model, banks engage in a high-wire act known as "maturity transformation": they accept short-term loans from customers in the form of deposits that can be withdrawn at any time, and extend long-term loans to businesses and consumers.[9] As long as customers have confidence in the safety of their savings, banks will have enough funds on hand to cover all withdrawals and the process of maturity transformation can continue without disruption. But if customers begin to doubt the solvency of a bank – perhaps because they fear that many of those 6 percent loans will not be repaid – they withdraw their funds in a so-called run and quickly exhaust the bank's supply of liquid assets. A run on one bank can lead to a run on another until the entire banking system is bankrupt.

In sophisticated banking systems, bank runs might not have the appearance of a mob of customers lined up outside, waiting anxiously to withdraw their funds. Instead, bank runs are often perpetuated by other financial institutions in a manner invisible to the person on the street. For example, when Lehman Brothers, formerly one of Wall Street's most prestigious investment banks, declared bankruptcy in 2008, other banks that conducted business with Lehman incurred substantial losses. Banks and hedge funds with large holdings of Lehman corporate bonds – which were virtually worthless after the bankruptcy – found themselves struggling to stay afloat, which in turn made their own banks wary of extending loans to them. As uncertainty about the stability of the financial system grew, banks became wary of providing support to each other. Banks with extra cash simply hoarded it rather than lend it to other banks with short-term funding needs, because they had scant confidence that

[7] Chinn and Frieden 2011.

[8] See footnote 6 for references. For research in political science on the causes of banking crises, see Bauerle Danzman, Winecoff, and Oatley 2017; Drezner and McNamara 2013; Jordana and Rosas 2014.

[9] See Rethel and Sinclair 2012, 16.

those other banks would still be standing the next morning.[10] As interbank lending plummeted, banks were forced to turn to their national central banks for emergency liquidity support. In the absence of angry customers queuing up outside their banks, a spectator walking down to Wall Street through midtown Manhattan would see no evidence that such a devastating bank run was in progress (except, perhaps, for an errant sweaty-palmed banker scurrying back from lunch).

The events that trigger a crisis of confidence in the banking sector are often the stuff of legend. Consider the Panic of 1907, in which the founders of United Copper Company tried to corner the market in their own stock and head off a speculative attack. During the summer of that year, copper magnate F. Augustus Heinze learned that speculators were selling United Copper's stock short – a strategy in which investors sell a borrowed stock at today's price with a commitment to purchase the shares at a later date, hopefully at a lower price. In essence, the market appeared to be betting that United Copper's shares would plummet. Heinze and his brother developed a scheme to bid up the price of the stock and thereby punish the speculators, turning their expected profit into a debilitating loss. With financing from New York banks, the Heinzes were initially successful in boosting United Copper's share price, but the scheme quickly fell apart as the stock plunged in value and the short-sellers happily reaped their expected gains. The banks that assisted the Heinzes in their ill-fated attempt at stock market manipulation suffered severe losses, and depositors rushed to withdraw their funds from any bank associated with the Heinze family. What began as a fiasco over a single traded stock turned into systemic nightmare as one bank run led to another, Wall Street became paralyzed, and the City of New York teetered on the brink of bankruptcy.[11]

Behind the sordid details, most crises have a common feature: banks fail because of their risky behaviors. The triggers of banking crises can vary from case to case, but rarely does confidence in the banking system evaporate without due cause. In 1907, banks collapsed because they were complicit in speculation and market manipulation that led to financial losses throughout the financial system. During the Asian financial crisis of the late 1990s, the trigger for the collapse of Thai banks was speculative lending to real estate developers that led to a boom and then a devastating bust in the real estate market. And in 2008, in the United States and Europe, after a decade of easy mortgages to borrowers with

[10] See Gorton and Tallman 2018.
[11] See Bruner and Carr 2008.

shaky credit histories and a growing bubble in the real estate market, investors grew fearful that banks and the holders of mortgage-backed securities might never get their money back.

Sordid details no doubt make for good reading, and this book makes an occasional attempt to indulge the reader accordingly. However, the goal of this book is explanation. We seek to understand why some countries are more prone to banking crises than other countries or at different times. Our focus sets us apart from much of the social science research that focuses on the consequences of banking crises rather than their causes. We zero in on the political decisions that shape the structure of financial markets and the international economic forces that make certain countries especially vulnerable to financial instability. Our approach is comparative and multimethod, relying on both statistical analysis and detailed historical case studies of two key countries: Canada and Germany. We draw upon data from the 1970s through the early twenty-first century for most of the world's developed economies, and we compile detailed historical narratives to explore how governments embark, often inadvertently, on divergent financial development paths.[12] Our quantitative empirical analyses include macro-level investigations of the correlates of banking crises across developed countries, as well as micro-level studies of the drivers of banks' risk taking.

By casting such a broad net, we deliberately part company with much of the existing case-study literature. There are plenty of books that chronicle the particular features of a notable crisis, including the Panic of 1907,[13] the Great Depression of the 1930s,[14] the US savings and loan crisis of the 1980s,[15] Britain's secondary banking crisis of the 1970s,[16] and the Great Recession since 2008.[17] By attempting to isolate the political and structural incentives that give rise to crises, we sacrifice the granular detail of these books in favor of developing an analytical explanation that can be applied across countries and time.

Some readers might question the timing of this book, which arrives (at least as of this writing) during a time of relative financial stability throughout the world. Bank supervision has been tightened since 2010,

[12] On inadvertency in financial development trajectories, see Krippner 2011, 2.
[13] Bruner and Carr 2008.
[14] Bernanke 2000.
[15] Lowy 1991.
[16] Reid 1988.
[17] See, e.g., Blinder 2013; Johnson and Kwak 2011; Lewis 2010; Sorkin 2010; Tett 2009; Tooze 2018.

and governments are generally unwinding their various bailouts and interventions – monetary and financial – which helped to contain the crisis.[18] In our view, this is an opportune time to write a book on bank failures, precisely because we are bucking the trend in the social sciences to react to current events rather than portend future ones. To be sure, we do not make specific predictions in this book; rather, we highlight the enduring features of financial systems and the sometimes volatile nature of global finance as triggers of bank failures. These triggers are just as relevant, and even more potent, today as they were five, fifty, or a hundred years ago.

Banking is an inherently political activity, but not in the way that many observers might imagine. Granted, bankers themselves have political preferences and may express them publicly, and some banks lobby for favorable public policies and donate to political campaigns and political action committees. But at a deeper level, banks are embedded in financial markets, which themselves reflect an accumulation of government choices. Banks today operate in an environment shaped by these choices, some of which make banks more resilient, others of which make them more prone to crisis.

We began this investigation of banking crises by exploring the influence of a number of variables that constitute the usual suspects in political economy research, including the partisanship of the government, the degree of fragmentation of decision making across the branches of government, the extent of state ownership of financial institutions, the scope and configuration of regulatory agencies, and the stringency of regulations themselves. We also explored exchange rate policy, capital account policy, and the applicability of national models of capitalism from the varieties of capitalism (VoC) literature.[19] The results from these early explorations were frustrating. Banking crises, like many forms of cancer, are a blight that afflicts victims without regard to their year-to-year or even decade-to-decade choices. Indeed, Reinhart and Rogoff call them an "equal opportunity menace."[20] They occur when pro-market governments are in charge, and when democratic socialists are at the helm.[21] The widely accepted categories from VoC scholarship are

[18] See Chinn and Frieden 2011, chap. 5.

[19] Hall and Soskice 2001.

[20] Reinhart and Rogoff 2009b, 147.

[21] Some evidence exists for a "partisan financial cycle" in which left-leaning parties tighten financial regulations and right-leaning parties loosen them. See Broz 2013.

similarly unhelpful in explaining variation.[22] Indeed, Canada and the United States – both liberal market economies with many other shared political attributes – are polar opposites when considering bank stability. Canada has not suffered a crisis in decades, whereas bank failures are a common, even mundane, occurrence in the United States.

Our investigation took us deeper into the structure of financial markets. Spurred by the story of the Heinze family's schemes in 1907 and similar historical episodes in Germany, we noticed that stock markets were implicated in many bank failures across countries and time, and we began to explore whether these markets had a systematic influence on bank behavior. We found that banking and securities markets are strange bedfellows. When securities markets are deep and sophisticated, banks often rely on them for financing and are enticed by new revenue streams, such as selling off mortgage loans that are bundled as securities. But banks also face competition from these markets as businesses choose to bypass traditional lending in favor of stock and bond offerings. These two influences – direct involvement in securities markets and competition from them – can lead banks to take on more risk.

Our investigation also centered on the main smoking gun in the economics literature on banking crises: capital inflows. A common precursor to crises is a sustained current account deficit, representing a surge in capital from foreign countries.[23] The link between capital and crises is complicated, involving an expansion of lending, rising asset prices – including real estate and stocks – and an eventual crisis of confidence in the banking system which causes the bubble to burst. As we learned from the existing literature, capital inflows are associated with various forms of financial mischief, but not always. Some banking systems seem capable of accommodating sustained surges without becoming riskier or more prone to failure. As we flesh out below, we argue that the relative prominence of securities markets is critical in determining whether foreign capital is channeled safely through the domestic economy, or whether it causes the various distortions that ultimately lead to a banking crisis.

[22] See Konzelmann, Fovargue-Davies, and Butzbach 2013.

[23] Reinhart and Reinhart 2008; Reinhart and Rogoff 2009b. See also Bauerle Danzman, Winecoff, and Oatley 2017; Jordà, Schularick, and Taylor 2011. On the link between capital inflows and the broader concept of "financialization," see Krippner 2011.

UNDERSTANDING BANKING CRISES: NATIONAL MARKET STRUCTURE AND INTERNATIONAL CAPITAL

To explain why banks fail, we must first understand their incentives to take on risk – or perhaps to take on too much risk. The fundamental purpose of any financial system is to channel funds from savers to borrowers, thereby enabling businesses, entrepreneurs, consumers, and sometimes governments to access capital for investment and consumption. Banks stand in the center of this process, providing savers a place to earn returns on their excess funds and offering borrowers access to much-needed financing. Regardless of the financial system, banks face a fundamental challenge known as "asymmetric information." Any potential corporate borrower is necessarily more knowledgeable about its own financial stability – including its income streams, market conditions, investment decisions, and managerial competence – than the bank's credit officers. As a result of asymmetric information, banks always face difficulties in discerning the ability and willingness of potential borrowers to repay their debts in the future. This leads to the possibility of a lending mistake of either the Type 1 or Type 2 variety: a non-creditworthy borrower could succeed in obtaining a loan and then fail to repay, or a creditworthy borrower could be denied a loan. Both types of errors are consequential. The first type is the more dramatic of the two, as multiple loan defaults could jeopardize the solvency of the bank. However, the second type reflects a societal deadweight loss, forgone revenue for the bank's managers, and (arguably) a failure to maximize shareholder value.

Banks must continually evaluate their risk appetites and lending criteria based on market conditions, corporate strategies, and prevailing regulations. As any homebuyer knows, some banks offer better mortgage rates than others, and the banks that offer the most competitive rates today might not be the most competitive in the future. This variation exists across countries as well. A borrower with a poor credit history who is precluded from obtaining a mortgage in Canada could be considered an acceptable candidate for a loan if she resided in the United States. Some banks take on substantial risk and accept the possibility of a default (a Type 1 error), all with the expectation of greater profits. Other banks err on the side of prudence and would rather make a Type 2 error if it ensures the bank's stability in the long run.

At the national level, what are the factors that determine how a bank will resolve this balancing act? In this book, we explore two dimensions of variation: the structure of national financial markets, which reflects a country's history of political decisions and rarely changes from year to year or even decade to decade; and the composition and magnitude of capital inflows from the rest of the world. In short, we argue that banks engage in riskier behavior when they compete alongside well-developed national securities markets. Capital inflows amplify this risk and increase the chance of a banking crisis.

The Structure of National Financial Markets

The first source of variation is what we label the structure of national financial markets. We use the word "financial" and not "banking" because we are interested in the characteristics of the entire system, not just banks. The landscape of national financial systems varies considerably from country to country across countless dimensions. For example, in Germany "universal banks" offer traditional banking services as well as stock and bond underwriting and insurance products, whereas other governments impose restrictions on the ability of any one firm to offer all of these services. Some countries have large, deep, and sophisticated markets for stocks and bonds, such as Finland and the United Kingdom, whereas traditional bank loans – fueled by bank deposits – dominate the financial landscape in countries such as Denmark and New Zealand. The relative degree of fragmentation is also highly variable across countries. Foreign visitors to the United States are often surprised to learn that there are nearly 7,000 federally insured banks in the country. In Canada, the so-called Big Five banks dominate the market.[24]

We argue that the relative size and depth of securities markets are of particular importance for bank stability.[25] These markets allow companies to seek capital directly from investors rather than rely on an intermediary. A firm can issue stock via an initial public offering or a secondary offering and thereby provide ownership rights in exchange for funds. Firms can also issue bonds, which promise payments and interest to the investor over a specific period of time. Securities can quickly

[24] On cross-national variation in banking systems, see Allen and Gale 2009; Demirgüç-Kunt and Levine 2004; Hardie and Howarth 2013.

[25] Note that the sophistication of securities markets is a more focused concept than financialization, which reflects a "broad-based transformation in which financial activities (rather than services generally) have become increasingly dominant." Krippner 2011, 2.

become complicated as financial markets develop: firms can issue hybrid securities with characteristics of stocks and bonds, and financial institutions can issue derivatives whose value is derived from an underlying asset or a previously issued security.

Companies issue securities and borrow from banks for similar reasons: to expand their operations, invest in infrastructure and human capital, and so on. For our purposes, it is reasonable to think of bank loans and securities as alternative methods of financing a business.

Businesses that wish to raise funds through securities markets may often do so without the assistance of a commercial bank. In contrast to bank loans, securities are highly impersonal and "arms-length."[26] Whereas a bank cultivates relationships with its depositors and borrowers, securities are often considered to be a manifestation of disintermediation in which banks are pushed aside in favor of direct transactions between investors and businesses. Banks sometimes play a role in this process as a broker, dealer, or underwriter, helping to match buyers and sellers of securities and maintaining a sufficiently liquid market for doing so. However, unlike a loan which inherently depends on a relationship between a bank and a borrower, a security does not require such a relationship. A holder of a company's stock has a direct (but largely impersonal) relationship with that company. Indeed, it is not uncommon in the United States for individual investors, especially of a certain age, to keep their company-issued stock certificates in a desk drawer. Only if they wish to sell the stock will they seek the services of a bank or broker.

The arms-length nature of securities markets has important implications for risk management. In highly liquid markets, investors can generally sell their financial instruments at the market-clearing price. The disparate holders of securities therefore have fewer incentives to monitor a firm's managers than a bank with long-term illiquid assets.[27] If new unfavorable information about a firm's prospects comes to light, investors can simply dump their shares and move on. This ease of exit suggests that investors will be relatively risk-acceptant in entering the market. Firms with high-risk, high-reward value propositions will realize better financing outcomes by issuing securities directly to investors rather than by seeking loans from conservative banks. The potential dangers are borne by the entire financial system. When investors are myopic because of their ability to exit, risk can accumulate throughout

[26] Rajan 1992.

[27] See Beck et al. 2001; Diamond 1991; Rajan 1992.

the financial system, and generally there is no agent responsible for overall management of "systemic risk."[28] The dangers are greater in more developed markets, as opaque chains of complex securities can impair the ability of even the most sophisticated investors to gauge the level of risk in the financial system.[29]

It would be unrealistic to expect that banks will stand aside insouciantly as firms bypass them in favor of securities markets, or what is often called the "non-bank financial sector." It seems more reasonable to expect that banks in countries with large financial markets will feel pressure to take on more risk in an effort to maintain their customer bases and their profits.[30] In other words, we expect the conservative bias in bank behavior to erode as securities markets become more prominent in the national financial system.

The increase in bank risk can take many forms. Most obviously, banks can make riskier loans, and more of them relative to their capital bases. As one example, consider the plight of the US banking industry in the 1980s, a time when companies were increasingly seeking the assistance of securities firms, finance companies, and other non-bank financial institutions for their financing needs. To maintain their profitability in the face of this stiff competition, banks extended increasing amounts of credit to real estate developers, historically considered a relatively risky industry, and other borrowers with shaky credit histories.[31] They allowed their loan-loss provisions – cushions of funds that support banks when borrowers fail to repay – to fall to precarious levels.[32] They also became more tightly tethered to stock markets by extending loans to support corporate takeovers and leveraged buyouts.[33]

As securities markets become a larger competitive threat, some banks – and some national banking systems – will begin to look more like securities firms. For example, banks can issue loans and then securitize those loans and sell them off to individual and corporate buyers. They can also derive more of their income from non-interest-income activities, also known as off-balance sheet activities, such as dealing in derivatives or investing their own funds in speculative investments.[34] These

[28] On systemic risk and macroprudential regulation, see, e.g., Borio 2003; Freixas, Laeven, and Peydro 2015; Tucker 2018.

[29] Gorton 2009.

[30] On competitive pressures from securities markets, see Porter 1993, 95.

[31] See, e.g., Sprague 1986.

[32] See Singer 2007, chap. 3.

[33] Edwards 1996, 38.

[34] Barth, Caprio, and Levine 2012, 66–7; Edwards 1996, 40.

"market-based banks" blur the line between commercial banking and securities markets, and therefore their fates – not just their profitability, but their stability – depend on securities market conditions.[35]

On the other hand, banks can also gamble for their profitability using traditional means. Wells Fargo, a long-standing California-based bank with a nationwide presence in the United States, had virtually no involvement in investment banking in the years up to the global financial crisis. To remain profitable, it extended real estate loans to risky borrowers and ultimately required a massive bailout by the US Treasury.[36] There was little about Wells Fargo's behavior that prima facie suggested that it was reacting to competition from the non-bank financial sector; indeed the bank had and continues to have a reputation as a relatively unsophisticated brick-and-mortar institution, not a high-flying financial innovator. However, the entire financial landscape is critical in explaining its behavior. As we argue in this book, securities markets can incentivize even the most traditional banks to take on more risks, even if those risks do not appear to be closely tied to securities markets.

A key contribution of this book is to highlight the political origins of financial market structure.[37] Both banking and securities markets require "affirmative acts of policy design."[38] During a banking system's formative years, government policy is particularly relevant for chartering – the process of granting an operating license to a bank and dictating the terms of its operation within the country. For securities, rules pertaining to disclosure of information, fraud, and exchange are most critical. To understand the relative prominence of banks vis-à-vis securities markets today, we must identify the key political decisions in these areas, which often occurred over a hundred years ago. The context of these decisions – or sometimes indecisions – differs from country to country but generally involves the thorniest challenges in a country's early political development, including the political and economic integration of subnational regions, the shedding of colonial rule, and the financing needs of the country's industries.

The reader should not take for granted our argument that government policies are critical for setting the groundwork for either a vibrant,

[35] Adrian and Shin 2010; Hardie et al. 2013.

[36] Johnson and Kwak 2011, 165–80.

[37] As Posner argues, "Arrangements for distributing capital, even when based on markets, are political institutions." Posner 2009, 6. On the connection between political science and securities market development, see Sobel 1994.

[38] Jacobs and Teles 2007, 158–9.

nationwide securities market or a limited, regionally fragmented one. There are indeed many studies of the politics of bank regulation, including the political economy of bank branch restrictions in the United States, which at least implicitly acknowledge that the government can either facilitate or hinder the development of a national banking market.[39] However, as we embarked upon the historical research for this book, we were frustrated to find a common assertion, especially in US economic history, that securities markets emerged and flourished because the banking system provided insufficient capital for industrialization.[40] To summarize these arguments more plainly, securities markets emerged and matured when they were needed. While there may be some truth to these functionalist accounts of markets, there is an inherent tension in scholarly research that privileges the role of politics in banking but downplays or ignores its role in securities. If the demand for capital by a country's industries is not, by itself, influential enough to overcome the political wrangling that splinters banking markets, why would that same demand so easily triumph over any political resistance to securities market development?

The contrast between the United States and Canada, which we delve into more deeply in Chapter 4, is instructive on this point. Both countries had similarly fragmented, thinly regulated stock markets leading up to the Great Depression, along with industries that were eager to attract capital directly from investors rather than banks. In the 1930s, the US government created the Securities and Exchange Commission, harmonized trading and disclosure rules across regional markets, and imposed strict anti-fraud requirements. At the time, these policies seemed punitive in their stringency, but they ultimately eased investors' concerns about the integrity of their investments and allowed securities markets to lower the cost of capital for industry in the ensuing decades. Canada, on the other hand, took no substantial steps toward reining in its disparate provincial stock markets. Its markets remain regionally fragmented today, and it has the dubious distinction of being the only industrialized country without a national securities regulator.

The importance of political history in the forging of national financial systems is important for us in two other ways. First, the path dependence

[39] See, e.g., Bordo, Redish, and Rockoff 2015; Bordo, Rockoff, and Redish 1994; Calomiris and Haber 2014; Kroszner and Strahan 1999.

[40] See most notably Allen and Gale 2000.

of financial markets challenges the common refrain that risk-hungry foreign investors trigger short-term domestic financial innovation.[41] In one variant of the "search for yield" story, domestic markets concoct suitably high-yielding investment products, like asset-backed securities, to satisfy the demands of investors who face an otherwise low-interest-rate environment. We argue instead that the stickiness of financial market structure makes the creation of new and riskier financial products far more difficult for underdeveloped securities markets. For example, Canada's financial system, with its provincially fragmented securities markets, will be relatively flat-footed compared to Britain's highly developed market in responding to investors' demands for higher-yielding products. It is for precisely this reason that the interaction between foreign capital and domestic financial structure is so critical for financial stability. A financial system dominated by banks will be a bulwark against the destabilizing influence of foreign capital, whereas a system with relatively prominent securities markets will amplify these risks.

The second reason why path-dependent financial trajectories are important to our study is that we are justified in using market structure as an exogenous explanatory variable in our quantitative analyses of contemporary banking crises. In other words, we take market structure as given because contemporary forces are unlikely to shift the landscape enough to jeopardize our inferences about the triggers of bank instability.

We delve deeply into two historical case studies to show how the accumulation of political decisions has led directly and sometimes inadvertently to markedly different financial systems. Our studies of Canada (Chapter 4) and Germany (Chapter 5) support the notion that financial market structure is historically contingent and slow to change. Interest groups based on industrial sector, geography, and sometimes cultural or linguistic heritage all jockey for position during a country's early economic history. Canada's natural resource industries were eager to maintain the flow of speculative capital for mining, oil prospecting, and other high-risk endeavors, and therefore resisted the imposition of onerous disclosure regulations and a national securities regulator, which later proved to be the sine qua non of modern securities markets. In Germany, banks initially had a privileged position as the sole providers of capital to businesses, with little reason to support the creation of

[41] On path dependence and development trajectories, see Levi 1997; Mahoney 2001; Pierson 2004; Thelen 2004.

regional or national securities markets. Interest groups, political parties, and anti-Semitism all played a role in restricting the development of stock markets from the late nineteenth century through World War II. These markets remained thin through the 1980s. However, in more recent times, as large banks faced a competitive threat from regional and foreign banks, they shifted their support in favor of financial market creation, spurring growth in Germany's stock markets.

In establishing the political history of securities market development, our case studies also cast doubt on alternative arguments about the causes of banks' risk taking and the determinants of banking crises. For example, some commentators point to Canadian banks' conservative culture as a reason for Canada's history of financial stability. We find, instead, that Canada's successive national and provincial governments since the late 1800s have enacted policies that hinder the development of the country's stock markets. Conservative behaviors that others attribute to culture we attribute to the structure of financial markets, which allows banks to maintain their dominant position in the financial landscape without taking on excessive risks.

The International Dimension: Global Capital

Foreign capital inflows are a mixed blessing. In theory, international financial integration brings similar benefits to the domestic allocation of capital between savers and borrowers. Countries can borrow from other countries to smooth their incomes, invest in infrastructure and other projects, and offset trade deficits. International investment also allows for diversification and optimization by sending capital to where it is most needed and most rewarded. Despite these theoretical benefits, global capital has a reputation for causing much strife in the world. Investors often reward countries for enacting unwise policies, and they are trigger-happy in pulling out their capital if a country faces an economic downturn. Curiously, as many scholars have noted, capital often flows uphill from emerging market countries (where capital is presumably scarce) to the industrialized world (where it is abundant).[42] What should in theory constitute a global stabilizing influence in fact becomes a force for instability and distortion.[43]

[42] See Lucas Jr. 1990; Prasad, Rajan, and Subramanian 2007.
[43] Borio 2014.

The dangers of foreign capital inflows can take many forms. For emerging market countries, foreign capital often arrives via a currency mismatch as banks borrow dollars (or another leading currency) from foreign banks in order to grant loans to domestic residents in the national currency. If the value of the national currency falls with respect to the dollar, banks on both sides of the transaction can suffer debilitating losses. For developed economies, exchange rate uncertainty is a less serious concern, but capital inflows are potentially destabilizing if they trigger a lending boom that causes an asset price bubble. Bankers themselves commonly describe an erosion of conservative risk management as capital flows in, often because a drop in interest rates prompts a precarious search for higher yields.[44] As the real estate market booms, commodity prices increase, and stock markets soar, banks tend to get swept up in the momentum and their choices come back to haunt them.

Many scholars believe that the malignancy of global capital – as reflected in current account deficits – is the most likely culprit behind banking crises.[45] In their analysis of the Great Recession, Chinn and Frieden point to the enduring prevalence of the capital flow cycle, in which "capital floods into a country, stimulates an economic boom, encourages high-flying financial and other activities, and eventually culminates in a crash."[46] They note that many previous crises fit this pattern, including the Mexican crisis of 1994, the Asian financial crisis of 1997, and dozens of others. Reinhart and Rogoff's *This Time Is Different* suggests that the pattern has deep historical roots.[47] One of their key findings, backed by data covering 800 years of financial crises, is that large current account deficits, asset price bubbles, and excessive sovereign borrowing are common precursors of crises across countries and throughout time. Moreover, bank failures were relatively rare during the Bretton Woods monetary system from the end of World War II to the early 1970s, when governments enacted strict controls on capital movements.[48] This overall finding – that foreign capital opens up a Pandora's box of financial distortions – now has the status of conventional wisdom in academic and policy circles.

44 Rajan 2005.

45 See Krippner 2011, chap. 4, for a discussion of the link between capital inflows and the financialization of the US economy.

46 Chinn and Frieden 2011, xiv.

47 Reinhart and Rogoff 2009b.

48 On capital controls during Bretton Woods, see Helleiner 1994, chap. 2.

The potential dangers of capital inflows are difficult to refute. However, existing research has failed to emphasize that foreign capital is not always destabilizing for the banking system. For every instance of a banking crisis preceded by a few years of substantial capital inflows, there are countless examples of capital inflows that are harmlessly – and even productively – channeled throughout the national financial system. For example, the Great Recession, the United Kingdom and the United States both experienced large current account deficits in the years preceding their respective crises. Australia and New Zealand also experienced substantial current account deficits, but their banking systems escaped relatively unscathed. Explaining this puzzle – why capital inflows lead to banking crises in some cases but not in others – is the central motivation of our book.

Summarizing the Argument

To address this puzzle, our approach to banking crises combines the domestic and international perspectives. We envision foreign capital as the fuel for a potentially destabilizing lending boom and a source of distorted bank risk management, but the actual effect of foreign capital depends on existing structures at the national level. When banks are conservative because of the relative absence of competition for financial intermediation, foreign capital can be safely channeled throughout the system without causing bank instability. On the other hand, when banks sit alongside viable securities markets, capital inflows exacerbate banks' risk taking and increase the probability of a crisis.

Our argument about the conditional impact of capital inflows – or of global market integration more generally – has a long lineage in political science. Geoffrey Garrett, for example, has argued that partisanship mediates the impact of global capital integration on domestic policy choices, whereas Duane Swank has argued that global capital's impact is conditional upon national welfare regimes.[49] Moreover, standard models from open-economy macroeconomics suggest that capital mobility exerts different constraints on national policy choices depending on the prevailing exchange rate regime.[50]

[49] Garrett 1998; Swank 2002.
[50] Clark and Hallerberg 2000.

Our key conditioning variable – domestic financial market structure – reflects a lengthy accumulation of government decisions, and in this sense is not dissimilar to national welfare regimes or other deeply rooted institutions. Early political coalitions form around particular configurations of banks and markets, with some political leaders in support of a dominant, monopolistic banking industry, and others in support of nationally harmonized securities markets. Governments that establish rules on disclosure, fraud, and supervision are likely to see the eventual rise of sophisticated securities markets, even if those rules seem punitive in their early years. Alternatively, government policy can favor the development of the banking industry by encouraging close ties between banks and industry, by imposing taxes that inhibit securities market development, or by refraining from providing the regulatory infrastructure needed for a nationally viable securities market.

Our historical analyses also inform our policy recommendations, which are discussed in Chapter 6. In light of the slow-moving nature of financial market structure, any policy proposal to fundamentally alter the shape and depth of financial markets will likely be dead on arrival. Proposals to re-introduce Glass-Steagall-type regulations that separate commercial and investment banking might be episodically popular in countries like the United States, but as our evidence suggests, they would fail to address the heightened risks that traditional brick-and-mortar commercial banks take as they compete with securities markets.

THE PLAN OF THE BOOK

In Chapter 2, we provide a fuller picture of the prevalence of banking crises in developed economies since the 1970s. We provide our working definition of the term "banking crisis" and review the available options for measurement. This section requires more ink than a typical book's discussion of measurement, because there is some inherent discretion in determining the threshold beyond which a bank failure, a government rescue, or a nationalization of one or more banks constitutes a crisis. We compare the most widely available crisis datasets, and throughout the remainder of the book we demonstrate how our results are robust (or sometimes not) to using these different measurements.

Chapter 2 also shows the reader how capital inflows and financial market structure vary across countries and time. As with our dependent variable, these explanatory variables can be measured in different ways. For capital inflows, we highlight the important distinctions between current account deficits and gross portfolio inflows. Our discussion of market structure focuses on the relative degree of competition between banks and securities markets, measured by the ratio of stock market size to bank credit. Simple graphs show how these variables vary across countries and also how they appear to be uncorrelated with each other: market structure changes only gradually, whereas capital inflows ebb and flow with greater intensity. This chapter concludes by articulating the motivation for the rest of our empirical analyses: past scholarship has identified foreign capital as a likely trigger of financial instability, but there are many examples of countries and time periods in which capital inflows are not destabilizing. When will foreign capital lead to bank failures, and when will it be productively and safely channeled through the banking system?

In Chapter 3, we provide our quantitative tests. Using datasets of banking crises covering the advanced industrialized countries from 1976 to 2011, we first explore the argument that capital inflows, conditional upon the presence of a relatively prominent securities market, are associated with a higher incidence of banking crises. Results from conditional logit and linear probability models suggest that national market structure is key to understanding when and why foreign capital is destabilizing. We demonstrate the robustness of these results to different measures of our dependent and explanatory variables and different model specifications.

We also present in Chapter 3 our second quantitative test, which focuses on the impact of capital inflows on banks' actual risk taking. Using measures of capital adequacy and insolvency risk, we find micro-level evidence that banks' protective capital cushions tend to decline with the combination of foreign capital and prominent securities markets.

Chapter 4 is a case study of Canada's financial development. Canada is often considered to be a paragon of bank stability, given that its history is virtually unblemished by bank failures. What is the secret to Canada's success? We explore the political origins of the country's conservative banking system, and the largely untold story of how political decisions rendered in the nineteenth and early twentieth centuries hindered the development of securities markets. Previous scholarship on Canada's financial system has emphasized its highly concentrated, well-managed banking industry but failed to notice that its securities markets are regionally fragmented and relatively backward.[51] Indeed, Canada is the only developed

[51] See Calomiris and Haber 2014, chap. 9.

country that does not have a national securities regulator (akin to the US Securities and Exchange Commission). We trace the underdevelopment of these markets to efforts by Canada's provinces to maintain regional control over regulation. Ironically, the interest groups in favor of light regulation, minimal disclosure requirements, and regional control were speculative industries like mining and oil exploration, which depended on a steady flow of funds from risk-acceptant investors. Stymying the creation of a national regulator and a unified national stock market may have been in these industries' short-term interests, but over time the lack of a national enforcer of disclosure and anti-fraud rules prevented Canada's securities markets from reaching the level of sophistication of markets in the United States, the United Kingdom, or Japan. Canada's banking system, which overshadows its relatively underdeveloped securities markets, therefore remains stable even in the face of persistent current account deficits.

In Chapter 5, we turn our gaze to Germany, which in its early years had a financial system that broadly resembled Canada's in both structure and stability. Banks were the primary source of capital for businesses, and close and enduring ties developed between firms and banks. Securities markets were small and regionally fragmented, and banks were generally stable. This chapter highlights how policy decisions in the aftermath of two major financial crises – the Panic of 1873 and the financial crisis of 1931 – arrested the development of German securities markets and solidified a heavily bank-centric financial system. Our historical narrative illustrates how interest-group and party politics, rising nationalism and anti-Semitism in the late nineteenth century, and the Nazis' ascendance to power in the 1930s all conspired to hobble the development of German stock markets prior to World War II, allowing banks to engage in long-term conservative lending with "patient capital" throughout the postwar era until the 1980s. In recent years, however, financial competitors from within Germany and from the European Union have prompted the large German banks to seek alternative sources of revenue. Deutsche Bank, Commerzbank, and the other large banks have become champions of *Finanzplatz Deutschland*, a single large securities market designed to compete with more established markets in New York and London. As this market has developed, the conservative bias of the large banks has eroded, and many required emergency bailouts in the early twenty-first century.

The final chapter summarizes our policy recommendations and reviews alternative arguments for bank instability. We address arguments about global imbalances, a global saving glut, and capital controls, and we weigh in on the merits of stricter capital requirements for banks, the "too big to fail" problem, and the return of Glass-Steagall regulations that separate commercial and investment banking. We also discuss the key political question of who should regulate, given the landscape of central banks, separate financial regulators, and national and regional agencies, each with varying degrees of independence from electoral politics.

2

Banking Crises, Capital Flows, and Financial Market Structure

The global and European financial crises since 2008 have made abundantly clear, once again, the extremely serious economic and political consequences of financial instability. In their study of the costs of systemic banking crises in industrialized and emerging markets since World War II, Reinhart and Rogoff (2009a) find that crises trigger "deep and prolonged" asset market collapses; on average, real estate markets collapse by 35 percent over six years, while stock prices fall by more than 50 percent, on average, over more than three years. The damage to the real economy from financial crises is even more severe: economic output in the wake of crises falls, on average, by 9 percent over two years, while unemployment rises by 7 percent over more than four years.[1] Similarly, Romer and Romer (2017) find that GDP in OECD countries is typically 9 percent lower five years after an extreme financial crisis.[2] In the United States, the most recent estimate suggests that "the 2007–08 financial crisis persistently lowered output by roughly 7 percentage points. This is a large number: In dollar terms, it represents a lifetime income loss in present-discounted value terms of about $70,000 for every American."[3] Crises also inflict massive damage on government budgets and debt, with government debt levels rising an average of 86 percent during post–World War II systemic banking crises.[4] Relatedly, the resolution costs of banking crises

[1] Reinhart and Rogoff 2009a, 466.
[2] Romer and Romer 2017.
[3] Barnichon, Matthes, and Ziegenbein 2018.
[4] Reinhart and Rogoff 2009a, 466.

are also substantial. In their dataset of systemic banking crises, Laeven and Valencia (2008) find that the average fiscal cost of adjustment to crises is 15 percent of GDP.[5]

As large as these economic costs are, perhaps the most serious and enduring effects of banking crises are their political consequences. A large and growing body of literature in comparative and international political economy highlights the massive impact of financial crises on political stability, government survival, and domestic politics. Crises are sometimes associated with the collapse of authoritarian regimes and are frequently associated with rising street protests, strikes, and electoral losses for incumbent parties in democracies.[6] A key finding in this arena is that crises lead to surges in political extremism. This manifests itself in the rise of new challenger parties on both the left and right, but especially in the rise of political support for right-wing parties.[7] These "hard right turns" are evident across space and time. In their study of more than 800 elections in 20 advanced democracies from 1870 to 2014, in the wake of over 100 financial crises, Funke, Schularick, and Trebesch (2016) find that far-right parties increase their vote share by about a third in the five years following systemic banking distress. They also find that government majorities in parliaments fragment and shrink in the wake of financial crises.[8]

Finally, banking crises inevitably spark domestic and international political conflict over government policy responses and the sharing of the burden of adjustment between different groups within countries and between creditor and debtor countries at the international level.[9] As in past crises, this conflict has been particularly evident within and between EU member-states during the Euro crisis.[10]

[5] Laeven and Valencia 2008.

[6] Chwieroth and Walter 2015b; Crespo-Tenorio, Jensen, and Rosas 2014; Funke, Schularick, and Trebesch 2016; Genovese, Schneider, and Wassmann 2016; Hernández and Kriesi 2016; Pepinsky 2009, 2012; Rosas 2006, 2009.

[7] Ahlquist, Copelovitch, and Walter forthcoming; de Bromhead, Eichengreen, and O'Rourke 2012; Hobolt and de Vries 2015.

[8] See also Trebbi, Mian, and Sufi 2012.

[9] Bechtel, Hainmueller, and Margalit 2014; Chinn and Frieden 2011; Copelovitch, Frieden, and Walter 2016; Dyson 2014; Fernandez-Albertos and Kuo 2016; Frieden 2007; Frieden and Walter 2017; Mosley and Singer 2009; Simmons 1994; Walter 2013.

[10] See Baerg and Hallerberg 2016; Blustein 2016; Copelovitch, Frieden, and Walter 2016; Jones, Kelemen, and Meunier 2016; Mody 2018.

Given these massive economic and political consequences, understanding and explaining why banking crises happen in some countries, at some times, but not in others is of paramount importance for scholars, policymakers, and the citizens of countries across the industrialized world. To explain why crises occur, however, one first needs to define what they are and how to measure them, and to understand how they vary in frequency across space and time. In this chapter, we provide a synoptic overview of the variation in banking crises across the advanced industrialized countries in the post–Bretton Woods era. We illustrate that banking crises are a central feature of developed countries' economies in the modern era of international capital mobility. We discuss the two most widely used metrics of banking crises in empirical research – the World Bank and Reinhart-Rogoff classifications – and we show that the incidence of crises in the industrialized world varies widely according to both of these metrics. Since the 1970s, some countries are far more prone to financial instability than others.

This chapter also shows how our two key explanatory variables – foreign capital inflows and domestic financial market structure – vary across the industrialized world in the post–Bretton Woods era. For capital inflows, we highlight the important distinctions between current account deficits and gross and net portfolio inflows. Our discussion of market structure focuses on the relative degree of competition between banks and securities markets, measured by the ratio of stock market size to bank credit. We discuss and illustrate how these variables vary across space and time and also how they appear to be uncorrelated with each other: market structure changes only gradually, whereas capital inflows ebb and flow with greater intensity.

The chapter concludes by articulating the motivation for the rest of our empirical analyses: past scholarship has identified foreign capital as a likely trigger of financial instability, but there are many examples of countries and time periods in which capital inflows are not destabilizing. The empirical analyses in Chapter 3 seek to explain this variation and identify the conditions under which foreign capital leads to bank failures, and when it is safely channeled through the banking system.

BANKING CRISES IN THE INDUSTRIALIZED WORLD

The globalization of finance is the defining feature of the contemporary world economy. From 1990 to 2005, cross-border capital flows increased from approximately $1 trillion to more than $12 trillion.

Although the global and Eurozone financial crises of the last decade have led to a partial retrenchment of financial globalization, today international capital flows still exceed $5 trillion.[11] This massive growth in international financial integration has brought many benefits in terms of growth, efficiency, and rising living standards. Nonetheless, the globalization of finance has come at a high price: the return of frequent, costly financial crises. Figure 2.1 illustrates the frequency and substantial variation in systemic banking crises across the industrialized world in the post–Bretton Woods era. It presents data from the World Bank *Global Financial Development Database*, which measures large-scale, systemic banking crises, defined as follows:

> Under our definition, in a systemic banking crisis, a country's corporate and financial sectors experience a large number of defaults and financial institutions and corporations face great difficulties repaying contracts on time. As a result, non-performing loans increase sharply and all or most of the aggregate banking system capital is exhausted. This situation may be accompanied by depressed asset prices (such as equity and real estate prices) on the heels of run-ups before the crisis, sharp increases in real interest rates, and a slowdown or reversal in capital flows. In some cases, the crisis is triggered by depositor runs on banks, though in most cases it is a general realization that systemically important financial institutions are in distress.[12]

The World Bank dataset identifies 131 crisis-years for the high-income OECD countries from 1976 to 2011 (out of 760 total country-years). Figure 2.1 clearly illustrates that banking crises are a feature, rather than a bug, of financial systems in modern industrialized countries. Indeed, the absence of banking crises is exceedingly rare; among OECD countries, only Australia, Canada, and New Zealand have not experienced a systemic banking crisis in the post–Bretton Woods era. In contrast, many of the world's richest and largest economies, including the United States, Japan, and the United Kingdom, have been rocked by multiple systemic crises since the 1970s. Even Germany, long held up as a paragon of banking stability in the postwar era, has experienced multiple years of systemic banking crisis in the last fifteen years.

The World Bank's classification is quite restrictive, however. It measures systemic crises – comprehensive problems in the banking system resulting in multiple bank runs and failures, or a systemic pattern of distress across a large number of institutions. Consequently, this definition

[11] McKinsey Global Institute 2017.

[12] Laeven and Valencia 2008, 5.

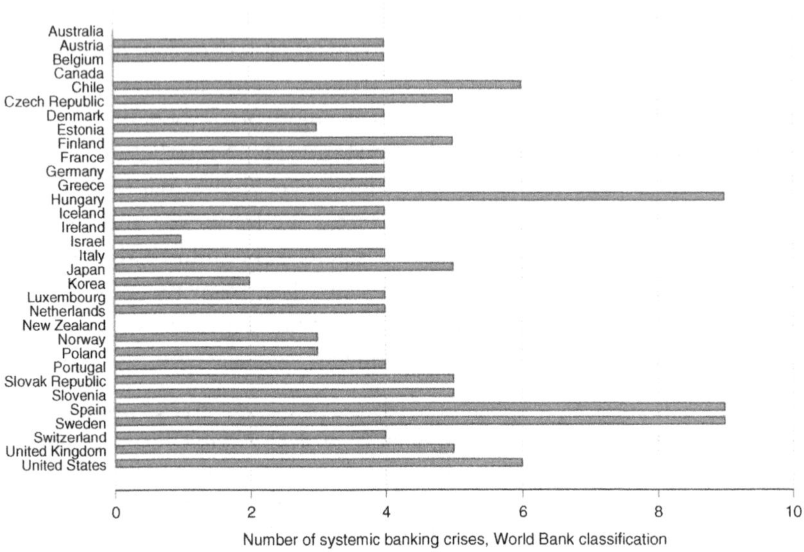

FIGURE 2.1. Total systemic banking crises (World Bank classification), OECD, 1976–2011. *Source:* World Bank, Global Financial Development Database.

does not capture all episodes of banking instability. For example, the World Bank classification codes the United Kingdom as experiencing a banking crisis only in the 2007–11 period, which overlooks major episodes of bank failures and instability in 1974–6, 1984, 1991, and 1995. Likewise, the World Bank classifies the United States as experiencing systemic banking crises only in 1988 (the height of the savings and loan crisis) and 2007–11, but overlooks the wave of major banking problems in the 1984–91 period, including the failure of Continental Illinois (the country's seventh-largest commercial bank) and substantial losses among the money-center banks stemming from the Latin American debt crisis.[13]

For this reason, many researchers also use Reinhart and Rogoff's (hereafter RR) classification of banking crises, which is broader and encompasses a wider range of cases. RR define a banking crisis as follows:

> We mark a banking crisis by two types of events: (1) bank runs that lead to the closure, merging, or takeover by the public sector of one or more financial institutions; or (2) if there are no runs, the closure, merging, takeover, or large-scale government assistance of an important financial institution (or group of institutions), that marks the start of a string of similar outcomes for other financial institutions.[14]

[13] See Singer 2007, chap. 4.

[14] Reinhart and Rogoff 2011, 1680.

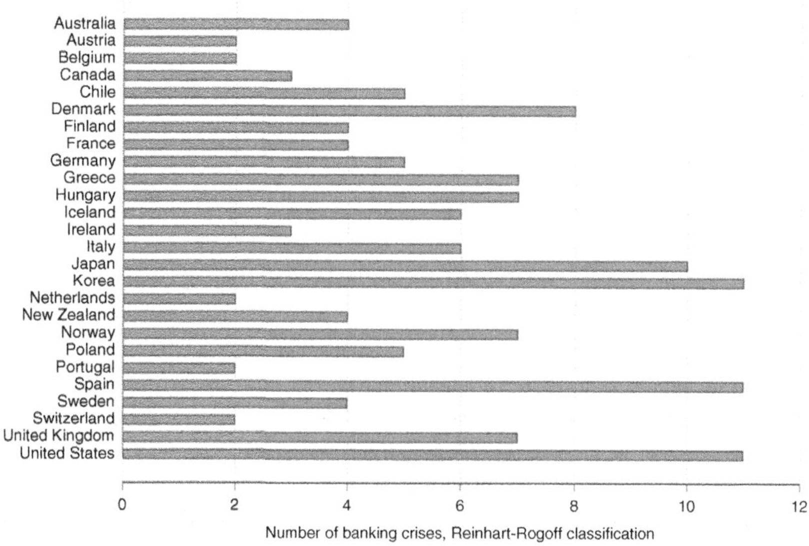

FIGURE 2.2. Total banking crises (Reinhart-Rogoff classification), OECD, 1976–2009. *Source:* Reinhart and Rogoff 2011.

RR's classification is a substantially more encompassing measure than the World Bank measure, which excludes "banking system distress events that affected isolated banks but were not systemic in nature."[15] Consequently, the frequency of RR crises is greater: from 1976 to 2009, there were 139 RR crisis-years across the OECD countries (out of 740 country-years). As Figure 2.2 illustrates, every single one of the OECD countries for which data are available experienced a banking crisis by the broader RR metric.[16] Once again, however, we observe substantial variation: crises are far more prevalent in some countries (e.g., the United States, United Kingdom, Japan, Spain, and Denmark) than others (e.g., Austria, Belgium, Canada, Netherlands, and Switzerland).

Figure 2.3 compares the World Bank and RR classifications across time. In general, as expected, the RR classification is more encompassing, coding crises in a larger number of country-years than the World Bank measure. Both measures, however, illustrate that – with the notable exception of 2003–6 – banking crises have been a regular feature of the

[15] Laeven and Valencia 2008, 6.

[16] The RR data ends in 2009, and data for Luxembourg and several newer OECD members (Czech Republic, Estonia, Israel, Slovakia, Slovenia) that joined the organization from the 1990s onward are missing for the entire period in the RR dataset.

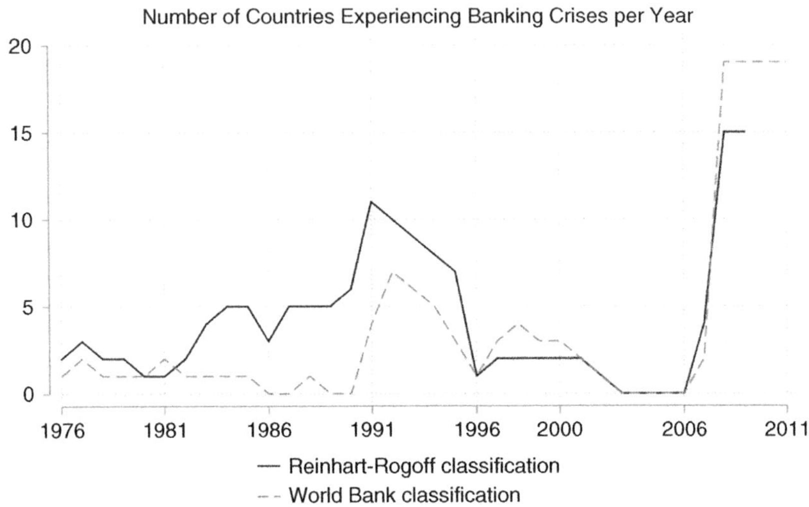

FIGURE 2.3. World Bank vs. Reinhart-Rogoff crisis classifications, OECD countries, 1976–2011. *Source:* World Bank, Global Financial Development Database; Reinhart and Rogoff 2011.

post–Bretton Woods era throughout the industrialized world. In addition to the wave of crises from 2007 onward, systemic banking crises were particularly prevalent in the first half of the 1990s in Scandinavia, Japan, and the post-Communist OECD member countries. While systemic crises were rare in the 1980s, a number of countries, including the United States, United Kingdom, Chile, Spain, Korea, and Iceland experienced smaller crises as measured by the RR classification.

WHAT CAUSES BANKING CRISES? CAPITAL INFLOWS AND FINANCIAL MARKET STRUCTURE

The literature on the determinants of financial crises in developing countries over the last four decades is vast.[17] Our focus is on the sources of banking instability in the industrialized world, where financial markets

[17] For example, Diaz-Alejandro 1985 links the 1980s crises in the Southern Cone to problems stemming from financial liberalization and a surge in foreign credit. Similarly, Calvo 1998 (on "sudden stops") and Kaminsky and Reinhart 1999 (on "twin" crises) identified the potentially destabilizing effects of current account deficits and capital inflows to emerging-market countries. See also Ghosh et al. 2014 on surges in emerging markets, and Efremidze et al. 2017 on the link between surges and sudden stops.

are deeper and securities markets more well-developed than in middle- and low-income countries. The central argument of this book is that variation in the incidence of banking crises can be explained by the interaction of two key variables: international capital inflows and the structure of domestic financial markets. In this section, we provide an overview of both variables across the industrialized world over the last forty years. The data illustrate the general increases in both the magnitude of capital inflows and the relative size of securities markets in industrialized countries in the post–Bretton Woods era. At the same time, we observe substantial variation across the OECD in both variables. We also show that the incidence of banking crises across the industrialized world does not correlate neatly with either capital inflows or financial market structure.

Capital Inflows: Net Flows

As we have discussed previously, the prevailing wisdom about modern financial crises links large capital inflows to domestic credit booms that eventually go bust, leaving banks in distress and inflicting damage on both the financial system and the real economy. Until recently most of this literature emphasized net capital inflows (inflows minus outflows), as measured by current account deficits.[18] According to standard balance of payments accounting, a country's capital account surplus is the mirror image of its current account deficit (mainly the difference between the value of exports and the value of imports), meaning that current account balances provide a readily available proxy for net capital inflows.[19] Figure 2.4 illustrates annual current account balances for the industrialized countries in the post–Bretton Woods era.

One key pattern visible in Figure 2.4 is the general increase in the size of current account balances (both surpluses and deficits) in the post–Bretton Woods era. This is indicative of the aforementioned exponential growth in cross-border financial flows – especially private portfolio capital flows – since the 1990s. With money moving rapidly and easily across borders, we have seen both larger current account deficits and larger surpluses, or what are frequently referred to as "global imbalances."[20]

[18] See Obstfeld 2012, 2.

[19] The current account also includes investment income (e.g., dividends of stock, interest on securities) and direct transfers (e.g., worker remittances and direct foreign aid).

[20] See, e.g., Chinn and Frieden 2011; Iversen and Soskice 2012; Obstfeld and Rogoff 2009; Reinhart and Reinhart 2008; Reinhart and Rogoff 2009b.

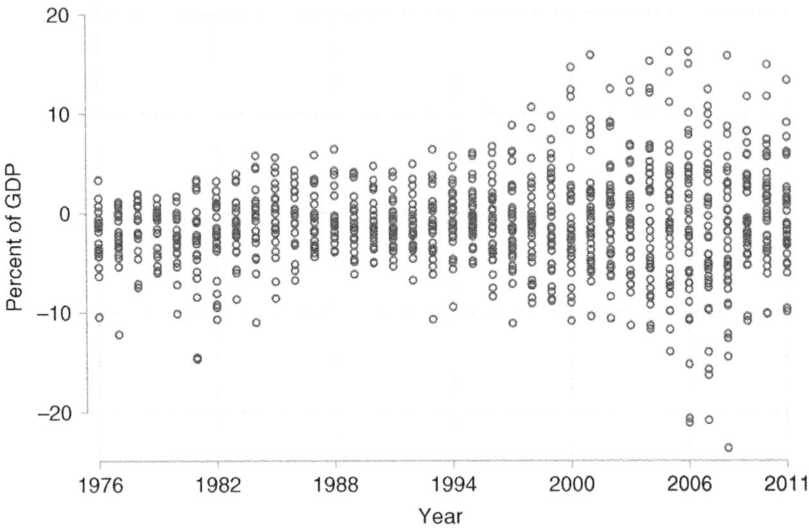

FIGURE 2.4. Current account balance, percent of GDP (net capital flows), OECD, 1976–2011. *Source:* World Bank, Open Data.

At the same time, there is substantial variation, both across countries and over time, in levels of current account imbalances.

As noted in the introduction, a potential problem with using current account balances as a measure of capital inflows is that capital does not always flow from surplus to deficit countries. In the case of the United States from 2002 to 2007, for example, approximately two-thirds of foreign capital inflows arrived from countries with which the United States was not running large current account deficits, such as the United Kingdom and certain Eurozone countries.[21] The primary source of the large US current account deficits prior to the Great Recession – its $300 billion bilateral trade deficit with China – had very little, if anything, to do with either the large influx of foreign capital into the United States in 2002–7 or the collapse of these flows in 2007–9. These facts challenge the "excess saving" view of the financial crisis, in which capital from surplus countries creates inherent distortions as it flows to vulnerable deficit countries.[22] Moreover, recent

[21] Borio and Disyatat 2011; Whelan 2010.
[22] Bernanke 2011.

work by Jordà, Schularick, and Taylor (2011), which examines a set of industrialized countries over 140 years, finds that current account deficits are not statistically significant correlates of banking crises in most of its model specifications.[23]

Capital Inflows: Gross Flows

Both our theory and a growing number of recent studies suggest that gross capital inflows, rather than net capital flows, are most closely associated with the risk of banking crises.[24] For example, Caballero (2016) finds that capital inflow "bonanzas" are strongly associated with banking crises, but that this effect is driven by portfolio equity and debt flows.[25] One key concern with using net capital flows, as measured via current account balances, is that countries may experience large gross inflows or outflows in a given year, even while net flows (as captured by the current account balance) are not particularly large as a share of GDP. In our sample of OECD countries from 1980 to 2011, the correlation between current account balances and gross inflows is only 0.01 (Figure 2.6). A second potential issue with using net capital flows is that they may be measuring productive foreign direct investment (FDI) rather than potentially destabilizing portfolio capital inflows. This is also true with aggregate gross capital inflow measures, which include both FDI and portfolio flows, along with other investments (bank flows, public loans, and trade credit).[26]

Figure 2.5 illustrates the variation across space and time in gross portfolio capital inflows in the industrialized countries since the 1970s. Once again, we see the broad increase in levels of capital flows as a result of financial globalization, as well as the substantial cross-national variation in levels of capital inflows, including the large surges and reversals associated with the Eurozone and global financial crises in the last decade.

Figure 2.6 presents a scatter plot of current account balances (net capital flows) against gross portfolio flows for the OECD countries from 1976 to 2011. The main takeaway from this graphic is that modest current account deficits often mask large gross portfolio capital inflows,

[23] Jordà, Schularick, and Taylor 2011. In a related study, Amri, Richey, and Willett 2016 find only a weak connection between capital inflow surges and credit booms for a sample of 46 countries from 1981 to 2010.

[24] See, e.g., Amri, Richey, and Willett 2016; Forbes and Warnock 2012; Mendoza and Terrones 2012; Rey 2015.

[25] Caballero 2016.

[26] Broner et al. 2013.

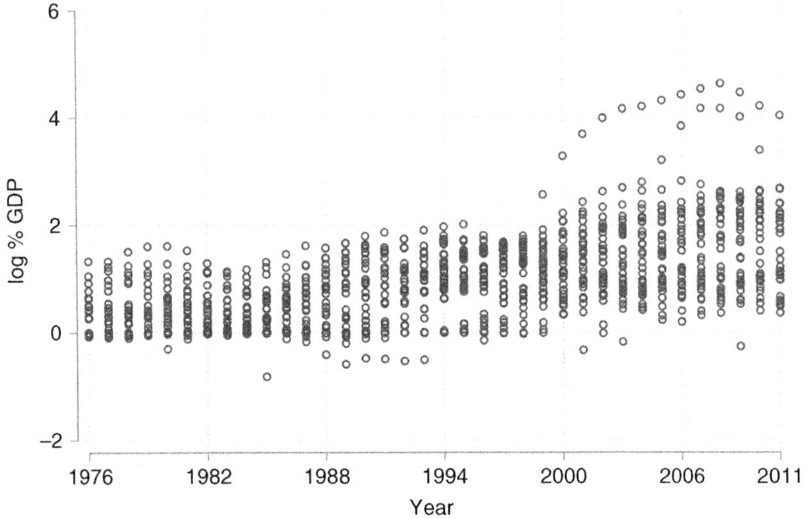

FIGURE 2.5. Portfolio gross inflows (log, % trend GDP, five-year moving average), OECD, 1976–2011. *Source:* Broner et al. 2013/World Bank Data Catalog.

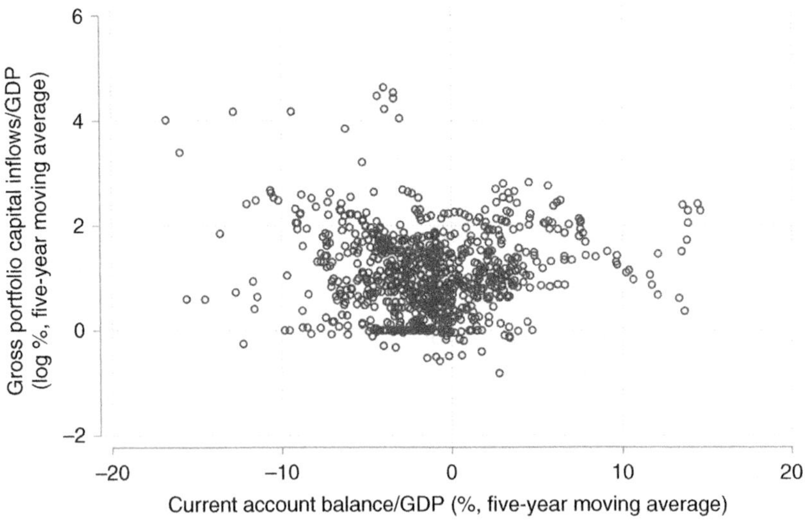

FIGURE 2.6. Gross portfolio and net capital inflows, OECD countries, 1976–2011. *Source:* Broner et al. 2013/World Bank Data Catalog.

as in the cases of Ireland and Iceland from 2005 to 2011 (the outlier dots at the top left of the scatter plot). This suggests that net inflows, as measured by current account deficits, may not capture the full story of the influence of capital inflows on financial stability. Large gross capital inflows, even if offset by equally large outflows, may still trigger banking crises under certain conditions.

Capital Inflows and Banking Crises

Figures 2.7 and 2.8 present box-and-whisker plots showing the distribution of gross portfolio and net capital flows (current account balances) in systemic banking crisis and non-crisis years across the OECD from 1976 to 2011. A box-and-whisker graph illustrates the center, spread, and overall range of data across distributions. The box consists of the observations ranging between the 25th and 75th percentile, with the line in the middle of the box indicating the median in the distribution. The whiskers are the two lines outside the box illustrating the maximum and minimum values, excluding outliers. Finally, the dots illustrate outlier cases in the distribution.

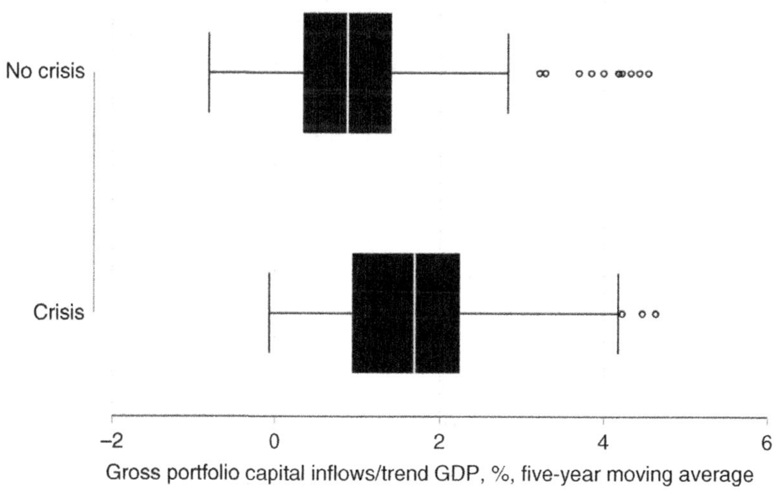

FIGURE 2.7. Systemic banking crises by gross portfolio capital inflows, OECD countries, 1976–2011. *Source:* World Bank, Global Financial Development Database; Broner et al. 2013.

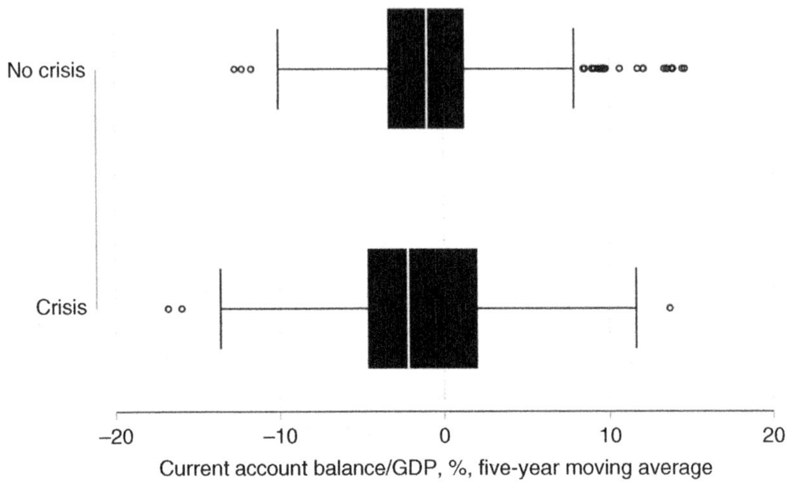

FIGURE 2.8. Systemic banking crises by net capital inflows, OECD countries, 1976–2011. *Source:* World Bank, Global Financial Development Database/ Open Data.

The patterns here suggest that large capital inflows – measured either as net or gross portfolio flows – are not always associated with banking instability. Some countries with low levels of gross inflows, such as Sweden, Hungary, and Spain, have experienced frequent banking crises, while others with relatively large gross inflows (e.g., Canada, Australia) have not experienced any systemic crises in the post–Bretton Woods era. Moreover, while Figure 2.7 suggests a positive correlation (0.26 in the sample) between gross portfolio flows and systemic banking crises, Figure 2.8 shows the extremely weak relationship between current account balances and financial stability (correlation of 0.06 in the sample). Regardless of which measure is used, capital inflows do not appear to have a straightforward relationship to banking crises. In some cases, inflows are correlated with crises, while in other cases, countries experience large capital inflows without any negative effect on financial stability.

Financial Market Structure

Why are capital inflows destabilizing in some cases but not others? To understand why this is the case, we must take into account the structure of domestic financial markets. A common assumption in the empirical literature on financial crises is that banking systems are all alike.

Scholars generally pay insufficient attention to the variation in national financial systems, including the relative importance of banks and non-bank financial institutions across countries and over time. Our central hypothesis is that banks take on more risk when they face competition from large, well-developed securities markets, and these risks are magnified in the face of capital inflows. Therefore, a national financial system with a large and deep securities market is more likely to experience a banking crisis in the face of capital inflows than a financial system with a relatively underdeveloped securities market. This argument helps to explain why capital inflows are sometimes, but not always, a source of instability for banking systems in the advanced industrialized countries.

The prominence of securities in finance is a central feature distinguishing financial systems in advanced industrialized economies from those in developing countries. Indeed, while securities play a role in the markets of all but the most primitive of developing countries, securities markets are far deeper and diverse in developed countries. Nonetheless, securities markets – both stock and bond markets – are more important in certain OECD countries than in others. Stock markets are, by a large margin, most developed in the United States. In 2011, the total value of shares traded on US stock markets, relative to GDP, was 251 percent, nearly 100 percent more than the second-highest value country, Korea (152 percent). In contrast, stock markets are far smaller in countries such as Germany (42 percent), France (48 percent), and Canada (82 percent). Private bond market capitalization also varies widely, with the largest markets in Denmark (168 percent of GDP), Ireland (113 percent), and the United States (91 percent) in 2012, dwarfing the relative size of those in France (56 percent), Canada (25 percent), and Germany (24 percent).

For the purposes of our argument, which emphasizes the degree of competition between banks and securities markets, the most relevant metric is not the absolute size of stock or bond markets, but rather the relative size of the securities and banking sectors in the financial system. Table 2.1 shows the substantial variation in the ratio of stock market trading volume to bank lending, which we label the market/bank ratio. The United States stands as an outlier among industrialized countries with its high market/bank ratio indicating the unmatched size of American securities markets. For this reason, scholars should exercise greater caution in drawing broad conclusions about the determinants of financial crises from the US case. Even beyond the United States, however, we see a high degree of variation in the relative size of banking and securities markets. In general, the newer, post-emerging-market OECD

TABLE 2.1. *Market/bank ratio, OECD countries, average, 1990–2011*

Country	Market/Bank Ratio
United States	1.94
Switzerland	0.94
Korea	0.85
Finland	0.81
Sweden	0.71
Australia	0.45
United Kingdom	0.45
Spain	0.43
Netherlands	0.43
Hungary	0.39
Japan	0.39
Canada	0.35
France	0.33
Greece	0.33
Italy	0.32
Germany	0.31
Israel	0.26
Iceland	0.25
Czech Republic	0.25
Norway	0.25
Denmark	0.24
Poland	0.22
Belgium	0.18
Portugal	0.16
Ireland	0.16
Chile	0.15
Estonia	0.14
New Zealand	0.11
Austria	0.07
Slovenia	0.07
Slovak Republic	0.05
Luxembourg	0.02

Source: World Bank Global Financial Development Database, calculated as the ratio of stock market trading volume to total bank lending.

countries have miniscule securities markets relative to the size of their banking sectors, mirroring the broader pattern we see when comparing developed and developing economies. At the other end of the scale, we see that countries with very high market/bank ratios include some of the world's largest and/or most sophisticated financial systems (Switzerland, Japan, United Kingdom), as well as those with large securities markets but relatively small banking sectors (Sweden, Finland, and Korea).

What explains this variation in the market structure of domestic financial systems? The importance of bank-based finance relative to decentralized securities markets has its roots in policy decisions and political battles often from the distant past. We explore these policy decisions and the political determinants of this variation in financial market structure in detailed case studies of Canada and Germany in Chapters 4 and 5 of the book.

For the moment, we note that trading in securities can only thrive in environments with strong rule of law and detailed regulations for information disclosure, accounting, and exchange.[27] Stock exchanges often emerge as modest subnational markets that cater to the needs of a specific industry, such as mining or heavy industry. For deep national markets to emerge, governments must take steps to harmonize the regulations across these regional markets – steps that may or may not be popular with industries and political leaders. For example, high-risk oil exploration companies might resist strict disclosure rules that could deter investors, whereas low-risk steel companies might be content to reveal a full range of financial information to investors. It might take an exogenous shock, like an economic recession, to spur governments to overcome these divergent interests and create a national stock market with a single set of regulations.

Moreover, the banking industry may, at times, feel threatened by growing securities markets that could constitute a threat to their core lending business. Our case studies reveal that bankers are often wary of stock markets, and sometimes determined to prevent them from expanding beyond their regional jurisdictions.

Our view of the politics of securities markets is often at odds with the literature on the development of financial markets. For example, a common refrain about banking markets in early US history is that their fragmentation led inexorably to a highly developed national securities market. The narrative includes President Jackson's veto of the

[27] Allen and Gale 2000.

re-chartering of the Second Bank of the United States, the longtime prohibition against interstate bank branching, and deeply held populist fears of large financial institutions, all of which hobbled banking markets for nearly two centuries.[28] Even the creation of the Federal Reserve System in 1913 solidified a regional, decentralized structure of bank governance and control.[29] In summing up the history of banking in the United States, Allen and Gale (2000) note that the weaknesses of US banks helped to strengthen the role of financial markets. They argue that securities, in a sense, filled a void that commercial banks were not able to fill, and the relative prominence of securities markets endures to this day.[30]

We are highly skeptical of these functionalist views of financial market development, which assert that they emerge due to an underlying national-level need. Scholars of banking markets agree that banks did not automatically settle their differences and join forces to create a concentrated, nationally diversified banking system in the United States, despite the overwhelming need for capital by a variety of industries. Why, then, should we believe that securities markets are immune from the political wrangling and regional discord that characterizes the banking market? In short, the need for capital does not trump all political resistance to securities market development or banking market development.

The accumulation of policy decisions, firm behaviors, and market decisions required to develop a thriving securities market implies a degree of path dependence in a country's financial market characteristics.[31] A financial system dominated by bank lending is unlikely to morph into a securities-based system in a short time, even though securities markets are gradually becoming more prominent in many countries around the world. Moreover, it is unlikely that foreign capital can, by itself, prompt such a transformation. Indeed, Figures 2.9 and 2.10 illustrate the relative stability of market characteristics over the last three decades, even in the face of large changes in current account balances (and resulting capital inflows or outflows), for Canada and Germany, respectively. The figures depict the current account deficit (in which higher numbers correspond to larger deficits) and levels of gross portfolio capital inflows to trend GDP. The figures demonstrate the relative stability of financial market

[28] See, e.g., Calomiris and Haber 2014; Roe 1994.
[29] Lowenstein 2015.
[30] Allen and Gale 2000, 34.
[31] Hall and Soskice 2001; see also Pierson 2004; Thelen 2004.

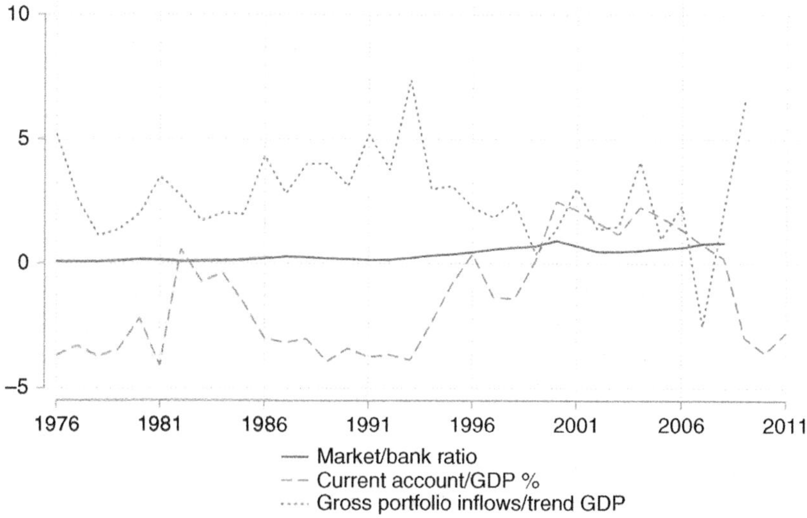

FIGURE 2.9. Capital inflows and financial market structure, Canada, 1976–2011. *Source:* World Bank Open Data and Global Financial Development Database; Broner et al. 2013.

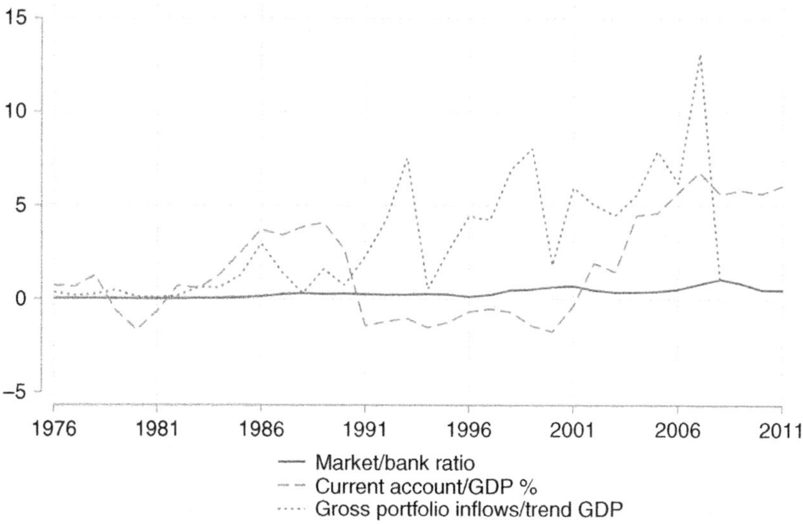

FIGURE 2.10. Capital inflows and financial market structure, Germany, 1976–2011. *Source:* World Bank Open Data and Global Financial Development Database; Broner et al. 2013.

characteristics from 1976 to 2011 even in the face of widely variable current account deficits and persistent gross portfolio capital inflows.

One potential alternative way to determine the relative importance of securities markets is to measure which activities are permitted by regulation and law, rather than relative market size. Currently, the best available source for this approach is the IMF's New Database on Financial Reforms, which contains information on a wide range of variables, including banking restrictions, financial liberalization, state ownership of banks, degree of securitization of the financial system, and the stringency of banking regulation for ninety-one countries from 1973 to 2005.[32] The database consists of a 21-point index of financial reform, with higher values generally corresponding to greater liberalization of the financial sector. Within this aggregate index, the authors code a 4-point index based on the question "Has a country taken measures to develop securities markets?" This subindex consists of four categories: 0 = no securities market exists; 1 = a securities market is starting to form with the introduction of auctioning of T-bills or the establishment of a security commission; 2 = further measures have been taken to develop securities markets (tax exemptions, introduction of medium- and long-term government bonds in order to build the benchmark of a yield curve, policies to develop corporate bond and equity markets, or the introduction of a primary dealer system to develop government security markets); and 3 = further policy measures have been taken to develop derivative markets or to broaden the institutional investor base by deregulating portfolio investments and pension funds, or completing the full deregulation of stock exchanges.

While this legal/regulatory-based index of securities market development is appealing in theory, it is less useful in practice for measuring the relative importance of securities markets in financial systems across the OECD countries. Indeed, there are at least two major problems with this alternative approach to measuring the structure of domestic financial markets. First, the data are not available for the last decade, and coverage within the OECD itself is spotty prior to that. Consequently, we cannot use this index to conduct quantitative analysis of the influence of financial market structure on banking crises for much of the post–Bretton Woods era. Second, there is extremely little variation in overall financial liberalization and effectively none in the subindex on securities market regulation. All countries within the high-income OECD group score

[32] Abiad, Detragiache, and Tressel 2008.

identically as having highly developed securities markets. Unfortunately, as the charts above illustrated, this uniformity masks substantial variation in the actual size and depth of stock and bond markets across the industrialized world. For this reason, we focus on the market/bank ratio as the best available empirical metric of the relative importance of banking versus securities markets in the financial system.

Financial Market Structure and Banking Crises

Figure 2.11 presents another box-and-whisker plot, this time showing the distribution of the market/bank ratio in systemic banking crisis and non-crisis years across the OECD from 1976 to 2011. As with capital flows, we see that the relationship between financial market structure and banking crises is not straightforward. In some cases, countries with more well-developed securities markets (larger market/bank ratios) experience crises, while in others, countries avoid financial instability. Although the median market/bank ratio is higher for crisis years, the overall distribution of financial market structure is quite similar in crisis and non-crisis cases. Thus, market structure alone does not seem to be a clear determinant of banking crises.

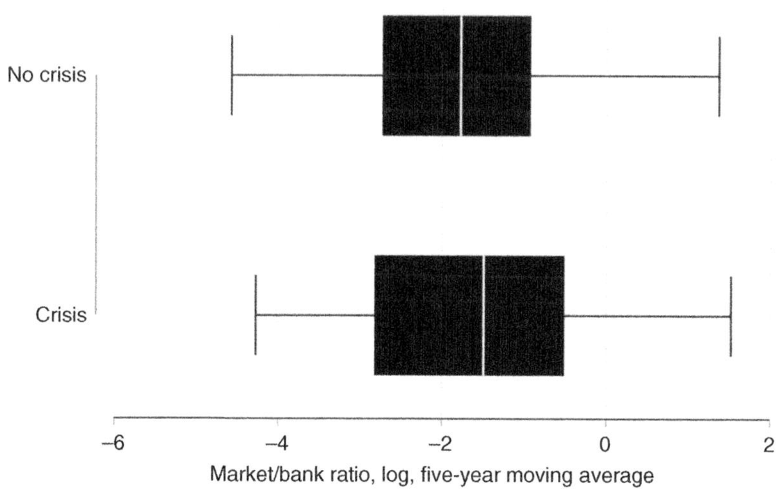

FIGURE 2.11. Systemic banking crises by market/bank ratio, OECD countries, 1976–2011. *Source:* World Bank, Global Financial Development Database.

Ultimately, neither capital inflows nor financial market structure alone are clear determinants of banking crises across space and time. Instead, as we have argued above, it is the combination of these two variables that triggers financial instability in some cases but not others. When large capital inflows meet a domestic financial system in which banks compete alongside large, well-developed securities markets, a country is at the greatest risk of experiencing financial instability.

CONCLUSION

In this chapter, we have provided an overview of banking crises in the industrialized world over the last four decades and highlighted the substantial variation in the two key variables – foreign capital flows and domestic financial market structure – that together determine why some industrialized countries have suffered banking crises while others have not. In the following chapter, we present statistical evidence demonstrating that this pattern holds across the OECD countries in the post–Bretton Woods era. Our results show that foreign capital is sometimes a trigger of banking crises, but only under certain conditions. The structure of domestic financial markets is a key mediating variable determining when global imbalances lead to financial instability.

3

Capital Inflows, Market Structure, and Banking Crises

Empirical Evidence

Thus far in the book, we have described the substantial variation in banking crises, capital inflows, and financial market structure across the industrialized world in the post–Bretton Woods era, and we have argued that the destabilizing impact of capital inflows is conditional on the relative prominence of banks versus non-bank financial markets. When banks compete with well-developed national securities markets to provide financing for businesses, their appetite for risk increases. As we discussed in Chapter 2, securities markets can incentivize even the most traditional commercial banks to take on more risks, even if those risks do not appear to be closely tied to securities markets. Capital inflows amplify this risk and increase the chance of a banking crisis. In contrast, when banks operate alongside relatively underdeveloped securities markets, they maintain their conservative bias and capital inflows are less likely to be destabilizing. Ultimately, it is the combination of foreign capital inflows and domestic financial market structure that tips the balance between banking stability and banking crises.

In this chapter, we present quantitative empirical evidence in support of this logic. At both the country- and bank-level, we find strong evidence in support of our book's central argument. The centerpiece of the chapter is a statistical analysis of the determinants of banking crises in the OECD countries from 1976 to 2011. The analysis shows that large international capital inflows are strongly correlated with banking crises, but only conditional on the structure of domestic financial markets. In contrast, other political factors, such as government partisanship and the size of legislative majorities, have relatively little influence on financial stability. In a series of robustness analyses, we also demonstrate that our key explanatory variables – capital inflows and financial market structure – are not simply serving as proxies for alternative explanations of banking crises, including levels of bank concentration and private credit growth.

The chapter also includes a second set of statistical analyses aimed at isolating the observable bank-level implications of our argument linking competition between banks and securities markets to an increased likelihood of banking crises. These results suggest that capital inflows are correlated with lower levels of bank capital and higher levels of insolvency risk, but only in financial systems where banks compete alongside large securities markets. Thus, capital inflows in more securitized financial systems adversely affect the *quality* of bank lending and the composition of balance sheets, rather than causing increases in the *volume* of bank credit. In other words, capital inflows appear to trigger banking crises not because they cause credit booms (surges in the amount of bank lending), but because they lead banks to reduce their capital holdings and lend to riskier customers. This decline in the quality of banks' loan portfolios, rather than an increase in the number and amount of loans, appears to be the smoking gun linking capital inflows to banking crises in industrialized countries.

DETERMINANTS OF BANKING CRISES IN OECD COUNTRIES

In order to test our argument linking capital inflows and financial market structure to the incidence of banking crises, we employ time-series cross-sectional analysis of data covering up to thirty-one OECD countries from 1976 to 2011.[1] Our unit of analysis is the country-year, and our dependent variables are a binary indicator of a banking crisis and country-level measures of bank capital and insolvency risk. We employ the following basic model:

$DV_{it} = \beta_0 + \beta_1$ *Capital inflows* $+ \beta_2$ *Financial market structure* $+ \beta_3$ *Capital inflows*Market Structure* $+ \beta_4$ *Private bank credit/GDP* $+ \beta_5$ *Per capita GDP growth* $+ \beta_6$ *Inflation* $+ \beta_6$ *OECD average per capita GDP growth* $+ \beta_7$ *US real interest rate* $+ \beta_8$ *Total global banking crises* $+$ *temporal controls* $+$ *country fixed effects* $+ \varepsilon$

In our banking crisis models, the main explanatory variables enter as five-year, lagged moving averages, rather than current-year observations

[1] Our banking crisis samples include all countries currently in the OECD, even if they were not members at the start of the sample. In the bank-level analysis below, our sample is restricted by data availability to twenty-nine countries from 1990 to 2009.

or one-year lags. Our aim is to ensure that we are picking up systematic trends in the explanatory variables, rather than year-to-year fluctuations in capital inflows, financial market structure, or major macroeconomic indicators.

The banking crisis models are estimated using both conditional (fixed effect) logit models and fixed-effect OLS (linear probability) models (LPM), in order to address issues of unobserved heterogeneity. Following Carter and Signorino (2010), we include the country-specific number of years since the last banking crisis, its square, and its cube, in order to control for temporal dependence in the data.[2] The bank capital and insolvency risk models employ OLS with country fixed effects. To address issues of heteroskedasticity, we estimate the logit models using robust standard errors clustered on country and the OLS models using Driscoll-Kraay standard errors, which also control for cross-sectional dependence in the data.[3]

Dependent and Independent Variables

Our dependent variables are the World Bank and Reinhart-Rogoff classifications of banking crises described in Chapter 2. *WB banking crisis* and *RR banking crisis*, drawn from these datasets, are binary variables that each take a value of 1 if country *i* experiences a banking crisis in year *t*. Our two key explanatory variables are international capital inflows and financial market structure, along with their interaction. Our theory and a growing number of recent studies suggest that gross capital inflows, rather than net capital flows, are most closely associated with the risk of banking crises.[4] For example, Caballero (2016) asserts that capital inflow "bonanzas" are strongly associated with banking crises, but that this effect is driven by portfolio equity and debt flows.[5] One key concern with using net capital flows (measured via current account balances) is that countries may experience large gross inflows or outflows in a given year, even while net flows (as captured by the current account balance) are not very large as a share of GDP. Indeed, in our sample of OECD countries from 1976 to 2011, the correlation between current account balances and gross inflows is only 0.01. A second potential

[2] Carter and Signorino 2010.

[3] Driscoll and Kraay 1998.

[4] See, e.g., Amri, Richey, and Willett 2016; Forbes and Warnock 2012; Mendoza and Terrones 2012.

[5] Caballero 2016.

issue with using net capital flows is that they may be measuring productive foreign direct investment (FDI) rather than potentially destabilizing portfolio capital inflows. This is also true with aggregate gross capital inflow measures, which include both FDI and portfolio flows, along with "other investments" (bank flows, public loans, and trade credit).[6]

For these reasons, our primary measure of capital inflows is *gross portfolio flows*, the five-year lagged moving average of gross portfolio capital flows as a share of trend GDP. This variable is calculated from a newly available World Bank dataset on gross capital inflows. It captures equity and debt inflows.[7] In our view, using gross portfolio inflows addresses these concerns and allows us to isolate in our models the sustained gross inflows from foreigners that are part and parcel of the dominant story linking capital inflows to banking crises. Nonetheless, while gross portfolio flows are our preferred measure of capital inflows, we also test models using net capital flows as a robustness check. For these models, we substitute the variable *net flows*, the five-year lagged moving average of the current account surplus/deficit in country i at time t, as a share of GDP. For ease of interpretation, we rescale this variable such that higher values of net flows indicate greater deficits, rather than surpluses. The current account balance is the mirror image of the capital account balance, so a current account deficit necessarily implies a capital account surplus, or net inflow of capital from the rest of the world. Current account data are taken from the World Bank.

Our second key independent variable is the domestic financial market structure of a country. This variable is a measure of the relative importance of securities markets relative to traditional banking in the domestic financial system in country i at time t. Identifying an optimal measure of bank-based versus market-based systems is difficult, given the diversity of financial instruments (stocks, bonds, derivatives) involved and because one must decide whether to measure the size and depth of securities markets or the degree to which financial regulations permit markets to thrive. No single metric captures both of these dimensions, but these variables are highly correlated. In this chapter, we focus

[6] Broner et al. 2013.

[7] The specific variable is the "portfolio investment liabilities" (PIL) component of CIF, the "aggregate gross inflows by foreigners" variable in the Broner et al. database. The authors scale PIL by trend GDP, using the Hodrick-Prescott filter and nominal GDP data from the World Bank's *World Development Indicators* and the IMF's *World Economic Outlook* (Broner et al. 2013, 5).

on *market/bank ratio*, the ratio of stock market volume traded to bank lending, expressed as a natural log.

To calculate market/bank ratio, we draw on two component variables from the World Bank's Global Financial Development Database.[8] The stock market variable, which equals total shares traded on domestic stock exchanges as a percentage of GDP, serves as a useful – albeit imperfect – proxy for the overall depth and liquidity of securities markets. It is theoretically possible for a country to have large and well-developed stock markets in the absence of similar bond markets. Historically, however, bond markets – driven initially in most countries by sovereign lending – have preceded stock market development. Moreover, in the contemporary global economy, the geographical correlation between the largest stock markets and the most complex derivatives markets is extremely high. For these reasons, we believe market/bank ratio to be a reasonable proxy of the size and depth of securities markets overall. The bank lending variable, which measures private credit extended by deposit money banks as a percentage of GDP, measures the size of the traditional commercial banking sector. Higher values of market/bank ratio indicate a more prominent securities market relative to traditional bank financial intermediation.

Control Variables

In addition to our main explanatory variables, we include several additional variables as controls for alternative factors that might influence the probability of banking crises. The first two variables, *per capita GDP growth* and *inflation*, control for country-specific macroeconomic conditions that might influence financial stability. Data for both variables are taken from the World Bank's World Development Indicators.[9] We also include *private credit by deposit money banks to GDP* as a control for both general financial market depth and level of development, and to ensure that market/bank ratio is capturing the relative size of banking and securities markets rather than simply the size of the banking sector or the baseline level of financial depth in a country.[10] This variable also enters as a natural log of the five-year moving average.

[8] Čihák et al. 2012. See http://data.worldbank.org/data-catalog/global-financial-development.

[9] GDP is measured in constant 2005 dollars.

[10] Private bank credit/GDP and liquid liabilities to GDP, another commonly used measure of financial development/depth, are correlated at 0.78. Our results are unchanged if we substitute the latter into our models as the control for financial depth.

In addition, we include several variables identified in the literature as year-specific global factors affecting financial stability for the countries in our sample.[11] The first of these is *OECD average per capita GDP growth*, the lagged average growth rate of GDP per capita (constant \$2005) in the OECD countries in year *t*. The second variable is *US real interest rate*, the lagged average on the yield on US short-term T-bills in year *t*. Past work has found that reductions in global interest rates and slower growth in the world's major economies are associated with increased probabilities of capital inflows in developing countries.[12] We also include the lagged number of banking crises in the world as a further control for the level of global financial stability. Table 3.1 presents summary statistics for all of the variables in our dataset.

Determinants of Banking Crises: Results

Table 3.2 presents the results of our regression analysis of the determinants of banking crises. We begin first with a baseline specification (Model 1) that includes only the control variables. In Model 2, we introduce gross portfolio inflows, which is positive and significant at the 95 percent confidence level, indicating a correlation between higher levels of capital inflows and an increased probability of banking crises. In Model 3, we introduce market/bank ratio and the multiplicative interaction between gross portfolio inflows and market/bank ratio. Model 4 replicates Model 3 but substitutes the RR crisis measure for the WB variable. Models 5 and 6, respectively, re-estimate the fully interactive model, for each crisis variable, using a linear probability model (LPM) in lieu of the conditional logit specification. Finally, Models 7 and 8 present the fully interactive models but substitute net flows (current account balances) for gross portfolio inflows.

In the baseline model, the results reflect past findings in the large literature on financial crises. Crises are strongly and positively correlated with private credit growth, inflation, and income growth, and negatively correlated with the average income growth rate in the industrialized countries. There is also strong evidence of temporal dependence in the incidence of banking crises among the OECD countries. These results on the control variables are broadly consistent across all of the specifications in Table 3.2.

11 Reinhart and Reinhart 2008.

12 Fernandez-Arias and Montiel 1996; Reinhart and Reinhart 2008.

TABLE 3.1. *Summary statistics*

Variable	Observations	Mean	Std. Dev.	Minimum	Maximum
Banking crisis (World Bank)	760	0.17	0.38	0	1
Banking crisis (Reinhart-Rogoff)	740	0.19	0.39	0	1
Tier 1 capital (log)	619	2.21	0.32	1.00	3.53
Z-score (log)	632	3.83	0.23	2.74	5.22
Gross portfolio inflows (log, % trend GDP)	760	1.12	0.85	−0.82	4.63
Current account deficit/GDP (%)	701	0.88	4.36	−14.61	16.79
Market/bank ratio (log)	760	−1.69	1.38	−4.44	1.52
Constant GDP per capita growth (%)	760	2.49	1.99	−7.35	10.94
Inflation (%, log)	760	9.57	18.55	−0.59	196.14
Private bank credit/GDP (%, log)	760	4.02	0.63	2.30	5.39
Total world banking crises (WB)	760	13.43	10.12	0	30
Total world banking crises (RR)	740	12.98	7.21	1	26
OECD average GDP growth rate (%)	760	2.22	1.75	−4.49	4.15
US real interest rate (%)	760	4.80	2.08	−1.28	8.72
Years since last banking crisis (WB)	760	13.43	10.12	0	30

TABLE 3.2. *Regression results, banking crisis models*

Model	1	2	3	4	5	6	7	8
Specification	*Logit*	*Logit*	*Logit*	*Logit*	*LPM*	*LPM*	*Logit*	*Logit*
Banking Crisis Variable	*World Bank*	*World Bank*	*World Bank*	*Reinhart-Rogoff*	*World Bank*	*Reinhart-Rogoff*	*World Bank*	*Reinhart-Rogoff*
Capital Flows Variable	*Gross Flows*	*Gross Flows*	*Gross Flows*	*Gross Flows*	*Gross Flows*	*Gross Flows*	*Net Flows*	*Net Flows*
Gross portfolio inflows/trend GDP (%, log)		1.180 [0.342]***	1.921 [0.519]***	1.672 [0.453]***	0.145 [0.041]***	0.143 [0.047]***		
Market/bank ratio (log)			−0.714 [0.348]**	−0.629 [0.272]**	−0.084 [0.023]***	−0.069 [0.034]***	−0.013 [0.241]	−0.258 [0.216]
Gross inflows*market/bank ratio			0.275 [0.188]	0.168 [0.159]	0.028 [0.016]*	0.016 [0.022]		
Current account (net inflows)/GDP (%, log)							0.460 [0.112]***	0.383 [0.100]***
Net inflows*market/bank ratio							0.059 [0.046]	0.041 [0.051]

Private bank credit/GDP (%, log)	7.678 [1.123]***	7.511 [1.176]***	7.550 [1.186]***	0.758 [0.586]	0.304 [0.059]***	0.725 [0.095]***	8.483 [1.201]***	3.279 [0.699]***
Inflation (%)	0.117 [0.024]***	0.131 [0.025]***	0.131 [0.026]***	0.031 [0.015]**	0.003 [0.001]**	0.003 [0.001]***	0.160 [0.027]***	0.041 [0.018]**
Per capita GDP growth ($2005, %)	0.463 [0.127]***	0.495 [0.129]***	0.533 [0.134]***	0.170 [0.103]*	0.012 [0.014]	0.018 [0.014]	0.611 [0.146]***	0.254 [0.125]**
US real interest rate (%)	0.093 [0.104]	0.135 [0.106]	0.098 [0.109]	0.247 [0.098]**	0.004 [0.014]	0.017 [0.013]	0.069 [0.110]	0.262 [0.103]**
OECD average per capita GDP growth (%)	−0.292 [0.111]***	−0.296 [0.115]***	−0.263 [0.116]**	−0.316 [0.123]**	−0.023 [0.009]**	−0.033 [0.012]***	−0.327 [0.117]***	−0.352 [0.132]***
Banking crises worldwide (count)	0.029 [0.020]	0.022 [0.021]	0.024 [0.022]	−0.065 [0.028]**	0.000 [0.003]	−0.009 [0.003]**	0.050 [0.023]**	−0.038 [0.030]
Years since last banking crisis	−0.643 [0.114]***	−0.685 [0.116]***	−0.630 [0.116]***	−0.851 [0.103]***	−0.073 [0.017]***	−0.115 [0.019]***	−0.525 [0.121]***	−0.725 [0.107]***
Years since last banking crisis^2	0.023 [0.006]***	0.025 [0.006]***	0.022 [0.006]***	0.045 [0.007]***	0.003 [0.001]**	0.006 [0.001]***	0.015 [0.007]**	0.035 [0.007]***

(continued)

TABLE 3.2 *(continued)*

Model	1	2	3	4	5	6	7	8
Specification	*Logit*	*Logit*	*Logit*	*Logit*	*LPM*	*LPM*	*Logit*	*Logit*
Banking Crisis Variable	*World Bank*	*World Bank*	*World Bank*	*Reinhart-Rogoff*	*World Bank*	*Reinhart-Rogoff*	*World Bank*	*Reinhart-Rogoff*
Capital Flows Variable	*Gross Flows*	*Gross Flows*	*Gross Flows*	*Gross Flows*	*Gross Flows*	*Gross Flows*	*Net Flows*	*Net Flows*
Years since last banking crisis[3]	0.000 [0.000]**	0.000 [0.000]***	0.000 [0.000]**	−0.001 [0.000]***	0.000 [0.000]*	0.000 [0.000]***	0.000 [0.000]	0.000 [0.000]***
Constant					−0.943 [0.318]***	0.104 [0.469]		
Observations	760	760	760	740	760	740	722	650
Countries	28	28	28	27	28	27	30	27
Log-likelihood	−118.972	−113.022	−110.993	−170.817	−76.010	−170.685	−108.212	−147.660
*AIC*n*	255.944	246.044	245.986	365.634	176.020	365.369	240.423	319.320
BIC	297.644	292.377	301.586	420.914	231.620	420.649	295.407	373.044

$^{*}p < 0.1$; $^{**}p < 0.05$; $^{***}p < 0.01$.
Models 1–4, 7–8: Conditional (fixed effects) logit.
Models 5–6: Linear probability models (OLS with country fixed effects & Driscoll-Kraay SEs).
2: Years since last banking crisis squared.
3: Years since last banking crisis cubed.

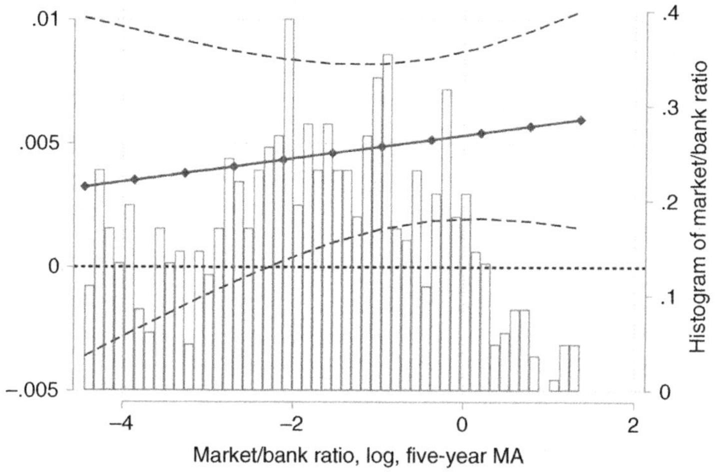

FIGURE 3.1. Average conditional marginal effect of gross portfolio capital inflows by market/bank ratio (World Bank banking crisis, Model 5, Table 3.2).

In Model 2, we add gross portfolio flows to the model. This variable is positively and significantly correlated with banking crises, as expected. In Model 3, we introduce market/bank ratio and its interaction with gross portfolio flows. As the goodness-of-fit statistics indicate, this specification is strongly preferred to the baseline Model 1, and also weakly preferred to Model 2. Moreover, the three components of the multiplicative interaction are jointly significant at the 99 percent confidence level. As noted above, Models 4–8 illustrate that this result is not dependent on the choice of specification (logit vs. LPM), banking crisis classification (WB vs. RR), or measure of capital flows (gross portfolio vs. net/current account).[13]

In these multiplicative interactive models, however, one cannot simply interpret the individual regression coefficients on the interaction terms and their components. Rather, as Figures 3.1–3.4 illustrate,

[13] There is an ongoing debate in economics and political science about the desirability of using probit/logit models versus OLS (linear probability models) for analyzing binary data. See Angrist and Pischke 2008; Beck 2015. Our results are robust to either approach. In generating the figures in this analysis, we employ the LPM specifications because of the greater ease of generating and interpreting marginal effects with this approach. These effects are "sample average" marginal effects (Beck 2015).

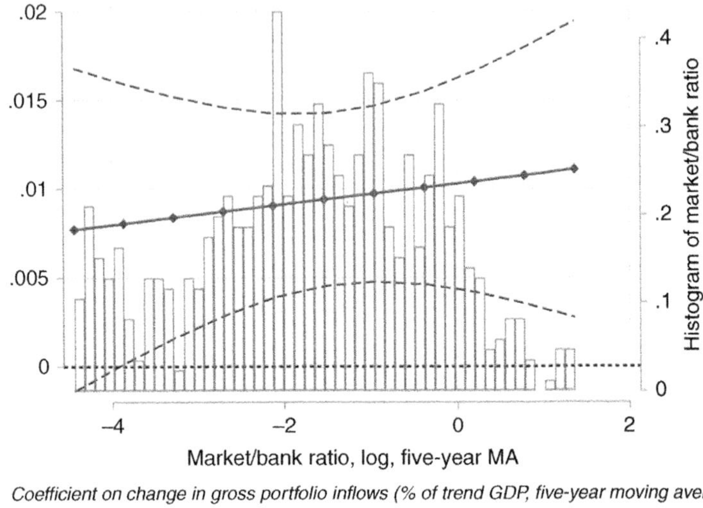

FIGURE 3.2. Average marginal effect of gross portfolio inflows by market/bank ratio (Reinhart-Rogoff banking crisis, Model 6, Table 3.2).

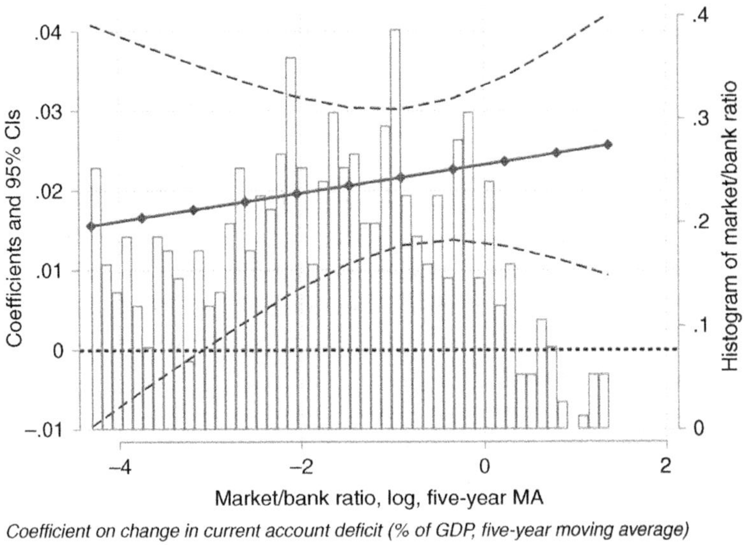

FIGURE 3.3. Average conditional marginal effect of net capital flows (Current account) by market/bank ratio (World Bank banking crisis).

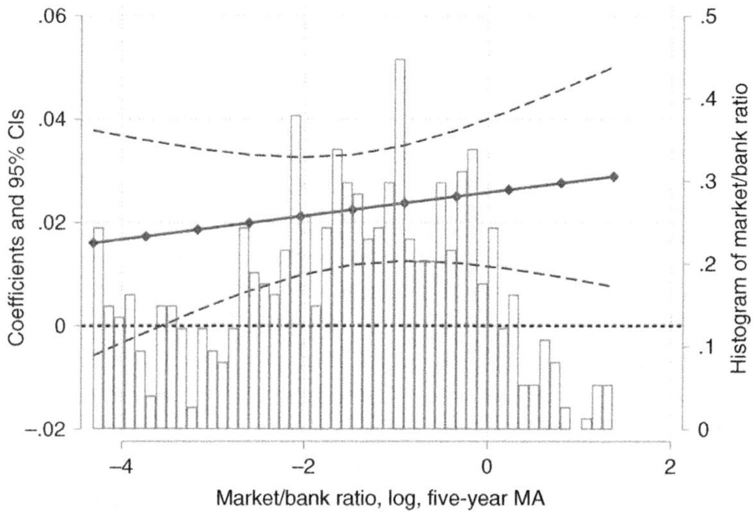

FIGURE 3.4. Average conditional marginal effect of net capital flows (Current account) by market/bank ratio (Reinhart-Rogoff banking crisis).

the coefficients on our measures of capital inflows must be assessed at different values of financial market structure (market/bank ratio). These models are generated using the LPM specifications (Models 5 and 6) and illustrate average conditional marginal effects. In each figure, we also include a histogram of market/bank ratio, to show the distribution of the variable that we are interacting with capital flows. This histogram shows that there is sufficient "common support" for reliably computing marginal effects across the range of X-axis values (Hainmueller et al. 2019).

As these graphs illustrate, our argument finds strong support in the data. In Figure 3.1, gross portfolio inflows have a positive and significant effect on the probability of a banking crisis only at high values of market/bank ratio. In contrast, the results suggest that external imbalances have no effect on the probability of banking crises in countries where the market/bank ratio is lower and financial systems consist primarily of traditional commercial banks. This finding is mirrored in Figures 3.2–3.4, which illustrate the corresponding average marginal effects for gross portfolio inflows (Reinhart-Rogoff crisis) and net flows (both WB and RR crisis classifications) across the range of values of market/bank ratio.

In order to illustrate the substantive significance of these results, we generate the predicted probability of a banking crisis using the specification of Model 5 (gross portfolio flows, WB crisis classification) from Table 3.2.[14] Setting all variables constant at sample means, the predicted probability of a banking crisis in this specification is only 1.0 percent. We then generate first differences calculating the effect of a 1.5 standard deviation increase in gross portfolio flows at both low and high levels of market/bank ratio, corresponding to 1.5 standard deviations below and above the sample mean of −1.69 (−3.8 and 0.38, respectively). The results are striking. At the "low" value of market/bank ratio, the increase in gross portfolio flows has no significant association with the probability of a banking crisis: the predicted change in probability is 17.8 percent, but the 95 percent confidence intervals overlap zero (−0.5%, 65.2%). In contrast, at the "high" value of market/bank ratio, the increase in gross portfolio flows has a large, positive, and significant correlation with the probability of a banking crisis (29.0%, 95% CIs: 3.7%, 74.3%).

To further illustrate the magnitude and conditional nature of these results, we zero in on two real-world country-year cases in our dataset: Sweden 1981 and Spain 2003. We choose these two observations because they correspond most closely to the low and high levels of market/bank ratio noted above: Sweden's (logged) market/bank ratio in 1981 was −3.75, while Spain's in 2003 was 0.39. Drawing once again on the specification of Model 5, Table 3.2, we set all variables in our analysis at the relevant values for these two country-year observations and calculate the predicted effect of a 1.5 standard deviation increase in gross portfolio flows on the probability of a banking crisis. The results provide further support for our theory that capital inflows are destabilizing only in more securitized financial systems. For Sweden 1981, the estimated first difference is 3.0 percent, which is substantively large given that the baseline predicted probability of a crisis for Sweden in 1981 is only 1.6 percent. However, this point estimate is not statistically significant and the 95 percent confidence intervals overlap zero (−0.1%, 19.3%). In contrast, for Spain 2003, the baseline predicted probability of a crisis is 3.2 percent, and the estimated first difference effect of a 1.5 standard deviation in gross portfolio flows is extremely large (48.0 percent) and significant at the 95 percent confidence level.

[14] Calculations done in Stata 15.1 using CLARIFY. (Tomz, Wittenberg, and King 2003).

Determinants of Banking Crises: Robustness

We estimate a range of additional models as robustness checks.[15] First, we re-estimate the models in Table 3.2, truncating our sample at 2006 to ensure that our results are not dependent on including the global wave of crises in the 2007–11 period. The goal here is to ensure that our findings are robust throughout the entire post–Bretton Woods era, rather than driven solely by the wave of country-level banking crises during the Great Recession. Our results here indicate that the relationship between capital inflows, financial market structure, and banking crises is not simply the product of the most recent global crisis. The conditional, interactive findings hold up in all of the gross portfolio flow models, using both classifications of banking crises. The pre-2007 results are mixed when using net flows, however, suggesting again that our argument is driven primarily by large gross flows, rather than large current account imbalances.

We also re-estimate our models using a "stripped" specification that removes all of the control variables except the controls for temporal dependence. The goal here is to ensure that our findings are not driven by the inclusion or omission of a key control variable. Once again, we find that our results are strongly robust in the specifications using gross portfolio flows but offer only mixed support when substituting net flows. Third, we conduct robustness checks to test different lag structures for our explanatory variables. We re-estimate the multiplicative interaction models using three-year moving averages on all of the independent variables, rather than five-year averages. In these specifications, the results are broadly robust. We also test models using one-year lags of the independent variables, but these models do not yield consistently significant results for the interactive marginal effects. This is not surprising, in our view, since our theory suggests that large capital inflows take time to work their way into the domestic financial system and through the banking sector. The lack of support for the one-year lag specifications also mirrors the indeterminacy of the existing literature on capital flow surges or bonanzas, which frequently uses one-year deviations in capital flows from its long-run trend.[16] This approach assumes that large sustained inflows – even massive ones – *within* the trend can be easily absorbed

[15] All results available on request.

[16] See, e.g., Crystallin et al. 2015.

without causing trouble in the financial sector, while a one-year spike can cause a crisis in the following year. In our view, this is far less likely than the potential destabilization resulting from a prolonged influx of capital, which our three-year and five-year trend variables better operationalize in the analysis.

Finally, we conduct robustness analysis to address the questions raised by Hainmueller et al. (2019) about the possibility of non-linearities in multiplicative interaction terms. The authors suggest this is a widespread problem in political science research and propose the use of a binning estimator that "allows researchers to estimate marginal effects without imposing the stringent linear interaction assumption."[17] We are skeptical of this approach unless it is firmly grounded in theory that justifies an expectation of non-linearity in the data. In our case, we have developed a clear theoretical expectation that capital flows will have a significant effect on financial stability at high values of market/bank ratio but not at low values, and we have no reason to expect there to be non-linear effects, in either the insignificant or significant ranges of Figures 3.1–3.4. Nonetheless, we run this diagnostic using the authors' *interflex* package in Stata as a robustness check.[18] In three of our four models (World Bank crisis/gross flows, RR crisis/gross flows, RR crisis/net flows) – including both using our preferred measure of gross portfolio capital inflows – the results confirm those in Figures 3.1, 3.2, and 3.4: the coefficient on capital flows is *only* positive and significant at high values of market/bank ratio, reinforcing our expectation of a linear interactive effect. In the fourth model (WB crisis/net flows, Figure 3.3), this robustness analysis finds evidence of positive and significant interactions in both the low and high (but not middle) values of market/bank ratio. We suspect this difference is primarily due to model dependence rather than non-linearities, since the *interflex* diagnostics do not allow us to control for spatial dependence in the LPM specification (as we did in Models 5 and 6 of Table 3.1), nor do they allow us to test the conditional logit specification (as we use in Models 1–4 and Models 7–8). Moreover, this final result appears to be highly dependent on the choice of "bins" in the analysis: our expected linear result is confirmed when using 2, 3, or 5 bins, but not 3. Thus, on the whole, non-linearity in the interaction terms does not appear to be an issue in our results.

[17] Hainmueller, Mummolo, and Xu 2019, 186.

[18] http://yiqingxu.org/software.html.

DETERMINANTS OF BANKING CRISES: TESTING ALTERNATIVE EXPLANATIONS

We also test a number of additional models to ensure that our results and main independent variables are not simply capturing alternative factors that might explain variation in financial stability across the industrialized world. Table 3.3 presents the results of these alternative specifications.

Size of the Banking System

First, we consider whether our results are driven not by the relative size of securities markets compared to commercial banking, but rather simply by the depth of financial markets or the amount of bank credit in the economy.[19] Our original analysis included bank credit as a share of GDP as a control variable. The results indicated that the size of the banking system in the overall economy is positively and significantly associated with banking crises. Here, we re-estimate our models substituting private credit by deposit money banks to GDP for the market/bank ratio to test whether our measure of market structure is simply picking up the level of financial depth or development in a country. The results clearly indicate that this is not the case.[20] There is no clear and statistically significant conditional relationship between capital inflows and levels of bank credit, in contrast to our clear and consistent findings of a conditional, interactive relationship between capital inflows and the market/bank ratio. Moreover, it is clear from our data that the market/bank ratio is not simply picking up overall variation in the amount of private credit in the financial system. The correlation between these variables is relatively small: 0.20. Thus, while countries with higher levels of bank credit (relative to GDP) are more crisis-prone, this is a separate factor, independent of the level of capital inflows or the relative size of banking and securities markets.

Bank Concentration

Second, we consider whether our results are affected by or driven by the degree of concentration in the banking sector affects financial stability. Table 3.3 shows mixed evidence that bank concentration, on

[19] Private bank credit to GDP and liquid liabilities to GDP – a widely used broader measure of overall financial liquidity or depth – are very highly correlated (0.83 in our sample, N = 760), whereas bank credit and market/bank are correlated only weakly (0.20).

[20] Graphs illustrating the average marginal effects from these alternative models are presented in the Data Appendix at the end of this chapter.

TABLE 3.3. *Regression results, banking crises: Robustness and alternative explanation models*

Model	1	2	3	4	5	6
Banking Crisis Variable	*World Bank*	*Reinhart-Rogoff*	*World Bank*	*Reinhart-Rogoff*	*World Bank*	*Reinhart- Rogoff*
Control Variable	*Size of Banking System*	*Size of Banking System*	*Bank Concentration*	*Bank Concentration*	*Partisanship and Legislative Majorities*	*Partisanship and Legislative Majorities*
Gross portfolio inflows/trend GDP (%, log)	−0.084 (0.195)	−0.097 (0.211)	0.124 (0.034)***	0.133 (0.052)**	0.132 (0.050)**	0.152 (0.046)***
Private credit by deposit money banks to GDP	0.272 (0.086)***	0.028 (0.086)	0.564 (0.095)***	0.565 (0.085)***	0.329 (0.067)***	0.083 (0.098)
Gross inflows*private credit by deposit money banks to GDP	0.031 (0.045)	0.041 (0.050)				
Bank concentration			−0.004 (0.002)	−0.005 (0.002)***		
Left executive					−0.062 (0.017)***	−0.023 (0.015)
Legislative seat share					0.116 (0.195)	−0.154 (0.201)

Market/bank ratio			−0.014 (0.026)	0.082 (0.059)	−0.086 (0.024)***	−0.072 (0.031)***
Gross inflows*market/ bank ratio			0.052 (0.019)**	0.027 (0.022)	0.025 (0.017)	0.021 (0.019)
Inflation(%)	0.004 (0.001)***	0.003 (0.001)***	−0.001 (0.003)	−0.002 (0.002)	0.002 (0.001)**	0.003 (0.001)***
Per capita GDP growth ($2005, %)	0.010 (0.017)	0.012 (0.015)	−0.025 (0.013)*	−0.041 (0.013)**	0.012 (0.014)	0.013 (0.014)
US real interest rate (%)	0.014 (0.017)	0.013 (0.014)	0.049 (0.031)	0.047 (0.023)*	0.011 (0.014)	0.013 (0.012)
OECD average per capita GDP growth (%)	−0.029 (0.017)*	−0.038 (0.016)**	−0.013 (0.030)	−0.006 (0.029)	−0.017 (0.013)	−0.032 (0.014)**
Banking crises worldwide (count)	−0.002 (0.003)	−0.006 (0.003)**	0.005 (0.005)	−0.000 (0.005)	0.000 (0.002)	−0.006 (0.002)**
Years since last banking crisis	−0.062 (0.017)***	−0.114 (0.018)***	−0.022 (0.019)	−0.058 (0.015)***	−0.056 (0.014)***	−0.112 (0.019)***

(continued)

TABLE 3.3 *(continued)*

Model	1	2	3	4	5	6
Banking Crisis Variable	*World Bank*	*Reinhart-Rogoff*	*World Bank*	*Reinhart-Rogoff*	*World Bank*	*Reinhart- Rogoff*
Control Variable	*Size of Banking System*	*Size of Banking System*	*Bank Concentration*	*Bank Concentration*	*Partisanship and Legislative Majorities*	*Partisanship and Legislative Majorities*
Years since last banking crisis[2]	0.002 (0.001)**	0.006 (0.001)***	−0.000 (0.001)	0.001 (0.001)	0.002 (0.001)**	0.006 (0.001)***
Years since last banking crisis[3]	−0.000 (0.000)*	−0.000 (0.000)***	0.000 (0.000)	−0.000 (0.000)	−0.000 (0.000)	−0.000 (0.000)***
Constant	−0.698 (0.372)*	0.441 (0.341)	−1.908 (0.441)***	−1.639 (0.334)***	−1.220 (0.355)***	0.129 (0.553)
Observations	704	740	358	344	685	720
Countries	28	27	28	27	28	27
Log-likelihood	−88.841	−179.129	−30.815	3.397	−51.236	−160.557
*AIC*n*	201.682	382.258	89.630	21.207	132.473	351.115
BIC	256.364	437.538	143.957	74.976	200.413	419.803

$^{*}p < 0.10$; $^{**}p < 0.05$; $^{***}p < 0.01$.
2: *Years since last banking crisis squared.*
3: *Years since last banking crisis cubed.*
Note: OLS regressions, country fixed effects, Driscoll-Kraay standard errors.

its own, affects financial stability: higher levels of bank concentration have no significant effect on the likelihood of systemic banking crises (World Bank classification) and a *negative* effect on the likelihood of a Reinhart-Rogoff crisis. We interpret these results cautiously, since limits on data availability for banking concentration reduce our sample to the 1997–2011 period. Nonetheless, it is clear that controlling for bank concentration does not alter the findings of our previous analysis about the conditional relationship between capital inflows, the relative size of the securities and banking sectors, and banking crises.

Moreover, it is clear that our market/bank ratio variable in the previous models was not simply a proxy for bank concentration. When we substitute bank concentration for market/bank ratio in our interactive models, there is no clear conditional relationship between capital inflows and banking crises. Given this, and the extremely low correlation between bank concentration and market/bank ratio in our data sample (0.09), the results strongly suggest that our argument is not simply picking up the effect of bank concentration on financial stability.

Partisanship and Legislative Majorities

We also consider the extent to which government partisanship and legislative politics shape financial stability and whether including these variables alters the substantive findings of our previous analysis.[21] We focus specifically on two variables: the partisan ideology of the executive (*left executive*), which takes a value of 1 if the chief executive is from a left-wing party), and the size of the governing coalition in parliament (*legislative seat share*), in terms of percentage seat share of the legislature. Both variables are drawn from the World Bank's Database of Political Institutions. The results provide limited evidence that these factors are key determinants of banking crises. Left executive is negative and significant in the World Bank crisis model but insignificant in the Reinhart-Rogoff specification. Legislative seat share is not significant in either specification. Moreover, we find no evidence of a conditional, interactive relationship between capital inflows and either government partisanship or legislative seat share. Although this is

[21] Bernhard and Leblang 2006; Leblang and Satyanath 2006, 2008.

not surprising, given the near-total lack of correlation between market/bank ratio and either left executive (–0.013) or legislative seat share (–0.011), this finding increases our confidence that market/bank ratio is not simply capturing aspects of the broader political/institutional context of the countries in our sample.

In sum, our banking crisis results are largely robust to, and not dependent on, the use of different lag structures, the inclusion or exclusion of the recent wave of global financial crises, and the presence or absence of control variables. Moreover, our robustness analysis clearly indicates that our measure of financial market structure is not driven simply by the denominator of the ratio (levels of bank credit or financial development). Across a wide range of specifications, we find similar results: capital inflows are correlated with an increased risk of banking crises, but only in financial systems where banks compete alongside sufficiently large and developed securities markets.

CAPITAL INFLOWS, MARKET STRUCTURE, AND BANKING CRISES: HOW AND WHY?

Thus far, our empirical analysis has treated banking crises as the dependent variable of interest. Our findings indicate that capital inflows are correlated with banking crises, but that financial market structure plays an important role as a mediating factor. As we expected, large capital inflows are only correlated with banking crises under certain conditions: namely, when they flow into a financial system in which commercial banks compete alongside large and highly developed securities markets. This conditional correlation between capital inflows, financial market structure, and banking crises is robust to a variety of alternative models and specifications.

In this section, we focus our analysis on identifying the *specific channels* by which capital inflows and financial market structure interact to trigger crises. As we discussed in Chapter 1, the conventional wisdom linking capital inflows to banking crises emphasizes distortions in the allocation of capital as it is channeled through banks and other financial intermediaries (Portes 2009). The question is precisely how this plays out and which distortions are most salient. Some scholars find a clear link between capital inflows and the *volume* of credit. For example, Jordà, Schularick, and Taylor (2011) and Schularick and Taylor (2012), in their groundbreaking work on the long-term patterns of financial instability in industrialized countries, find that (1) domestic credit growth is the single most important determinant of banking crises; and (2) capital inflows, as measured by current account deficits, go hand in hand with credit booms, especially in the post–Bretton Woods era.[22] In contrast, other scholars, such as Amri, Richey, and Willett (2016), find only a weak relationship between capital inflows and domestic credit growth and note that this connection is diminishing over the last two decades.[23] If this is the case, then capital inflows may not be connected to banking crises through an increase in credit volume, but rather through some other channel.

We explore this issue in the remainder of the chapter. First, in this section, we test whether there is empirical evidence in support of the credit boom/volume channel. To do this, we re-estimate our models of banking crisis from above, but substitute domestic bank credit growth as an alternative dependent variable in place of the World Bank and Reinhart-Rogoff crisis variables. If capital inflows lead to banking crises by triggering changes in the *volume* of domestic lending, then we should find a similar conditional, interactive relationship between capital inflows, financial market structure, and credit growth as we did above in our banking crisis models. Such evidence would suggest that the key channel by which capital inflows lead to banking crises is through credit booms.

If this were the case, then one could argue that our theory is simply a modification of the existing conventional wisdom linking credit booms to banking crises. In this case, financial market structure might be a key mediating variable, but our theory would simply be introducing a qualifying condition to the existing literature's core finding linking credit growth to financial instability. However, this is not the case. In a further set of robustness checks, we employ the same specifications as in Table 3.2 to test for a conditional interactive relationship between capital inflows and bank credit growth.[24] Our sample, as above, is the high-income OECD countries from 1976 to 2011, and we test models using both gross portfolio flows and net flows (current account deficits). However, in these models, we replace banking crisis with an alternative dependent variable: *domestic credit growth*, the year-to-year change in domestic bank credit provided by deposit money banks, as a share of GDP. Data are taken from the World Bank's Global Financial Development Database. The results cast doubt on the argument that

[22] Jordà, Schularick, and Taylor 2011; Schularick and Taylor 2012.
[23] Amri, Richey, and Willett 2016.
[24] See Figures 3.A11 and 3.A12 in the Appendix.

the causal chain linking capital inflows to banking crises runs through increases in the volume of domestic credit. In these models, we find no statistically significant relationship – either unconditionally or in the multiplicative interactive models – between either gross portfolio flows or net flows and the aggregate growth rate of domestic bank credit.

While we find no significant correlation between capital inflows and bank credit, the results of this additional analysis do indicate that market/bank ratio is positively and significantly correlated with domestic credit growth. This reinforces our argument and earlier finding that banks behave differently when they compete alongside large and highly developed securities markets in a country's financial system. However, the aggregate level of credit banks provide is not conditional on the size of capital inflows into the country.

Ultimately, while capital inflows are conditionally correlated with banking crises, the relationship does not appear to operate through a simple increase in the volume of bank loans. This is not to say that credit booms are unimportant precursors to banking crises. Indeed, we find the existing literature compelling in this regard. But credit booms appear to be a separate channel of financial instability from the one we identify in our analysis.

BANK-LEVEL ANALYSIS: CAPITAL ADEQUACY AND INSOLVENCY RISK

If capital inflows are correlated with banking crises but not increases in aggregate domestic credit growth, the question remains: Why and how do capital inflows interact with financial market structure to trigger banking crises? In order to answer this question, we attempt to isolate bank-level behavior in industrialized countries in the remainder of this chapter. Our goal is to identify whether, and to what extent, capital inflows influence the propensity of banks to take on greater risk, through a reduction in capital reserves and/or the assumption of greater insolvency risk, and to see whether this varies depending on a country's domestic financial market structure.

We employ two national-level measures of bank capital adequacy and solvency, respectively. The first variable, *Tier 1 commercial bank capital*, is the asset-weighted Tier 1 capital ratio of commercial banks headquartered in each country in our sample. Tier 1 capital encompasses loss-absorbing capital including common stock and disclosed reserves; as Tier 1 capital increases, banks are generally more resilient to shocks. The data to construct this variable are taken from the firm-level BankScope dataset. The second variable, *Z-score* is a widely used measure of bank-level insolvency risk. It is defined as follows:

> The z-score ... compares buffers (capitalization and returns) with risk (volatility of returns) to measure a bank's solvency risk. The z-score is defined as $z \equiv (k + \mu)/\sigma$, where k is equity capital as percent of assets, μ is return as percent of assets, and σ is standard deviation of return on assets as a proxy for return volatility. The popularity of the z-score stems from the fact that it has a clear (negative) relationship to the probability of a financial institution's insolvency, that is, the probability that the value of its assets becomes lower than the value of its debt. A higher z-score therefore implies a lower probability of insolvency.[25]

As with our measure of Tier 1 capital, we aggregate the bank-level data from BankScope to develop an asset-weighted, national commercial bank *Z*-score for each country in our sample. Our data sample for the bank-level analysis runs from 1991 to 2011 for Tier 1 commercial bank capital, and from 1991 to 2010 for *Z*-score.

We focus here on national-level aggregates of bank-level behavior because of the many unique determinants of variation – and year-to-year fluctuations – in individual bank's balance sheets and lending behavior. Moreover, in the BankScope data, many large banks and bank holding companies have dozens of individual entries for state- and local-level branches. For example, J.P. Morgan has over thirty unique line items in the 2010 data. As a result, it is difficult, if not impossible, to develop good empirical estimates of the overall balance sheet behavior of a single bank. However, these detailed data, once aggregated at the level of country-year observations, provide a clear and comprehensive picture of levels and changes in the balance sheet behavior of banks across time and space.

National-level aggregates also provide an appropriate test of our theoretical predictions. Our goal with these analyses is to explore the behavior of the national banking system in the aggregate, rather than hone in on the risk taking of any particular bank. Certainly, some banks will be riskier than others within a country, but exploring this variation is beyond the scope of our analysis and data. Indeed, we do not have a theory about which individual banks will change their behavior in the face of capital inflows and competition from securities markets; rather, our argument is an "on average" one about the relative stability of national-level banking systems. If our argument is correct, we should observe not only a greater incidence of banking crises in countries where large capital inflows enter a financial system characterized by large national

[25] From "Key Terms Explained," available at www.worldbank.org/en/publication/gfdr/gfdr-2016/background/financial-stability. Accessed August 26, 2019.

securities markets, but we should also observe changes in national-level aggregates of bank capital adequacy and insolvency risk.

Results: Tier 1 Bank Capital and Commercial Bank Z-Scores

To test this hypothesis, we employ the two national-level, asset-weighted measures of bank capital adequacy and solvency described earlier: Tier 1 commercial bank capital and Z-score, both of which enter our regressions as natural logs. For each of these dependent variables, we include specifications using the two different measures of capital inflows (gross portfolio inflows, net flows) and the multiplicative interactions between capital inflows and market/bank ratio. In contrast to the banking crisis models, here we employ one-year lags of our independent variables. As noted above, there are strong theoretical and empirical reasons to employ five-year moving averages in the crisis models, given the time lag between large capital inflows and the actual outbreak of a systemic crisis. In contrast, we expect banks' actual behaviors to change incrementally and quickly in the presence of large capital inflows; the accumulation of banks' risky behaviors is likely to trigger a systemic crisis only after a period of years.

Table 3.4 present the results of this additional analysis. Once again, the results provide strong support for our hypotheses. As illustrated in Figures 3.5 and 3.6, the conditional marginal effect is clear in both Tier 1 capital models: larger capital inflows – measured either as gross or net flows – are associated with reduced bank capital levels but only at high levels of market/bank ratio. At low levels of market/bank ratio, however, capital inflows have no significant correlation with bank capital levels. The results for the two models measuring insolvency risk (lower Z-scores) are mixed. In Figure 3.7 (Z-scores, gross portfolio inflows), the three component terms of the multiplicative interaction are jointly significant at the 90 percent level ($p < 0.073$), but the graph of the average conditional marginal effect overlaps zero at all values of market/bank ratio. However, In Figure 3.8, we once again see the conditional and significant marginal effect, as expected: net capital flows are positively correlated with insolvency risk (lower Z-scores), but only at high levels of market/bank ratio. Thus, while the Z-score analysis provides only qualified support for our argument, these findings, in tandem with the strong and clear results on the Tier 1 capital analysis, suggest that banks do behave differently in the wake of large capital inflows in different types of financial systems.

TABLE 3.4. *Regression results, Tier 1 capital and Z-score models*

Model	1	2	3	4
Capital Flow Variable	*Gross Portfolio*	*Net (Current Account)*	*Gross Portfolio*	*Net (Current Account)*
Dependent Variable	*Tier 1 Capital (log)*	*Tier 1 Capital (log)*	*Z-Score (log)*	*Z-Score (log)*
Capital flows (% GDP)	−0.002 (0.001)**	−0.009 (0.003)***	−0.001 (0.001)	−0.005 (0.002)**
Market/bank ratio	0.070 (0.020)***	0.059 (0.020)***	0.024 (0.011)**	0.032 (0.011)***
Capital flows*market/bank ratio	−0.001 (0.000)**	−0.001 (0.003)	−0.000 (0.000)	−0.002 (0.002)
Lagged dependent variable	0.588 (0.092)***	0.578 (0.072)***	0.450 (0.076)***	0.441 (0.063)***
Private bank credit/GDP (%, log)	0.059 (0.028)**	0.079 (0.022)***	0.018 (0.028)	0.032 (0.020)
Inflation (%)	0.008 (0.005)*	0.010 (0.005)*	0.013 (0.006)*	0.013 (0.006)**
Per capita GDP growth ($2005, %)	−0.009 (0.006)	0.002 (0.011)	0.003 (0.004)	0.007 (0.006)

(continued)

TABLE 3.4 *(continued)*

Model	1	2	3	4
Capital Flow Variable	*Gross Portfolio*	*Net (Current Account)*	*Gross Portfolio*	*Net (Current Account)*
Dependent Variable	*Tier 1 Capital (log)*	*Tier 1 Capital (log)*	*Z-Score (log)*	*Z-Score (log)*
US real interest rate (%)	−0.016 (0.005)***	−0.013 (0.004)***	−0.011 (0.007)	−0.019 (0.005)***
OECD avg. per capita GDP growth (%)	0.000 (0.007)	−0.014 (0.012)	−0.018 (0.009)*	−0.016 (0.008)**
Number of banking crises worldwide	0.002 (0.001)	0.003 (0.001)***	−0.000 (0.001)	0.001 (0.001)
Constant	0.777 (0.253)***	0.699 (0.203)***	1.708 (0.676)**	2.102 (0.247)***
Observations	484	505	490	512
Countries	29	31	29	31
Log-likelihood	250.026	190.311	283.183	252.740
*AIC*n*	−478.052	−358.623	−542.366	−483.481
BIC	−432.049	−312.153	−492.033	−436.859

$^{*}p < 0.10$; $^{**}p < 0.05$; $^{***}p < 0.01$.

Note: OLS regressions, country fixed effects, Driscoll-Kraay standard errors.

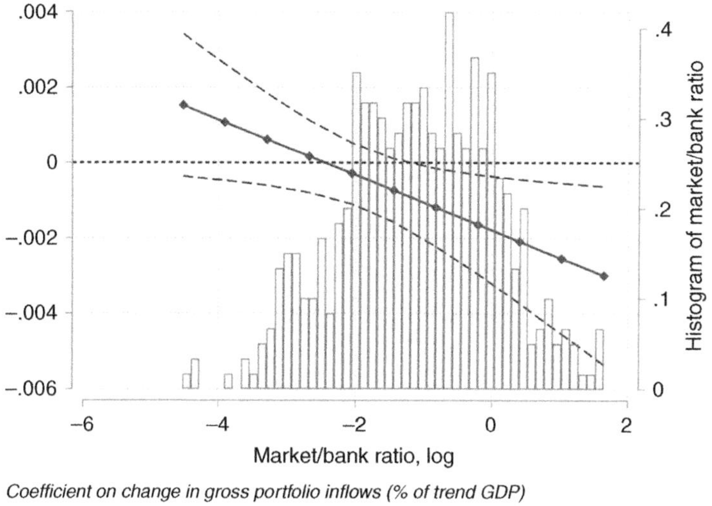

FIGURE 3.5. Average conditional marginal effect of gross portfolio inflows by market/bank ratio (Tier 1 commercial bank capital ratio, Model 1, Table 3.4).

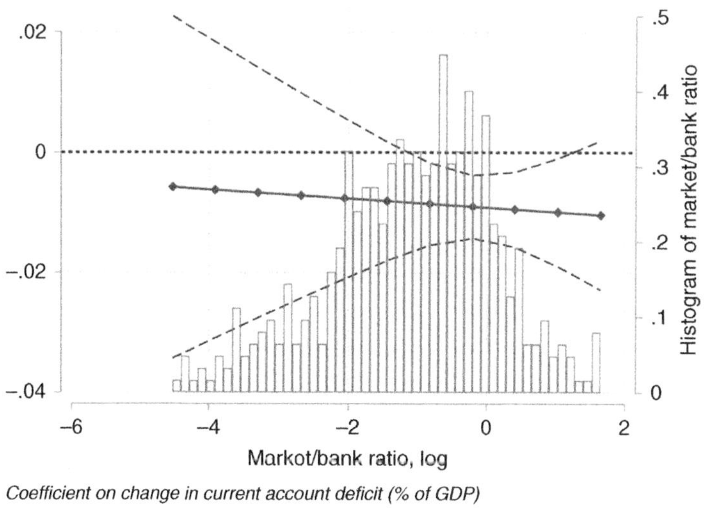

FIGURE 3.6. Average conditional marginal effect of net capital inflows by market/bank ratio (Tier 1 commercial bank capital ratio, Model 2, Table 3.4).

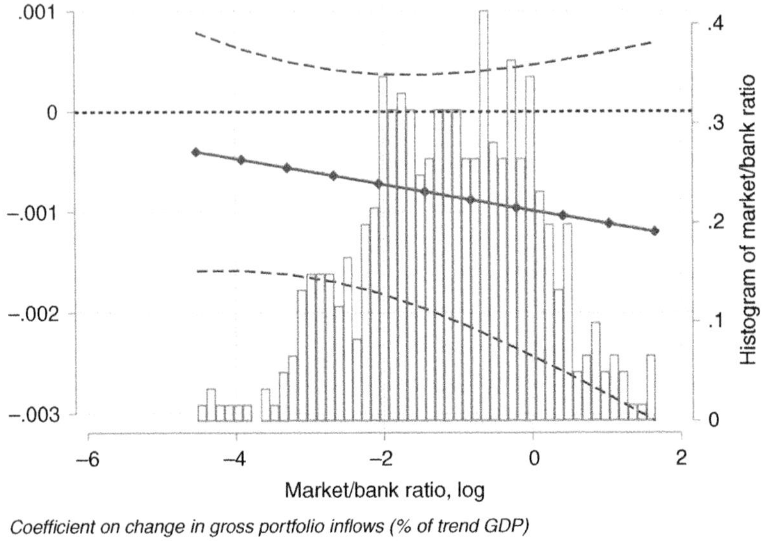

FIGURE 3.7. Average conditional marginal effect of gross portfolio inflows by market/bank ratio (Commercial bank Z-score, Model 3, Table 3.4).

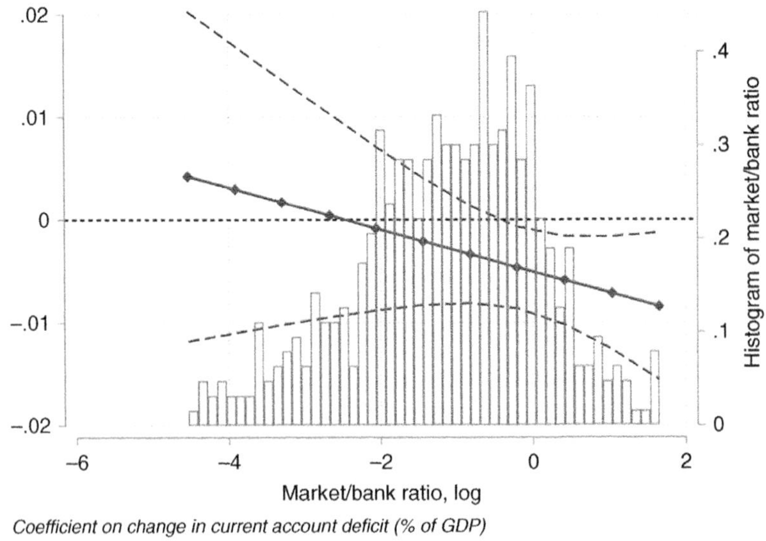

FIGURE 3.8. Average conditional marginal effect of net capital inflows by market/bank ratio (Commercial bank Z-score, Model 4, Table 3.4).

These results further clarify the channel by which capital inflows and market structure come together to increase the probability of banking crises. In the previous section, we found no significant link between capital inflows and domestic credit growth, either unconditionally, or interactively with financial market structure. In this section, we find that bank capital adequacy and insolvency risk are conditionally correlated with capital inflows. These findings, taken together, suggest that this relationship does not exist because of increases in the *volume* of bank credit. Rather, capital inflows – in financial systems where banks complete alongside large securities markets – affect the *quality* of bank lending and the composition of bank balance sheets. In short, these results strongly suggest that capital inflows trigger banking crises not because they cause credit booms (surges in the amount of bank lending), but because they lead banks to reduce their capital holdings and lend to more risky customers. This decline in the quality of banks' loan portfolios, rather than an increase in the number and amount of loans, appears to be the smoking gun linking capital inflows to banking crises in industrialized countries.

CONCLUSION

In this chapter, we conducted a battery of statistical tests of the observable implications of our theory and argument. In the wake of the Great Recession, observers in both policy and academic circles have pointed to global imbalances as the main perpetrator of financial crises. As we have argued here, we believe this view is only partially correct. The statistical analyses presented in this chapter suggest that the prominence of securities markets relative to commercial banking is the critical factor that tips the balance between benign and destabilizing capital inflows. One interpretation of our results is that bank-dominated financial sectors act as a "financial levee" that insulates countries from the destabilizing influence of capital inflows. Our results suggest that scholars would be well served to shift their attention from global imbalances and current account deficits toward developing richer explanations of causal pathways linking financial intermediation to financial stability.

To be clear, we do not argue that capital inflows and external imbalances are unimportant or benign. Rather, our argument is that these factors' importance has been overstated in the recent crisis literature, at the expense of other factors – most notably, financial market structure – of equal importance for financial stability. Taken together, the results of our banking crisis and bank capital/insolvency risk analyses paint a clear picture about the relationship between capital inflows, financial market structure, and financial stability. Large capital inflows are – as the literature argues – frequently destabilizing for banking and financial stability. Yet our empirical analysis shows that this relationship is clearly conditional. In financial systems where banks compete alongside (and directly) with large securities markets, capital inflows lead banks to engage in riskier behavior. Ultimately, this behavior and enhanced financial vulnerability lead to a higher incidence of banking crises. In contrast, where banks face less competition from nonbank actors in equity and debt markets, the clear relationship between capital inflows and financial instability is no longer evident.

These results raise questions about precisely which aspects of securities markets are most important for financial stability. Our measures of financial market structure do not gauge the relative prominence of different types of securities. Better historical data on derivatives such as mortgage-backed securities, credit default swaps, and other asset-backed securities could help us determine whether certain financial products are particularly influential in amplifying the destabilizing effects of capital inflows. Also omitted from this chapter is an empirical analysis of the role of regulation as a buffer against crises; indeed, regulation might be a second financial levee that buffers the impact of imbalances on financial stability.[26] A number of regulatory dimensions may be important, including the degree of government ownership of the banking sector, rules about financial transparency, capital adequacy requirements, regulator independence and mandate, and the specific modalities of bank inspections.[27] We return to further discussion of the policy and regulatory implications of our argument and this analysis in Chapter 6.

Ultimately, our analysis in this chapter makes clear that financial market structure – specifically, the relative size of securities markets compared to commercial banking – has important implications for financial stability. The structure of financial intermediation determines how capital inflows are channeled into the domestic political economy and how banks' lending behavior varies across time and space. When banks operate in a financial system marked by the relative absence of competition for financial intermediation, foreign capital is more frequently channeled

[26] See Amri and Kocher 2012 for a cross-national empirical study covering the three decades before the global financial crisis, and Helleiner 2014; Quaglia 2012; and Young and Park 2013 for analyses of postcrisis regulatory response.

[27] See, e.g., Copelovitch and Singer 2008, 2017; Gandrud and O'Keeffe 2017; Singer 2007; Tsingou 2015; Young and Park 2013.

safely throughout the system without causing bank instability. On the other hand, when banks operate alongside larger and deeper securities markets, capital inflows exacerbate banks' risk taking and increase the probability of a crisis. Our quantitative analysis in this chapter provides substantial evidence that banks' behavior has varied according to this pattern across the industrialized world in the post–Bretton Woods era, and it illustrates that this variation is also strongly correlated with variation in the incidence of banking crises.[28]

Thus far, however, we have only touched on the origins of securities markets and the sources of variation in the relative size of banking and securities across countries. In the statistical analysis in this chapter, we used financial market structure as an exogenous independent variable and demonstrated that its interaction with variation in capital inflows explains patterns of banking crises across space and time. Given the persistent stability in the rank-ordering of market/bank ratios among the industrialized countries since the 1970s, this was a reasonable empirical strategy in our analysis here. Nonetheless, the question remains: How, when, and why did this variation in domestic financial market structure emerge? If, as our quantitative analysis demonstrates, structural variation in domestic financial markets that developed over the long term are as important for contemporary financial stability as short-term foreign capital inflows, then we need to understand the sources of national variation and the reasons for its persistence into the twenty-first century.

Statistical analysis is not well-suited to answering this question, in part because high-quality, cross-national quantitative data on financial market structure is generally not available prior to the 1970s, but more importantly because the development of modern national variation in market structure is a complex, path-dependent process that occurred over more than a century in most industrialized countries, from the 1800s until World War II. In order to trace this process and understand the complex, step-by-step chain of events explaining the long-term development of national variation in financial market structure, we turn to historical case-study analysis in the next two chapters. We delve into the welter of historical policy decisions and political battles that helped to determine the relative strength of traditional banking in modern, industrialized economies and why large, deep, and centralized securities markets developed in some countries but not others.

[28] In contrast, there is some evidence that securities markets might reduce the output costs of banking crises. See DeLean and Joyce 2014.

We focus, in particular, on two key country cases: Canada and Germany. These cases highlight the political debates and decisions, primarily in the nineteenth and early twentieth centuries, that have had long-term implications for financial stability in the industrialized countries. We have chosen these two countries for several reasons. First, Canada stands out as one of the rare exceptions in the contemporary global economy: a beacon of banking stability in a global financial system beset since the 1970s by near-constant crises and instability. Indeed, in sharp contrast to its southern neighbor, which has been wracked by banking crises throughout American history, Canada has not experienced a systemic banking crisis in its entire history. At the same time, Canada stands out for another reason: its securities markets are surprisingly underdeveloped and highly fragmented, even today. While many analysts have looked to Canada in order to understand how its highly concentrated banking system remains stable, we focus instead on how the historical and political decisions resulting in Canada's underdeveloped securities market have actually had salutary effects on the stability of its banking system and enhanced its resilience in the face of large capital inflows over the last forty years.

Second, we have chosen Germany because it presents both clear parallels to Canada and stark differences. For most of German history, from its nineteenth century unification until the 1980s, Germany's story closely mirrored that of Canada's. Historical political battles and decisions in the 1870–1945 period led to the emergence and persistence of a financial system dominated by traditional banking, with securities markets relegated to a secondary role. During this period, Germany enjoyed a level of banking stability similar to Canada's. Unlike Canada, however, larger and centralized securities markets did emerge in Germany in the 1990s, and the German financial system is now far more securities-centric than it was in previous decades. This transformation, as we expect, has had substantial negative consequences for financial stability in Germany. For the first time in the postwar era, Germany has experienced a wave of banking crises in the last two decades, culminating in a series of high-profile bank failures during the Great Recession. As we discuss in the Chapter 5, the development of large national securities markets played a key role in this shift by altering banks' behavior and transforming Germany's staid but stable financial system into a more crisis-prone one in the twenty-first century.

Comparing the long-term development of Canada and Germany in these case studies makes clear that variation in domestic financial market structure is a complex and often acrimonious historical and political process involving both intentional policy decisions and unintended consequences over the long term. At the same time, the case analysis also highlights how this process had largely played out by World War II in both Canada and Germany, leading to distinct and persistent national variation in market structure through the postwar era into the modern post–Bretton Woods period. Thus, in the chapters that follow, we bridge the gap between the statistical analysis of banking crises over the last four decades presented here and the historical factors contributing to modern-day financial stability. Both approaches, we contend, are essential to understanding the sources of banking crises. Indeed, it is the combination of short-term foreign capital inflows and the substantial variation in domestic financial market structure forged over the historical long run that determines why some countries find themselves more vulnerable to banking crises today.

DATA APPENDIX

Variable	Source	Construction
Banking crisis (RR)	Reinhart and Rogoff (2009b); available at www.carmenreinhart.com	1 if major bank run, public takeover of major financial institutions, or large-scale public assistance; 0 otherwise.
Banking crisis (WB)	World Bank Global Financial Development Database (GFDD 2016), building on Laeven and Valencia (2008)	1 if systemic crisis characterized by a large number of defaults, a sharp increase in non-performing loans, and exhaustion of bank capital; 0 otherwise.
Tier 1 capital	BankScope	Loss-absorbing capital including common stock and reserves; national asset-weighted bank average.
Z-Score	BankScope/World Bank GFDD	Defined as $z \equiv (k+\mu)/\sigma$, where k is equity capital as percent of assets, μ is return as percent of assets, and σ is standard deviation of return on assets as a proxy for return volatility. National asset-weighted bank average.
Market structure	World Bank Global Financial Development Database (GFDD 2016)	Total shares traded on domestic exchanges as share of GDP, divided by private credit extended by money banks as a share of GDP.

Variable	Source	Construction
Gross portfolio flows	Broner et al. (2013), World Bank	Capital inflows by foreign agents (foreigners' holdings of domestic assets), equity and debt flows.
Per capita GDP growth	World Bank World Development Indicators	Annual growth in real GDP per capita ($2005).
Inflation	World Bank World Development Indicators	Inflation calculated using the GDP deflator.
Bank credit	World Bank Global Financial Development Database (2016)	Financial resources provided to the private sector by domestic money banks as a share of GDP. Domestic money banks comprise commercial banks and other financial institutions that accept transferable deposits, such as demand deposits.
OECD average GDP per capita growth	World Bank World Development Indicators	Average annual real per capita GDP growth rate ($2005) of OECD member countries.
US real interest rate	World Bank World Development Indicators	Nominal interest adjusted for inflation measured by the GDP deflator.

DATA AND COUNTRY SAMPLES

Crisis sample, 1976–2011

N = 760 (World Bank crisis models); for *Reinhart-Rogoff* models, *N* = 740 (1976–2009)

Country	Year
Austria	1976–2011
Chile	1981–2011
Czech Republic	1995–2011
Denmark	1976–2011
Finland	1983–2011
France	1976–2011
Germany	1993–2011
Greece	1981–2011
Hungary	1993–2011
Iceland	1994–2011
Ireland	1996–2011
Italy	1976–2011
Japan	1978–2011
Korea, Republic of	1980–2011
Latvia	1997–2011
Mexico	1980–2011
Netherlands	1976–2011
Norway	1981–2011
Poland	1992–2011
Portugal	1990–2011
Slovak Republic	1995–2011
Slovenia	1997–2011
Spain	1976–2011
Sweden	1976–2011
Switzerland	1982–2011
Turkey	1990–2011
United Kingdom	1990–2011
United States	1976–2011

Bank-level sample, 1991–2009

N = 484 (Tier 1 capital); N = 490 (Z-score)

Country	Year
Australia	1991–2009
Austria	1993–2010
Canada	1996–2009
Chile	1998–2010
Czech Republic	1995–2009
Denmark	1991–2010
Estonia	1999–2010
Finland	1991–2010
France	1991–2009
Germany	1993–2009
Greece	1992–2009
Iceland	1994–2010
Ireland	1996–2010
Israel	1994–2010
Italy	1991–2010
Japan	1992–2009
Korea, Republic of	1993–2010
Netherlands	1993–2010
New Zealand	1992–2009
Norway	1991–2007
Poland	1994–2010
Portugal	1991–2010
Slovak Republic	1995–2009
Slovenia	1997–2009
Spain	1991–2010
Sweden	1991–2009
Switzerland	1992–2010
United Kingdom	1991–2010
United States	1993–2010

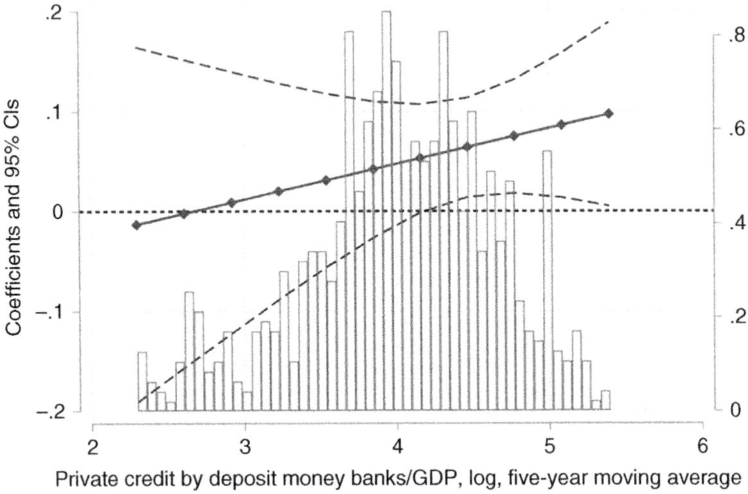

Gross portfolio inflows, WB crisis

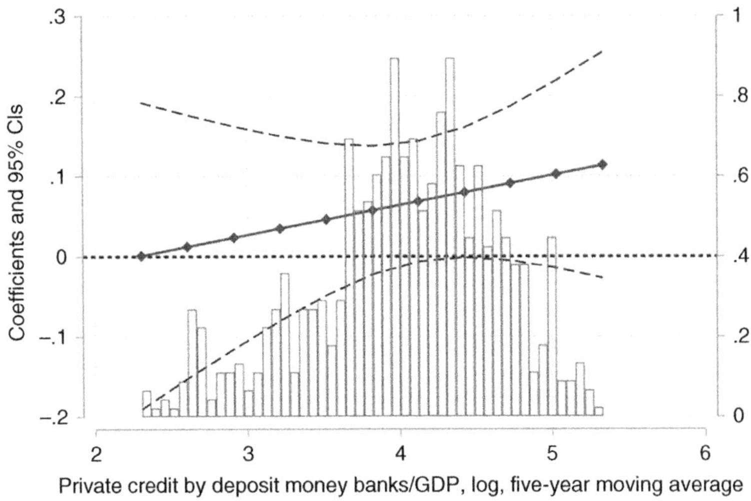

Gross portfolio inflows, RR crisis

FIGURES 3.A1–3.A4. No clear conditional relationship between capital inflows, bank credit/GDP, and crises.

(continued)

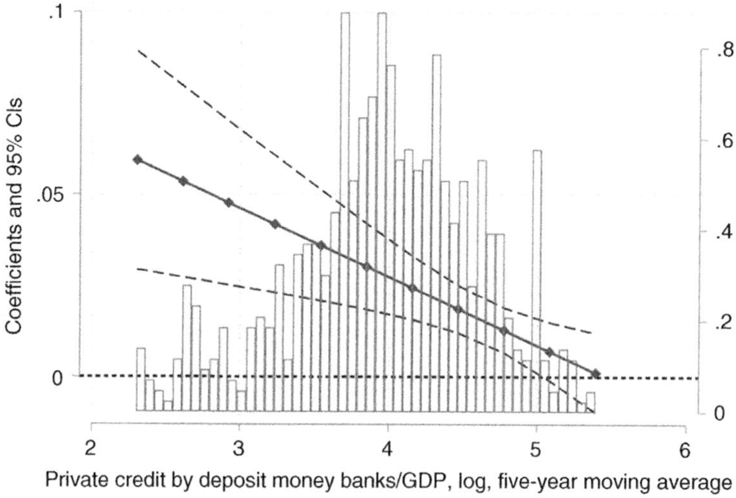

Current account (net flows), WB crisis

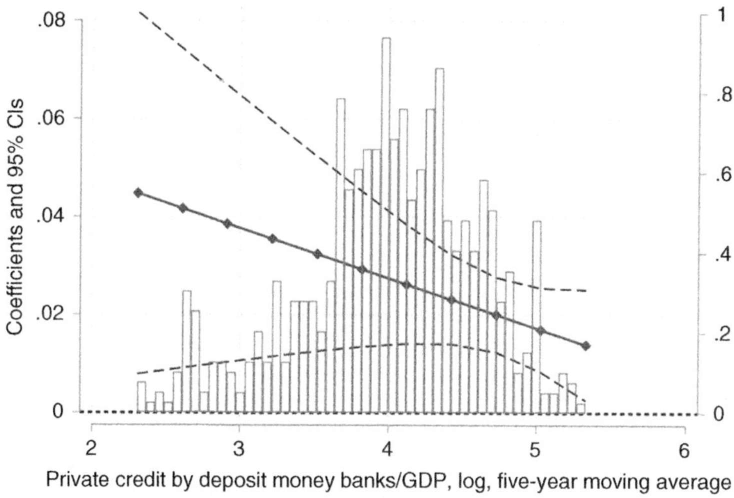

Current account (net flows), RR crisis

FIGURES 3.A1–3.A4 *(continued)*

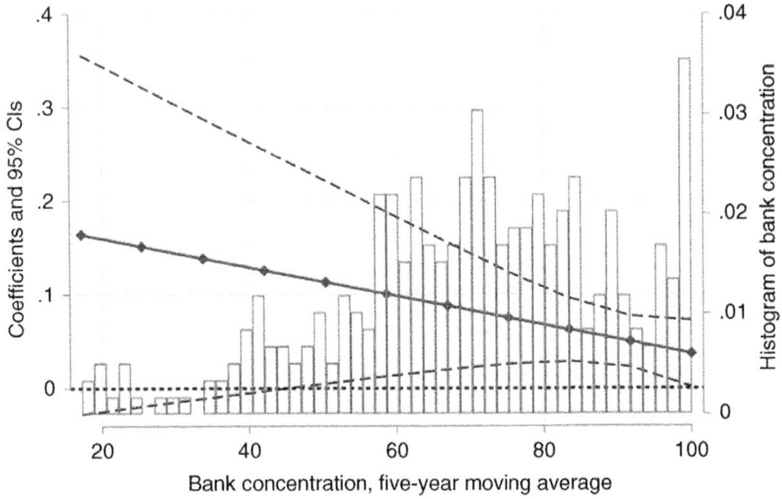

WB crisis, gross flows

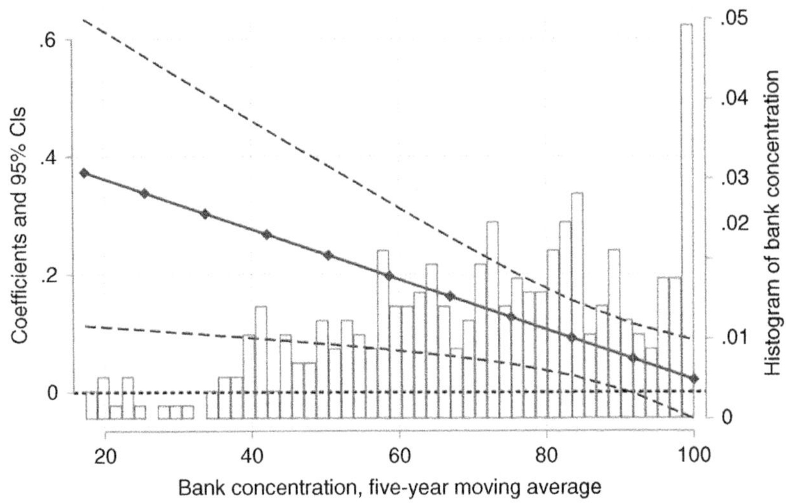

RR crisis, gross flows

FIGURES 3.A5–3.A8. No clear conditional relationship between capital inflows, bank concentration ratios, and crises.

(continued)

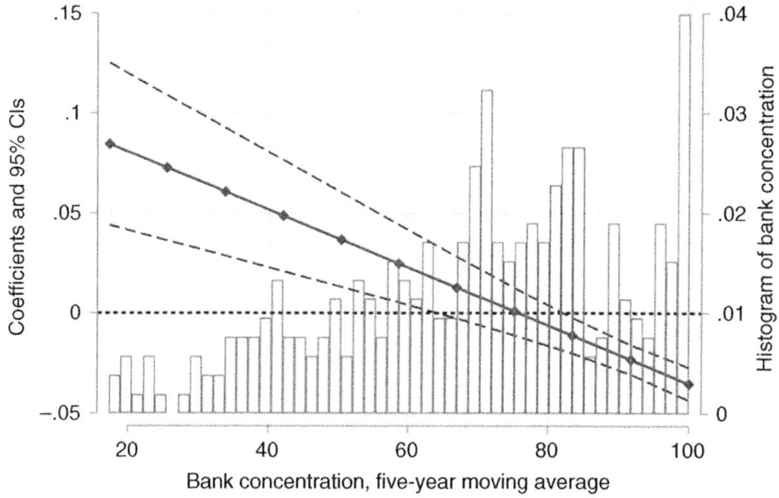

WB crisis, net flows

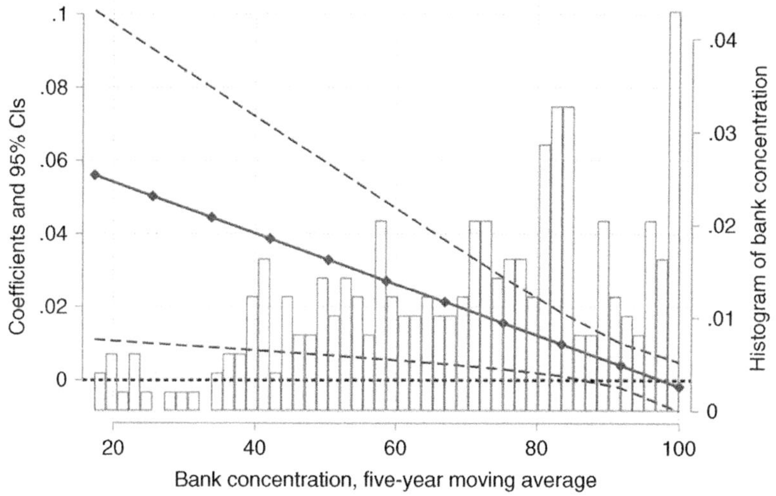

RR crisis, net flows

FIGURES 3.A5–3.A8 *(continued)*

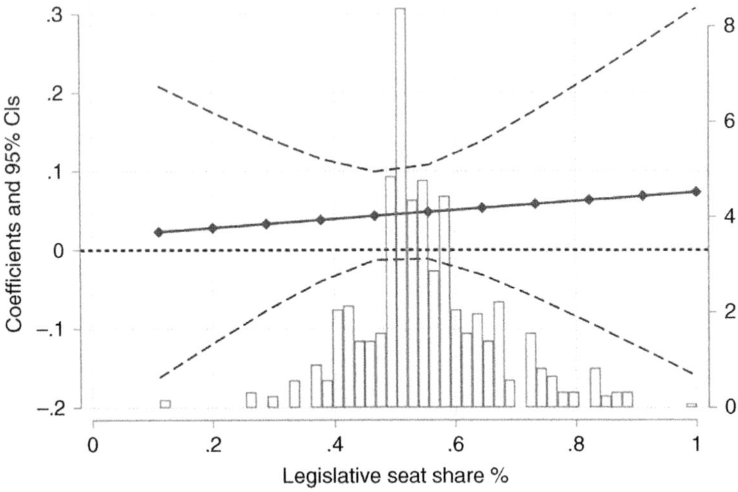

WB crisis, gross flows, interaction with legislative seat share

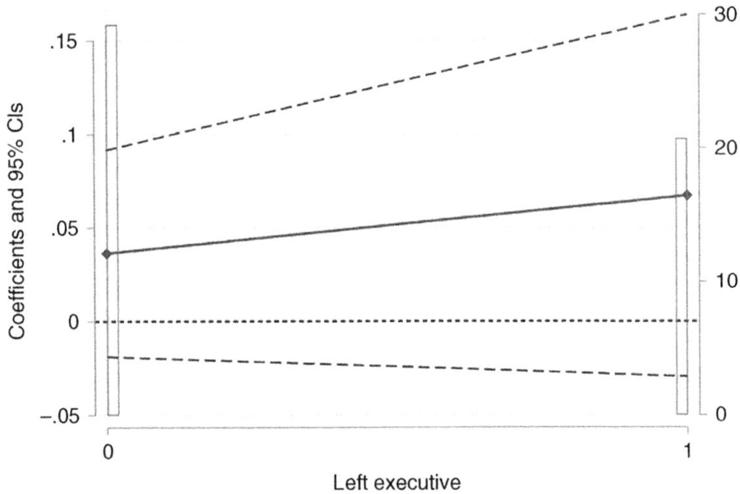

WB crisis, gross flows, interaction with left executive

FIGURES 3.A9 AND 3.A10. No clear conditional relationship between capital inflows, left executive/parliamentary seat share, and crises.

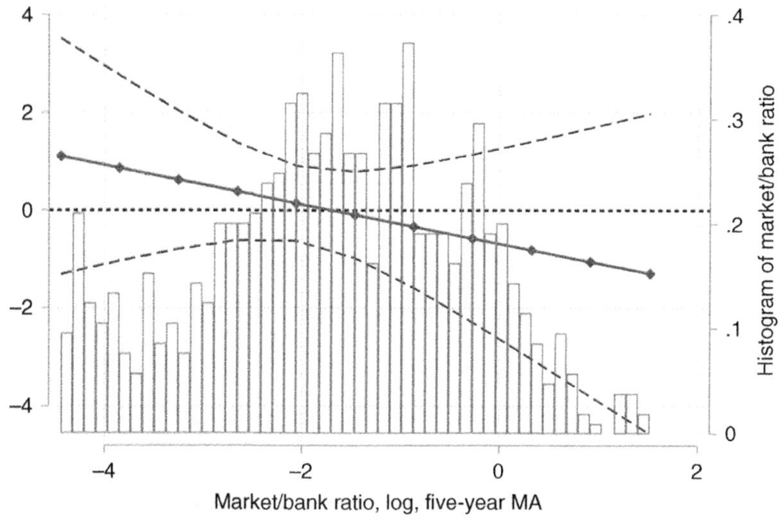

Coefficient on change in gross portfolio inflows (% of trend GDP, five-year moving average)

FIGURE 3.A11. No conditional effect of capital inflows on bank credit growth (Dependent variable: annual percentage change in private domestic credit growth as % of GDP).

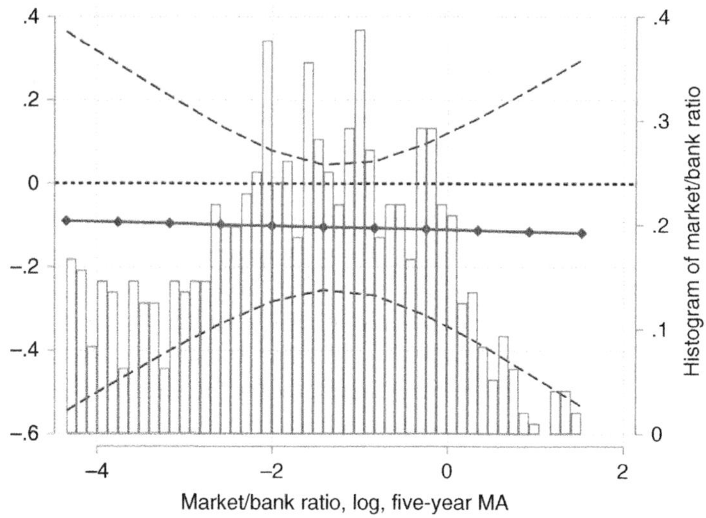

Coefficient on change in current account deficit (% of GDP, five-year moving average)

FIGURE 3.A12. No conditional effect of capital inflows on bank credit growth (Dependent variable: annual percentage change in private domestic credit growth as % of GDP).

4

O Canada? Unraveling the Mystery of Canadian Bank Stability

O Canada! This is the national anthem of Canada, of course. But lately these words have been uttered in the most unlikely of contexts. Residents of countries around the world who have experienced the anguish of banking crises have looked at Canada's remarkably stable banking system with awe and envy. Beginning in 2008, a global financial crisis swept North America and Europe, and several long-standing financial institutions with prestigious names – Lehman Brothers, Bear Stearns, Northern Rock, Merrill Lynch, Wells Fargo, and Fortis, to name a few – collapsed or required emergency bailouts. The crisis hit the United States the hardest, but the United Kingdom, Switzerland, Germany, Belgium, and many other countries faced debilitating bankruptcies and bank runs through 2010. Canada was different. No Canadian bank failed or required emergency funding from the government. Some Canadian banks even posted healthy profits during the height of the crisis, seemingly in proud defiance of their southern neighbor's faltering financial system.[1] Unsurprisingly, policymakers and social scientists around the world have wondered whether Canada holds the secret to financial stability, and if so, whether it can be replicated elsewhere.

Canada's banking stability is not a new phenomenon. During the Great Depression of the 1930s, not a single Canadian bank failed.[2] Throughout the turbulent 1980s, the United States slogged its way through the infamous savings and loan crisis, the failure of Continental Illinois (then one of the ten largest banks in the country), and hundreds

[1] Bell and Hindmoor 2015, 126.
[2] Bordo, Redish, and Rockoff 2015.

of smaller bank failures, but Canadian banks pushed forward with no substantial disruptions. The rare exceptions highlighted just how unaccustomed the Canadian authorities were to dealing with bank instability. In 1985, two obscure Alberta-based banks – the Canadian Commercial Bank and Northland Bank – surprised the residents of Edmonton and Calgary by abruptly shuttering their doors after just ten years in operation. In response, an alarmed Canadian government initiated a formal high-level inquiry headed by a justice of the Supreme Court of Canada, culminating in a ponderous 600-page report on the causes of the bank failures.[3] In contrast, collapsing banks are a relatively mundane occurrence in the United States. If the energies of the US Supreme Court were similarly diverted toward bank failure investigations in 1985, the justices would have been forced to suspend their normal judicial duties to handle the enormous workload of analyzing 120 failures.[4]

Why are Canadian banks so stable relative to those in the United States and elsewhere? Recent scholarship suggests that the answer lies in the structural characteristics of the banking sector.[5]

Political decisions made by British colonizers in the 1800s and by Canadian leaders after independence sent the country down a path toward a centrally controlled banking system governed by a single set of rules for all the provinces. Today, the banking landscape is noted for its high concentration, long history of nationwide branching, culture of conservatism, and simple regulatory structure headed by a single national regulator. In contrast, the United States resembles a Jackson Pollock painting with its 8,000 banks, a confusing splatter of overlapping national and state regulators, and a history of restrictions on nationwide branching.[6] Based on the prevailing scholarship, the secret to stability seems clear: keep the banking industry simple with a small number of nationally diversified banks and a unified regulatory structure.

Yet scholars have overlooked a critical feature of the Canadian financial system, a feature that is central to the argument of this book: Canada's securities markets are surprisingly underdeveloped and provincially fragmented. Canada is the only major industrialized country

[3] Crow 2002, 72; Puri 2013, 168–72.

[4] Bank failure data from FDIC 1998.

[5] Bell and Hindmoor 2015; Bordo, Redish, and Rockoff 2015; Bordo, Rockoff, and Redish 1994; Calomiris and Haber 2014.

[6] See Kroszner and Strahan 1999.

without a national securities regulator. The Canadian constitution did not specifically stipulate how securities markets would be organized or governed, which means that these issues are left to the individual provinces to decide. Thirteen provincial and territorial regulators representing a mix of British common law and French civil law all participate in supervising the issuance and exchange of stocks and bonds.[7] Throughout the twentieth century, shares traded hands in independently supervised exchanges in Toronto, Montreal, Vancouver, Calgary, and Winnipeg. Today, a firm that wishes to raise capital through an issuance of stock must comply with the rules of every province and territory in which its stock will be sold. The costs of doing so could make issuing stock less appealing than securing a traditional bank loan, even with recent efforts to harmonize the rules across the provinces. Moreover, the absence of a national enforcer of rules on insider trading, fraud, and disclosure casts a pall over a market completely dependent on integrity and transparency.[8] Two prominent analysts noted in 1995 that Canada – a fully industrialized country – was home to stock markets that were systematically less developed than those in several *emerging-market* countries, including Malaysia, South Korea, and Thailand.[9]

We argue that Canadian banks' famous conservative bias and history of stability are attributable primarily to weak competitive pressures from underdeveloped securities markets rather than from the concentrated nature of the Canadian banking system or the structure of Canadian banking regulation.[10] Firms in need of capital understand that offering stock to Canadian residents is fraught with costs and inefficiencies. Some firms take their chances by issuing shares on foreign exchanges, especially in the United States or Britain, in the hope of receiving more favorable valuations, while others use national exchanges and tolerate the high costs. But typical Canadian firms rely primarily on longstanding relationships with national banks for their financing needs.

7 Puri 2010, 608.

8 See Puri 2013, 164–5.

9 Demirgüc-Kunt and Levine 1996.

10 There is an ongoing debate about whether bank concentration is itself a determinant of the probability of crises. Some evidence suggests a link for developing countries, where the presence of small locally focused banks could reflect an absence of financial expertise and a heightened chance of mismanagement. However, when economists have examined only developed economies, no link emerges between concentration and the likelihood of banking crises. See Beck, Demirgüç-Kunt, and Levine 2006. Our analysis does not consider Canadian credit unions which are member-owned and constitute a very small percentage of total banking assets.

Banks need not take on undue risk to maintain their client bases, nor are they tempted to dabble in asset-backed securities and other instruments for which markets are relatively shallow. In short, bank lending remains conservative and banks themselves remain stable.[11]

If Canadian banks have a stability-enhancing conservative tilt due in part to the relatively weak pull of securities markets, then by the same logic, US banks are more risk-acceptant due to the depth and sophistication of US securities markets. Unlike the banking industry, US securities markets have been governed by a single regulator – the Securities and Exchange Commission (SEC) – since 1934. The fifty states play only a minor role in the governance of these markets. The early national harmonization of rules on disclosure and fraud allowed these markets to grow unfettered by subnational governments and are now deemed to be the most efficient and well-governed in the world.[12] The experience of post-1970 bank instability in the United States is more likely attributable to the growth of sophisticated securities markets rather than the byzantine structure of the banking industry itself, especially in light of increasing national consolidation of the banking system. We return to the issue of US financial instability in the book's concluding chapter.

Governments are key players in the creation or hindrance of securities markets. Policy decisions rendered during the very early days of a country's financial sector development have enduring effects on regulatory structures, national harmonization or fragmentation, and market depth and sophistication. The primacy of government policy choices is often lost in popular commentary on financial markets. During the Great Recession of 2008–10, commentators frequently referred to the needs of foreign investors, especially those in a desperate "search for yield," as the driving force behind the creation of a welter of risky financial instruments like asset-backed securities and other derivatives. But these instruments only materialized in countries that already possessed well-functioning and sophisticated financial markets.[13]

The goal of this chapter is to isolate the political decisions that shaped the trajectories of Canada's banking system and securities markets, and

[11] On Canadian banks' conservative bias, see Puri 2013.

[12] On the growing centralization of US securities markets since the 1930s, see Michie 2006, 216–19.

[13] See Butzbach, Konzelmann, and Fovargue-Davies 2013, 235.

to emphasize that financial liberalization does not automatically lead to well-functioning markets. Jacobs and Teles provide an elegant summary of our thinking:

> [M]arket creation entails not merely a negative choice to get the state out of the way, but an affirmative act of policy design. All markets exist within institutional structures shaped by public policy: with any decision to decollectivize, privatize, or deregulate, policymakers must necessarily make a host of additional choices about how to configure, and perhaps even direct, the new market. These choices are not simply dictated by an objective, self-evident logic of the "invisible hand": they are political decisions among alternatives – and will have major, and imperfectly foreseeable, consequences for market dynamics.[14]

We further argue that the development trajectory of the securities market influences the behavior of the banking system. In the case of Canada, the relative absence of "affirmative acts of policy design" for securities markets rendered those markets fragmented and underdeveloped, thereby providing space for banks to remain dominant and conservative providers of capital.

We begin with a historical narrative of the development of the banking industry, highlighting the critical decisions codified in Canada's Constitution Act of 1867, which minimized provincial influence on bank chartering and supervision and gave the industry its current national shape. We then continue with a parallel historical analysis of securities markets. The provinces and even the stock exchanges themselves retained control over regulation and governance up to the Great Depression. During the economic crisis of the early 1930s, while the US government seized the opportunity to create a national securities regulator and to minimize the role of state regulatory agencies, Canada made few changes to its regulatory system. The government took no steps to create a national regulator, instead reaffirming the authority of the provinces to supervise their stock exchanges in accordance with their particular needs.

Having established the political origins of Canada's current financial landscape, we then explore the causes and consequences of recent foreign capital inflows. As noted in Chapter 1, capital inflows are a primary trigger of banking instability in developed economies. We demonstrate how Canadian banks have channeled foreign capital to borrowers without taking on undue risk or otherwise changing their lending behavior.

[14] Jacobs and Teles 2007, 158–9; see also Posner 2009, 6.

While this chapter is focused on Canada, we cannot resist the temptation to make comparisons to the United States at various points in the text. Canada and the United States are an ideal duo for comparison. Both countries are former British colonies with federal systems, and they share an enormous border, a common language, and arguably a common culture. Both are "liberal market economies" in the varieties of capitalism nomenclature.[15] Banking markets in both countries were similarly fragmented through the 1860s, as were securities markets through the Great Depression. But certain policy decisions enabled financial markets to unify and thrive, while others caused them to splinter and stagnate. These decisions had, and continue to have, profound implications for bank stability in the twentieth and twenty-first centuries.[16]

THE POLITICAL ROOTS OF THE CANADIAN BANKING MARKET

Our story begins before Canada was Canada. In the 1700s, British and French settlers descended on the eastern regions of New Brunswick and Nova Scotia and further westward toward the areas near the formidable St. Lawrence River. The region bordering Lake Ontario, where the river begins its several-hundred-mile journey eastward to the Atlantic Ocean, came to be known as Upper Canada (modern-day Ontario) in honor of its prime location at the top of the river. The region further downstream and extending far to the north became known as Lower Canada (modern-day Quebec). These areas, along with the territory spanning all the way west to the Pacific Ocean, constituted an enormously attractive target for European settlers. The vast countryside, more than forty times the acreage of the United Kingdom, contained fertile farmland, abundant timber, valuable furs, and almost unfathomable quantities of iron ore, coal, oil, silver, and other natural resources. The St. Lawrence River, anchored by one of the largest estuaries on the planet, provided a convenient channel from the ocean into the territory, ultimately joining five enormous interconnected freshwater lakes.

[15] Hall and Soskice 2001.

[16] This chapter and the next follow the guidance from Gourevitch 1996, 241–2. "If we are to understand the micro-institutions that influence national economic behavior, we must therefore seek to understand the political processes that make these policies, sustain them, produce change, and deter change." We also explore the political economy widely for relevant interest groups, rather than focus on a narrow set of financial institutions. See Pagliari and Young 2014.

And to Canada's south, of course, was another large region with similarly abundant resources, under British control until the United States declared independence in 1776.

Canada's geography and the origins of its early settlers created enormous problems for British colonizers. The remote interior location of some of the region's valuable natural resources, such as coal in Alberta and various minerals in Manitoba, generated great demand for efficient transportation.[17] Large amounts of capital were needed to build railroads and widen waterways, and to finance the highly capital-intensive activities of mining and oil exploration. Moreover, the prominence of French settlers in Quebec prompted the British to think strategically about governance and representation as its colony began to grow.

During the early 1800s, economic development proceeded in the context of a highly fragmented political and financial structure. Upper Canada, Lower Canada, New Brunswick, and Nova Scotia were home to provincial legislatures, each with its own rules reflecting a mix of British and French influences. Merchants in each province banded together and created banks with the blessing of these legislatures, and with highly variable capital structures and business models.[18] For example, the Bank of Upper Canada, which received its charter from the Upper Canada legislature in 1819 and royal assent in 1821, was formed with the expectation that the provincial government would be a prominent holder of the bank's stock.[19] In contrast, the Bank of Montreal, chartered by the legislature of Lower Canada and granted royal assent in 1822, had fewer formal ties to the government and no regular schedule for disclosing its balance sheet and other financial information. Moreover, its charter permitted the establishment of branches in both Upper and Lower Canada.[20] By the middle of the nineteenth century, a patchwork of banks operated throughout Canada, each with its own idiosyncratic procedures for issuing bank notes and backing those notes with gold or government bonds. The fledgling federal government experimented with new legislation, including the Free Banking Act of 1850, which attempted to minimize the influence of provincial legislatures in the bank chartering process. However, the end result was to encourage the establishment of unit

[17] Easterbrook and Aitken 1956, 397–400.

[18] See Breckenridge 1910, 15–37.

[19] Binhammer 1968, 70.

[20] McKeagan 2009, 63.

banks – those with just a single location – and potentially exacerbate the fragmentation from earlier in the century.[21] The act was repealed in 1880 after just five banks were created under its auspices.

The provinces had good reasons for jealously guarding their exclusive control over bank chartering. In addition to receiving a steady flow of chartering fees, provincial legislatures also enjoyed a quid pro quo with the banks that they helped to create. A bank's founders would implicitly pledge their support to the government in exchange for a charter; and those banks whose managers were less than supportive of key political leaders might find their charter applications denied without explanation. Banks could also be privileged partners in the politically fraught process of government finance. A bank charter could come with strings attached, including a requirement to hold government bonds as backing for the issuance of bank notes. If a province could rely on banks as captive buyers of its bonds, then it could issue more debt at lower interest rates. As a result, throughout much of the nineteenth century, bankers and politicians were inextricably linked at the provincial level, and provincial leaders generally had little incentive to permit the entry of banks chartered by other provinces.[22]

In this sense, the banking landscapes in Canada and the United States looked similar by the middle of the nineteenth century.[23] Banking was a subnational phenomenon. The provinces – or in the case of the United States, the state governments – had the sole authority to grant bank charters. Unit banking was more common in the United States than in Canada, but both systems were highly fragmented with limited involvement of the national government.

One important consequence of a geographically fragmented banking system was that banks faced difficulty in diversifying their loan portfolios. A bank in Prince Edward Island in the 1850s could offer loans to potato farmers but not to heavy industry or other sectors that were absent from the small island. Similarly, banks in the Western provinces catered to the needs of regional businesses, including miners, timber producers, and railway operators. The relatively tight relationships forged between bankers and borrowers helped to mitigate the problem

[21] Binhammer 1968, 73; Easterbrook and Aitken 1956, 458.

[22] Easterbrook and Aitken 1956, 453.

[23] On US bank branching regulations and their relaxation in recent times, see Kroszner and Strahan 1999.

of asymmetric information, which might otherwise prevent a bank from issuing a loan to a borrower with an uncertain future. However, the lack of diversification also made the banks highly vulnerable to economic swings and sector-specific shocks. A drought could trigger the downfall of a bank with high loan exposures to farmers; likewise, a period of bad luck in prospecting for gold, silver, or coal could cause a bank in a Western province to falter.

A second consequence of the provincial organization of the banking system was that corruption and collusion were rampant. Politically connected elites formed banks in each province, and invariably they made lending decisions with an explicitly political calculus.[24] The Bank of Upper Canada, formed by a group of elites known derisively as the Family Compact, provided a steady stream of funds to merchants and others who supported the maintenance of a British aristocratic class within the legislative system. A parallel group of mostly British merchants and landowners in Lower Canada, known as Chateau Clique, helped to establish the Bank of Montreal in 1817 and subsequently maintained oligarchic control over the financial system.[25] As discussed later, the collusion between bankers and politicians caused considerable political tension among settlers who felt disenfranchised and marginalized.[26] The links between the Bank of Upper Canada and the government ultimately led to the bank's demise during the economic downturn of the late 1850s. The Bank of Montreal, however, evolved throughout the nineteenth century and now exists proudly as Canada's fourth largest bank, boasting that it has never missed a dividend payment since 1829.[27]

One particularly notable bank that failed just before confederation was the Commercial Bank of the Midland District. Eventually known as the Commercial Bank of Canada, the bank had the auspicious features of many prominent banks in this period: a prestigious group of founders, abundant political connections, and a prime location – in this case, the city of Kingston, perched at the northeast corner of Lake Ontario at the mouth of the St. Lawrence River. The bank proved to be a reliable source of funding for area businesses, including breweries and railroads.

[24] Calomiris and Haber 2014, 287–96.

[25] On the Bank of Montreal's charter, see Breckenridge 1910, 9.

[26] See, e.g., Calomiris and Haber 2014, 299.

[27] See www.bmo.com/home/about/banking/investor-relations/shareholder-information/dividend-information.

In the late 1850s, after the collapse of the Bank of Upper Canada, the Commercial Bank took on the accounts of the Great Western Railway and provided substantial funding for the construction and operation of the Detroit & Milwaukee Railway.[28] When the railway hit hard times, Great Western found itself unable to pay its debts. As rumors began to fly, depositors rushed to withdraw their funds from Commercial Bank, ultimately causing it to collapse in 1867. The bank's failure was devastating to the community. Queens University, established by a royal charter issued by Queen Victoria in 1841, lost two thirds of its endowment in the fiasco.[29]

As the provinces and territories of Canada entered the second half of the nineteenth century, the banking "system," if such a word applies, was in shambles. The Family Compact's famed Bank of Upper Canada had collapsed, leaving only its beautiful three-story limestone building in the Old Town district of Toronto. Commercial Bank soon closed its doors as well, leaving businesses scrambling for capital and financial services. Merchants squabbled about appropriate rules for new banks and were stymied by conflicting interests across provinces. Canada, in short, faced a critical juncture in the evolution of its banking system.[30]

The Birth of a Modern Banking System

The British North America Act of 1867, also called the Constitution Act, marked the birth of modern Canada. The new country, called the Dominion of Canada, comprised the provinces of Ontario, Quebec, New Brunswick, and Nova Scotia. With the blessing of the British crown, Canadian political leaders agreed to create a national government with sweeping powers over economic and commercial policy. The act also formalized the establishment of provincial governments and delegated a number of important functions to them. Canada was still under the rubric of the British Empire, but it became a self-governing entity, clearly on a path to becoming a fully sovereign country.

The compromises inherent in the act reflected both international and domestic influences. Internationally, there is no underestimating the impact of the early tumultuous years of the United States on Canadian thinkers.

[28] Breckenridge 1910, 82.

[29] See www.queensu.ca/encyclopedia/c/commercial-bank-midland-district.

[30] On critical junctures, see Mahoney 2001; Thelen 2004.

Lord Durham, governor-general of the Province of Canada in the late 1830s, wrote of the ordinary Canadian resident:

> The influence of the United States surrounds him on every side and is forever present ... it is felt in all the transactions of commerce, from the important operations of the monetary system down to the minor details of ordinary traffic; it stamps, on all the habits and opinions of the surrounding countries, the common characteristics of the thoughts, feelings, and customs of the American people.[31]

When Canadian leaders sat down at the negotiating table at the Quebec Conference of 1864, the US Civil War was in full swing, and the prospects for holding the nascent American federation together were uncertain. Wary Canadian leaders like John A. MacDonald, who would become Canada's first prime minister, favored a strong national government to avoid the regional displays of power and leverage that seemed to be tearing apart the United States.[32] Unlike the US Constitution, in which any unspecified policy realm was assumed to be within the jurisdiction of the individual states, the Constitution Act stipulated that any power not specifically delegated to the provinces was retained by the national government.

Canada had its own struggles on the domestic front that affected the character of its new confederation. The 1830s were a particularly difficult time as settlers grew increasingly frustrated with the unelected legislative councils that made rules in each province. The famous Rebellions of 1837 occurred when settlers grew dissatisfied with the Tory-affiliated oligarchies that governed Upper and Lower Canada and engaged in armed uprisings. Lord Durham, tasked by Britain to investigate the causes of the rebellions, advocated for the unification of Upper and Lower Canada in his *Report on the Affairs of British North America*.[33] He also recommended the establishment of a "responsible government" for the unified province, a not-so-subtle dig against the Family Compact and Chateau Clique oligarchies. To be clear, Lord Durham's motivation was to keep the peace and to ensure a loyal British ruling class in the provinces, not to impose representative government for its own sake. But the idea that the union of the provinces was tenuous, and that political discord could rip it apart, endured through the 1860s and beyond.[34]

French settlers in Canada posed a particular concern for Lord Durham and other British loyalists. As Calomiris and Haber (2014)

[31] Quoted in Hammond 1957, 631.
[32] Armstrong 1981, 8–14.
[33] Durham 1839.
[34] Armstrong 1981, 9.

note, the vast majority of Canada's residents in the late 1700s were of French origin, no doubt a source of dismay to provincial leaders who wished to keep the colony firmly in the hands of the British Empire.[35] The institutional strength of the newly created national government in 1867 was in part attributable to the goal of limiting the power of the French population. Seats in the upper house of the new government were allocated by province, not by population, thereby minimizing the influence of French-controlled Quebec and favoring sparsely populated British-controlled regions. The addition of three new British-dominated provinces to the country – Manitoba (1870), British Columbia (1871), and Prince Edward Island (1873) – helped to tilt the balance away from the French by the mid-1870s.

The British North America Act granted the newly created federal government exclusive control over banking, but the details were left for future legislation. The Bank Act of 1871 formalized all of the details and established a foundation for Canadian banking, parts of which endure to this day.[36] The most important rule was that all new banks would require national charters granted by the Parliament. Any bank created under the previous system would be allowed to operate under its existing provincial charter until 1881, after which it would be required to apply for a new national charter. A second important rule was that new banks required a relatively large amount of capital to secure a charter. The bank's managers had to show subscribed capital of at least $500,000, with at least $100,000 in hand before the bank could open its doors.[37] This high capital requirement ensured that banks would be fairly large, and it encouraged, if not required, banks to open branches over large areas to secure adequate deposit and lending bases. It also served as a de facto restriction on entry; some observers have gone as far as to call the system a "cartel backed by the federal government."[38]

As admirers of the Canadian banking system have long noted, economies of scale and nationwide branching help to ensure a stable financial system.[39] Consider the experience of the Bank of Nova Scotia, which began in the 1830s as a modest bank with branches in the Maritime towns of Halifax, St. John, Pictou, and others.[40] The demand for capital

35 Calomiris and Haber 2014, 285.
36 Binhammer 1968, 76; For a full discussion of the 1871 banking law, see Smith 2012.
37 Waite 1971, 78.
38 Bordo, Redish, and Rockoff 2015, 224.
39 See Bordo, Redish, and Rockoff 2015; Calomiris and Haber 2014.
40 This section relies on Frost 1982.

from cotton mills, sugar refineries, timber producers, and other industries led to the bank's steady growth up until confederation. A period of extraordinary expansion began in the 1880s – just after the passage of the Bank Act – as the bank added branches in Montreal, Toronto, and eventually all the way to Vancouver. By 1910, the bank had a total of ninety-eight branches spanning the entire country. The economic downturn in Nova Scotia in the 1880s and 1890s would have doomed a bank that catered exclusively to local industries, but the Bank of Nova Scotia's extensive network of branches ensured that its lending portfolio was highly diversified. Weaknesses in the seafaring communities of the Maritimes could be comfortably offset by strengths in manufacturing and agricultural industries in Toronto, Calgary, and Edmonton.

The Bank Act set the country on a path toward a highly concentrated banking system. Smaller banks like the Bank of Nova Scotia either scaled up their branching in the early twentieth century or shuttered their doors. The banking system condensed from a high of fifty-one banks during the 1870–1920 period to less than ten throughout the rest of the century.[41]

It would be an exaggeration to claim that Canadian banks were uniformly stable during the early twentieth century. While prevailing legislation encouraged geographic diversification, it was still possible for bankers to get themselves into trouble for reasons other than the narrowness of their loan portfolios. Ontario Bank, for example, which had a prominent branch in Toronto and twenty-nine others throughout Ontario and Quebec, failed in 1906 due to fraud by the bank's managers and catastrophic bets on the US stock market.[42] Home Bank failed in 1923 for similar reasons, and although it accounted for just 1 percent of national bank capital at the time, it helped to spur the creation of a national bank regulator just two years later.[43] The Office of the Inspector General of Banks, renamed the Office of the Superintendent of Financial Institutions in 1987 after taking insurance under its jurisdiction, has been the sole regulator of banks for nearly 100 years.

In previous studies of Canadian banking stability, the narrative generally stops here. As Bordo, Redish, and Rockoff argue, "In Canada the banking system was created as a system of large financial institutions whose size and diversification enhanced their robustness. Moreover, it evolved into an oligopoly, which was tightly regulated in a grand

[41] Bordo, Rockoff, and Redish 1994, 326–7.

[42] www.thestar.com/news/gta/2008/02/19/the_ontario_banks_1906_collapse.html.

[43] Bordo, Rockoff, and Redish 1994, 329.

bargain whereby the chartered banks would provide financial stability in exchange for the Canadian government limiting entry to the industry."[44] Diversification and sensible regulation no doubt enhanced banks' stability, but as Ontario Bank's failure in 1906 indicates, even large banks can make mistakes and take on excessive risk. Moreover, there is scant evidence that developed-economy banking systems composed of large, diversified banks are more stable than those with a larger number of smaller banks.[45] In recent times, nationally diversified banks like Wells Fargo in the United States and Northern Rock in the United Kingdom required emergency assistance after becoming insolvent. To flesh out a more compelling explanation for bank stability, our narrative continues with an analysis of the development of securities markets in Canada.

POLITICAL ORIGINS OF CANADA'S SECURITIES MARKETS

As with the history of banking discussed earlier, we can usefully begin the history of Canadian securities markets in the nineteenth century. Demand for capital was acute during Canada's early years largely as a result of a daunting variety of transportation and infrastructure challenges.[46] One of the great promises of the colony was the St. Lawrence River, which proved to be a partially navigable and partially treacherous channel from the Great Lakes to the Atlantic Ocean. An early nautical challenge was to allow ships to bypass the Lachine Rapids – the turbulent waters of the St. Lawrence around the southern curve of the island of Montreal – by carving out a ten-mile canal running northeast through the island. The Lachine Canal opened in 1825, coincidentally the same year as the christening of the enormous Erie Canal throughout the State of New York in the United States.[47] Additional projects followed, including the Welland Canal connecting Lake Ontario and Lake Erie, the Cornwall Canal midway between Montreal and Kingston, and the Beauharnois Canal that bypassed a smaller set of rapids just southwest of Montreal.[48] Canada's vast landscapes proved to be an even greater challenge, both logistically and financially. The territory spanned, at its extremes, well over 3,000 miles from east to west and nearly that

[44] Bordo, Redish, and Rockoff 2015, 219.
[45] Beck, Demirgüç-Kunt, and Levine 2006.
[46] See, e.g., McKeagan 2009; Tucker 1978.
[47] See Sobel 1965, 32–8.
[48] www.greatlakes-seaway.com/en/seaway/history/.

distance from north to south. Investors funneled millions into railroads from the 1830s through the 1900s in an attempt to develop the territory's interior regions and facilitate the cross-country movement of natural resources, manufactured goods, and residents.

Mining was a particularly important capital-intensive undertaking during Canada's early years.[49] Unlike the process of building a railroad, in which the engineering challenges are straightforward to predict, the process of prospecting for gold, coal, and diamonds was fraught with uncertainty. There was no foolproof method of detecting the location of precious minerals; instead, prospectors used their best estimates and then began the arduous and often expensive process of dredging, sluicing, blasting, and digging underground. Whoever provided the capital for such an undertaking bore the risk that the process could be categorically unsuccessful.

The nascent banking industry of the 1830s and 1840s, along with wealthy businessmen, cobbled together as much capital as they could for infrastructure and mining projects. Business leaders were particularly interested in developing Canada's transportation system. For example, John Molson, founder of the Quebec brewery that bears his name, was eager to create a transit link between his operations on the shore of the St. Lawrence to the Richelieu River to the east. He led the financing for the Champlain and St. Lawrence Railroad – Canada's first – which opened in 1836. Molson's brand of single-handed financial leadership, however, became less common as the century progressed. The scale of the investments required to develop the country's interior and extract its natural resources quickly eclipsed the ability of individual businessmen and even banks to provide adequate financing.[50]

Scarce capital prompted businesses to form joint-stock companies that could tap into the excess savings of disparate investors around the country and overseas.[51] The bearer of a stock certificate had an ownership claim on the company and could receive dividends or other payouts. Investors were passive (except for a select few who owned large percentages of outstanding shares), so no business acumen was required to invest. Shares of stock could be bought and sold in the open market, thereby shifting the ownership stake from one investor to another. Banks were early adopters of this form of enterprise given the large sums of capital required to obtain a charter, but railways, mining companies, and other industrials quickly followed suit.

[49] See Smith 1986.
[50] Michie 1988, 40.
[51] Ibid., 38.

The rise of joint-stock companies created two key challenges for Canadian financial development. The first was that buying and selling securities required markets in which participants could transact. An investor in, say, a mining company who wished to sell his shares needed to find a willing buyer; and similarly, an investor who wished to hold shares in a railroad company had to find a seller – either the company itself or a current shareholder. Stockbrokers helped to fill these roles for investors but they faced similar problems with each other. A broker in Kingston with shares to offload might struggle to find a broker elsewhere in the province who was willing to purchase them for his clients. At stake was nothing less than the viability of this system for raising capital: if securities could not be freely bought and sold, investors would have little incentive to participate and businesses would have to seek capital through other channels.[52]

It is difficult to pinpoint the exact date of the establishment of Canada's first stock exchange because it most likely emerged in a coffee shop.[53] In the 1830s, brokers began to congregate in the Exchange Coffee House on St. Paul Street in Montreal. Businessmen from all over the region would arrive via stagecoach to check into the attached hotel or to have a meal in the restaurant. At first the buying and selling of stock was limited to shares in the Champlain and St. Lawrence Railroad, which John Molson and his co-investors were eager to offload at a healthy profit. Eventually, trading expanded to include shares in banks and other railroads, and the nascent stock market outgrew the confines of the quaint coffee house. In 1863, market participants created a Board of Stock Brokers with rules governing membership, commissions, and other fees, and in 1874 they obtained a charter for the Montreal Stock Exchange.[54]

The other Canadian exchanges had similar origins. In Toronto in the 1850s, a small group of businessmen gathered for thirty minutes each morning to swap information and rumors and to connect buyers and sellers of bank and railroad shares.[55] By the 1860s, the *Toronto Leader* was publishing weekly stock prices for the Bank of Upper Canada, the Bank of Montreal, the Toronto Gas Company, and several other companies.[56] The informal gathering of brokers received formal recognition as the Toronto Stock Exchange in 1878 with a special act of the Ontario

[52] See ibid., 36.

[53] Edgar Andrew Collard, "From Coffee House to Tower," *Montreal Gazette*, January 21, 1984, B2.

[54] McKay 1964, 37.

[55] Whiteside 1985.

[56] McKay 1964, 35.

legislature.[57] The western exchanges emerged early in the twentieth century, starting with Winnipeg in 1903, Vancouver in 1907, and finally Calgary in 1913. Vancouver in particular grew quickly as a trading venue for shares in oil and mining companies and remained Canada's third largest exchange throughout most of the century.[58]

The second key challenge, which these exchanges only partially addressed, was building trust in the integrity of securities markets and in securities themselves. It was all too easy for a con artist to concoct a fictitious company and peddle its stock to citizens with the promise of great rewards. Investors with modest incomes, lured by shares costing only a few pennies each, could subsequently find that their investment was completely worthless. Mining companies in particular had incentives to make lavish promises of discoveries in order to accumulate the large sums of capital needed for prospecting. If a mining company went bankrupt or if its managers disappeared without further communication, the disparate investors in its stock had little recourse – and given the relatively small sums involved per investor, the costs of collective action precluded any follow-up with the judicial system.

Managing a stock exchange is a delicate balancing act. Unlike a bank that cultivates a long-term relationship with a borrower and monitors its finances, stock investors are often driven by speculation. There is nothing inherently unethical about a high-risk, high-reward investment. Regulators would agree that in a well-functioning financial system, an investor who wishes to gamble on a highly uncertain mining company should be allowed to do so as long as there is no criminal deceit underpinning the transaction. The delicacy arises because there is a fine line between risk and deception. The asymmetry of information between a stock investor and a company's managers is extremely high, especially when the investor is an ordinary citizen with no business training. The ideal balance from a commercial perspective is to disclose enough information about the enterprise to enable investors to make informed decisions, but not to close off the inflow of capital simply because an investment is highly speculative.[59]

The early stock markets approached regulation gradually and idiosyncratically. In practice, the precise balance of risk and regulation

[57] Ibid.

[58] Armstrong 1997.

[59] On the importance of information in capital market development, see Sylla and Smith 1995.

depended on the characteristics of the dominant sector in the province. Each stock exchange adopted a practice of self-regulation. Exchanges that catered to highly speculative stocks in the natural resource sector, like Vancouver, imposed few restrictions on listed companies or brokers. Brokers in Vancouver routinely made fraudulent claims about mining companies with little fear of criminal sanctions. With evidence consisting only of verbal commitments and passionate sales pitches, fraud was nearly impossible to substantiate in the courts.[60] Criminality aside, the Vancouver board of directors had little incentive to impose stringent rules on a market that was celebrated for its risk. In contrast, the Toronto and Montreal exchanges had more sectoral diversification, including the finance and transportation industries, and enforced somewhat tighter disclosure rules for listed firms and transaction standards for brokers.[61]

Canada's response to these key challenges – creating formal stock markets and enacting appropriate regulations – was to allow a highly fragmented stock market system to emerge.[62] The geographic fragmentation occurred as a result of the high transaction costs of trading stock in the nineteenth and early twentieth centuries. The absence of modern communications infrastructure meant that securities transactions were conducted in person. Brokers needed a physical place to gather and share information about the companies whose shares were trading hands. Given the vastness of Canada's territory and the likelihood that rumor mills were most active within provinces rather than across them, exchanges formed at the provincial level and specialized in trading shares in the province's most prevalent site-specific sectors.[63] Regulatory fragmentation flowed naturally from this geographic separation as each exchange catered its rules to the risk appetites of investors and sectors in that region.

The British North America Act did little to offset these trends toward fragmentation. At the time of the act, stock exchanges were in their infancy in Ontario and Quebec and there was no sense among political leaders that securities markets would require national regulation or supervision. Unlike banking, in which legislators could reap great financial rewards and political connections as gatekeepers of bank charters, there were no discernible rents to be gained by restricting the chartering

[60] Armstrong 1997, 6.

[61] See Cruise 1987.

[62] See Michie 1988, 54–61.

[63] See, e.g., Cruise 1987.

of stock exchanges.[64] Toronto's and Montreal's original fifteen-seat exchanges – each literally a single room with fifteen chairs – hardly seemed like targets of political opportunism for national leaders, or a cause for concern by broader segments of society. The Constitution therefore omitted any mention of securities regulation or stock market supervision. Normally this omission would have paved the way for national regulation in the future, because the Constitution Act granted the national government all powers that were not specifically delegated to the provinces. However, as capital markets expanded in the twentieth century, each province or territory invoked the "property and civil rights" clause of the act to justify the maintenance of self-regulation at the provincial level.[65]

Canadian Capital Markets from 1900 to the Great Depression

Canadian and US stock markets developed in parallel during the early 1900s, and Canada's policy choices mirrored those of its southern neighbor. Securities fraud was the most important issue during this period. Historical accounts of financial markets in the early twentieth century are rife with colorful expressions of criminality: swindlers, flimflammers, con artists, hustlers, and fleecers were eager to separate naïve investors from their money.[66] In the US State of Kansas, deceptive brokers would allegedly peddle schemes that had no more basis than "so many feet of blue sky."[67] The Kansas banking commissioner initiated an investigation into securities fraud in 1910, and a year later the state legislature passed a set of rules governing the offering and sale of securities. Later dubbed the first blue-sky law, the legislation required all stock issuers to obtain a permit from the state banking commissioner before offering securities to any resident of Kansas.[68] The permit application required the issuer to provide, under oath, a variety of information about finances and manager qualifications. This information would, in theory, allow the commissioner to determine whether the stock peddler had a bona fide investment opportunity worthy of careful consideration by the investor.

[64] On the limited interest-group environment for financial regulation more generally, see Pagliari and Young 2016; Rosenbluth 1989.

[65] Puri 2009, 1690.

[66] See, For example, Cruise 1987.

[67] Neufeld 1972, 535.

[68] For a summary, see Seligman 1982, 44.

Blue-sky laws, in addition to addressing a serious problem with stock peddlers, were also a manifestation of early competition between banks and the non-bank financial sector. It is not a coincidence that a bank commissioner led the charge for more stringent rules for securities markets. In the few years before World War I, the turbulent US economy led to stubbornly high inflation that threatened the ability of banks to attract and retain deposits.[69] Higher-yielding securities were a potentially attractive alternative for investors eager to earn a reasonable rate of return in a high-inflation environment. Bank commissioners were natural advocates for legislative efforts to suppress securities markets and to prevent stockbrokers from siphoning away banks' scarce deposits.

Kansas's blue-sky law created an international and domestic domino effect of legislative adoption. By 1913, twenty-three US states had enacted securities regulation statutes, with all but six of them either identical to the Kansas law or modeled on it.[70] By 1933, every state but Nevada had securities legislation on its books. Blue-sky laws also spread quickly throughout Canada. The Province of Manitoba was the Canadian pioneer, having adopted a Sale of Shares Act in 1912 that was taken almost verbatim from the Kansas legislation. Saskatchewan and Alberta enacted similar legislation in 1915 and 1916, respectively, and New Brunswick followed suit in 1923. Quebec introduced an information disclosure rule in 1924 and Ontario followed with more wide-ranging anti-fraud protections and rules for stockbrokers in 1928.[71]

Despite some early boasting by local officials, blue-sky laws were largely ineffective in both the United States and Canada.[72] As Seligman notes, "Rarely have statues enacted with such fanfare and general support subsequently been so universally deprecated."[73] The legislation delegated enforcement responsibilities to a disparate group of unskilled government workers in banking commissions, railroad commissions, and state and provincial audit and other agencies.[74] State and provincial officials had wide latitude to interpret the rules and to accept or reject stock issues for personal or political reasons.[75] As political leaders changed, so too did the agents responsible for law enforcement.

[69] Macey and Miller 1991, 350.
[70] Seligman 1982, 45.
[71] Neufeld 1972, 535.
[72] See Keller 1988, 332; Neufeld 1972, 539; Seligman 1982, 45.
[73] Seligman 1982, 45.
[74] Keller 1988, 332.
[75] Macey and Miller 1991, 350.

Some regions were deliberately lax in their enforcement efforts in order to attract business and investment. And finally, state- and provincial-level laws were easy to evade via cross-state business dealings.[76] An investment firm could simply make an offering across state or provincial lines through the mail and bypass any blue-sky licensing or disclosure requirements. In Canada, so-called Dominion companies – those with national charters – were largely exempt from provincial regulations. Regional laws were simply ill-equipped to address a national phenomenon.

The rollout and subsequent foundering of blue-sky laws coincided with a dramatic increase in the number of Canadian residents entering the market for securities. The Canadian government borrowed heavily to finance its involvement in World War I with much of the borrowing coming directly from ordinary citizens. The government issued so-called Victory Bonds in small denominations, thereby enabling modest investors to participate. As Armstrong notes, "For many citizens the purchase of a Victory bond marked their first foray into such an investment. When prosperity returned in the 1920s, Canadians in all walks of life plunged enthusiastically into stock speculation, especially in mining shares."[77] Part of their enthusiasm came from their experience not just with purchasing war bonds, but with selling them on the secondary market. Individual investors learned that securities need not be held for the long haul; even a ten-year bond could be traded at any time on the Montreal or Toronto exchanges. Similarly, investors grew accustomed to the idea that shares in a mining company could be offloaded, sometimes at a handsome profit, well before the outcome of the company's mineral prospecting was made public. The liquidity of markets formed part of a virtuous circle: as more investors purchased their first shares, securities became easier to trade on secondary markets, thereby attracting more investors who were otherwise wary of the costs of exiting the market. The number of stocks traded on the Toronto Stock Exchange increased from 80 to over 200 between 1900 and 1914. Total shares traded per year in Toronto and Montreal expanded from around 45 million in 1919 to 350 million in the late 1920s. By 1929, the price of a seat on the Montreal Stock Exchange had reached a whopping $225,000.[78]

[76] Seligman 1982, 45.

[77] Armstrong 1997, 7.

[78] McKay 1964, 34. This is more than $3 million in today's dollars.

As markets broadened and deepened, the failings of market regulation grew more pronounced.[79] Fraud continued to drag down investor trust. Provincial regulators had inadequate staffs and financial resources to fulfill their obligations. Only superficial rules existed for the form, content, and distribution of prospectuses and for the types of information that firms were required to disclose in their financial statements. It was not uncommon for bankrupt companies to issue shares and to obfuscate their dire financial circumstances from potential buyers. Moreover, there were virtually no regulations pertaining to the ethics of stock exchanges themselves. Managers of companies with inside information could trade on their knowledge, manipulate share prices, and reap huge rewards at the expense of ordinary investors. Insiders could also bypass the will of shareholders by manipulating the voting process, such as failing to send proxy statements or neglecting to disclose all pertinent information in proxy solicitations. Perhaps the most pressing problem of all was that regulations were not uniform throughout the country or even within provinces. Shares that traded on certain exchanges were exempt from consumer protection rules, and every province and territory had its own system of regulatory oversight.

The Great Depression: A Window of Opportunity Closes for National Securities Regulation

In the first decades of the twentieth century, the stock markets in the United States and Canada were similarly fragmented. In the United States, thirty exchanges operated in cities throughout the country, ranging from San Francisco and Seattle on the West Coast, to Cleveland and Detroit in the Midwest, to Boston and New York on the East Coast.[80] Each exchange catered to firms with headquarters in the region. The Cincinnati Stock Exchange, for example, was the marketplace for shares in Procter and Gamble, Kroger, and Goodyear Tire, all prominent local firms.[81] In Canada, exchanges in Montreal, Toronto, Vancouver, Calgary, and Winnipeg served as marketplaces for shares of regional companies. Each exchange had its own set of rules for brokers, investors, and listed shares, and had to abide by prevailing state or provincial blue-sky laws.

[79] This section relies on Neufeld 1972, 539.

[80] Kaltenborn 1964, 26–8.

[81] See www.cincinnatistockexchange.us/kroger-and-the-cincinnati-stock-exchange/.

The 1920s were boom years for all of these exchanges. Buoyant corporate profits, relatively cheap credit, and a feeling of euphoria after the end of World War I combined to boost share prices and investor interest. From 1921 to 1929, the year-to-year trend in stock prices in Canada was consistently upward; investors who purchased a diversified portfolio of stocks at the start of this period would have seen their account value triple by the end of the period.[82] But as with US markets, these gains did not reflect the underlying reality of firm performance or the overall health of the economy. Compared to corporate earnings, share prices were unusually high; and in light of falling prices for goods and services and a slowdown in export growth, stock market euphoria seemed oddly misplaced, at least in retrospect.

The collapse came suddenly in the autumn of 1929. A wave of selling began on October 28, overwhelming the ability of stock tickers to record all the transactions. Throngs of brokers and investors descended upon the financial districts in Montreal and Toronto as banks and brokerage offices struggled to keep up with the paperwork.[83] The manic selling continued the next day – Black Tuesday – as investors struggled to pull their funds from a crashing market. In the ensuing days and weeks, the exchanges enacted a range of short-term crisis management strategies. The Toronto Stock Exchange shortened its trading hours to 10 a.m. to 1 p.m.[84] Other exchanges imposed floors for stock prices, automatically ceasing trading if a share price touched the floor. Trading volumes plummeted as liquidity dried up. The Alberta Stock Exchange, a previously vibrant marketplace for shares of mining and resource exploration companies, experienced a 60 percent decline in volume during the first half of 1930.[85] By the end of the year, stock indexes experienced a historic decline: nearly 30 percent for industrials, utilities, and banks, and 25 percent for mining shares.[86]

The crisis shed light on the seedy underbelly of stock exchanges as observers wondered whether the crash was due in part to the unethical activities of traders. One strategy that grew in prevalence throughout the 1920s was called "pooling," a form of collusion in which a small group of investors, often working in partnership with a staff

[82] Bothwell, Drummond, and English 1987, 221.
[83] Armstrong 1997, 146.
[84] Ibid.
[85] Ibid., 169.
[86] Ibid., 146; 180.

member of the stock exchange, would bid up a stock's price to generate attention from other investors. Once an investor purchases shares, the insiders would offload their positions at a large profit. Shares in mining companies were particularly susceptible to this type of market manipulation, partly due to the power of rumor to generate investor interest, and partly because the relatively small number of outstanding shares (called "floats") allowed for easy manipulation of prices by a small group of investors.[87] A second form of manipulation, also most applicable to mining shares and other stocks with small floats, was "wash trading": investors purchases shares from one broker and sells the shares immediately through another broker. The insiders incur no risk but the market activity provides a false sense to other investors that the stock is actively traded, thereby luring them to purchase the stock and bid up its price.[88] The insiders, having amassed a sizable holding of the stock before the manipulation, can then offload their shares at a profit.

Stockbrokers were complicit in the unethical strategies of their clients and also engaged in a few strategies of their own. The market for penny stocks was particularly ripe for exploitation. Investors in these highly speculative shares would often place orders on margin, borrowing from the broker at a high rate of interest with the hope that the shares would increase in value. Some brokers would fail to execute orders for penny stocks and instead pocket the proceeds, knowing that their clients were likely to be delinquent in their loan payments. In the off chance that clients successfully paid off the loan and wanted to claim their shares, the broker would quickly buy the stock at the prevailing price. The discrepancy between clients' purchases and brokers' actual activity led to a stark conflict of interest: brokers would often "short" (sell on margin) the stock that was supposed to be held on behalf of clients.[89] In essence, brokers manipulated the market for their own gain at the expense of their clients' welfare.

Investors whose savings were wiped out in the crash inveighed against the lack of a level playing field with market insiders and unscrupulous brokers. Provincial leaders took notice, but their subsequent policy

[87] See Cruise 1987.

[88] As quaint as this manipulation sounds, it remains a serious problem today, even in the most sophisticated stock markets. See www.wsj.com/articles/SB10001424127887323639604578366491497070204. Wash trading is explicitly prohibited by the Securities and Exchange Act of 1934.

[89] Armstrong 1997, 147.

proposals were modest. Led by Ontario Attorney General William H. Price, representatives from the provinces met in Toronto in early 1930 to discuss the failings of stock market regulation.[90] Provincial leaders came to a series of agreements, all of which re-emphasized the primacy of regional, as opposed to national, supervision of exchanges. The leaders agreed that legislatures should amend their existing market rules to formally prohibit the practice of stockbrokers going short against their customers' holdings. They also agreed, at least in principle, that the individual stock exchanges should tighten their listing requirements, maintain better records, and expel members who failed to abide by the rules. But the policymakers also made it clear that extreme caution was warranted for even these incremental regulatory adjustments. Their report concluded with the following revealing statement: "The development of mining and other natural resources of the country must always be kept in mind, and care must be taken in remedying of abuses not to create others, which would only stifle business and not advance the general interests of the public."[91]

The market crash and Great Depression constituted a nationwide shock that could have triggered a national policy response. And for banking, in fact, the government responded a few years later by establishing the Bank of Canada, the country's first central bank.[92] But compared to the banking industry, which was governed by a single set of rules and supervised exclusively at the national level, the securities industry remained a patchwork of idiosyncratic markets with widely varying rules. In this context, it is all the more surprising that the national government was an advocate of regulatory forbearance. In the early 1930s, federal policymakers in Ottawa were primarily concerned about protecting Dominion companies – those with national charters and governed by national rules. Provincial leaders wanted to subject these companies to blue-sky laws and ensure a level playing field with provincially chartered firms. Conservative Prime Minister Richard Bennett's government clamored for an exemption. A prominent court case, *Lymburn v. Mayland*, eventually settled the issue on appeal, granting the provinces the right to apply fraud-protection rules to Dominion companies that wished to sell shares.[93] By the mid-1930s, the federal government stood aside as the provinces assumed unequivocal

[90] Ibid., 159–60.
[91] Quoted in ibid., 160.
[92] Crow 2002, 6.
[93] Armstrong 1997, 217.

control over securities markets. Regulators invoked the "property and civil rights" clause of the Constitution Act of 1867 as justification for keeping securities regulation in provincial hands.[94] A new Companies Act, passed during the 1934 session of Parliament, required promoters of nationally chartered companies to disclose certain financial data to the public, but this legislation simply brought national companies up to provincial disclosure standards. Canada therefore entered the 1940s with a securities industry that was virtually unchanged from the 1920s, at least in terms of its regulatory structure. The absence of a push toward national harmonization after the Great Depression helped to solidify a fragmented securities market for the decades that followed.

Canada's Underdeveloped Securities Markets Endure

To this day, despite consolidation of the stock exchanges themselves,[95] Canada has not enacted national securities legislation of the type that exists in most other industrialized countries. The first earnest attempt to create a national securities commission, akin to the US Securities and Exchange Commission, came only in 2003 with a federal report ironically entitled *It's Time*. The report cited inadequate enforcement, unnecessary duplication, high bureaucratic costs, and inconsistent investor protection across the provinces.[96] The report received endorsements from the Investment Dealers Association of Canada and the Canadian Bankers Association but mixed support from the provinces. Ontario, home to Canada's largest exchange, generally favored the creation of a national regulatory regime that would most likely reflect prevailing regulations in the province. Quebec, with its French-speaking population and civil law system, was opposed. The Alberta and British Columbia regulators echoed the sentiments of the provinces in 1930 by expressing strong reservations about imposing a uniform set of rules that could hamper the ability of natural resource companies to raise capital.[97]

94 Puri 2009, 1690.

95 In 1999, the Vancouver, Alberta, and Winnipeg exchanges merged to form the Canadian Venture Exchange, later renamed the TSX Venture Exchange, which is now part of the Toronto Stock Exchange (TSX). Today, Canada is home to three exchanges: TSX, TSX Venture, and Bourse de Montréal.

96 Kitching 2009, 5.

97 Resistance by the provinces to national integration is similar to European states' resistance in the late twentieth century to pan-European stock markets with harmonized regulations. See Posner 2009.

Throughout the twentieth century, a firm that wished to raise capital through a public offering across Canada had to abide by the licensing and disclosure requirements of every province and territory in which its stock would be made available.[98] More recently, the Canadian Securities Administrators (CSA), an umbrella organization of the thirteen provincial and territorial regulators, developed a "passport" system in 2004 to allow a market participant to access all markets in participating jurisdictions by complying with the rules of a single provincial regulator. The passport system has been in place for more than a decade, but Ontario – the country's largest and most important securities jurisdiction – has chosen not to participate. In practice, participating jurisdictions accept the rulings of the Ontario Securities Commission (OSC), but the OSC requires non-Ontario market participants to seek its approval through a special interface system.[99] The passport eased some of the costs of raising capital on stock markets, but issuing firms must still pay hefty fees to specialized lawyers and accountants in each province and listing fees to each regulator. The delays associated with provincial approval of an issuing company's prospectus constitute an additional cost.[100] Moreover, certain regulatory areas remain beyond the scope of harmonization, such as derivatives and enforcement actions.[101]

Advocates for a single national regulator noted these high costs during the legislative debates of the early 2000s, continuing more recently with the report of the Expert Panel on Securities Regulation in 2009.[102] The Investment Funds Institute of Canada argued that Canadian capital markets "as a result of our grossly inefficient regulatory model, must bear costs that are completely out of proportion to any potential benefit that can be derived from participating in the Canadian market. The unfortunate combination of small size and high regulatory compliance and transactional costs is inherently unattractive as it renders the cost of raising capital prohibitively high."[103] The expert panel spelled out the problem starkly in its introduction: "If Canada is to realize its potential in the global economy, the regulation of its financial markets must be among the world's best. At the moment, it is not."[104]

[98] Kitching 2009, 4.

[99] See the CSA's summary at www.securities-administrators.ca/aboutcsa.aspx?id=96.

[100] MacIntosh 1997, 210.

[101] Anand and Green 2010, 665.

[102] Hockin 2009.

[103] Hockin 2003, 4–5.

[104] Hockin 2009, 1.

High costs aside, market participants also perceive weaknesses in the enforcement of securities law due to the fragmented regulatory structure.[105] Provincial securities commissions conduct regulatory and enforcement functions and are solely responsible for investigating regulatory misconduct and presiding over adjudicative proceedings.[106] Some provinces place greater emphasis on investor protection than others; moreover, many jurisdictions do not have sufficient staffs or budgets to perform their duties adequately.[107] Enforcement of securities law often requires coordination among disparate provincial regulators, a process characterized by delays and inefficiencies. Global best practices, as represented by International Organization of Securities Commissions (IOSCO) standards, are not easily implemented in Canada due to its fragmentation; in fact, Canada is the only developed country not represented by a national regulator in IOSCO, an organization representing securities markets in 115 member jurisdictions.

The expert panel summarized its concerns about Canada's current regulatory structure as follows:

> We believe that the fragmented structure, requiring decisions to be coordinated across up to 13 jurisdictions, makes it difficult for Canadian securities regulators to react quickly and decisively to capital market events. One illustration of this difficulty is the adoption in September 2008 by our international counterparts, including the United States and United Kingdom, of restrictions of short-selling of certain stock as a temporary stability measure. The Canadian response lagged behind the coordinated efforts of the United States and the United Kingdom, and was not uniform across the provinces. A second illustration is the delay between the freezing of the non-bank Asset Backed Commercial Paper (ABCP) market in August 2007 and the release of a consultation paper by the Canadian Securities Administrators to seek input on a number of proposals that aim to prevent similar capital market failures in the future. We find that the fragmented securities regulatory structure is prone to foster slow securities regulatory responses, which makes Canada vulnerable to market and reputational risks.[108]

Weak enforcement of market rules casts a pall over the disparate provincial stock markets. As Randall Morck derisively points out in a review of Canadian securities markets, "It's nice to be an insider in Canada."[109] Insider trading prohibitions are so weakly enforced that convictions are extremely rare; there is no evidence of anyone being

[105] Puri 2010, 611.
[106] Hockin 2009, 29.
[107] Anand and Green 2010, 18; Puri 2009, 1691.
[108] Hockin 2009, 40.
[109] Morck 2010, 9.

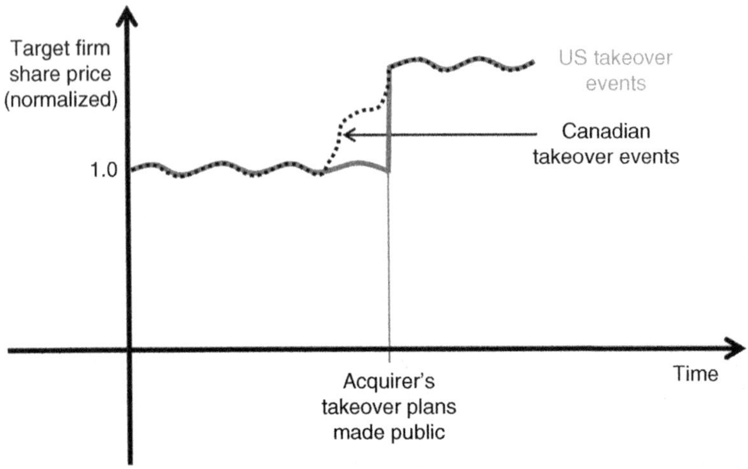

FIGURE 4.1. Corporate takeovers in Canada and the United States. *Source:* Stylized example derived from Morck 2010, 10.

convicted of this crime before 2009.[110] In the United States, the SEC strictly enforces insider trading laws, and several celebrities and high-profile business leaders have been arrested and served jail time for their crimes, including Martha Stewart, Ivan Boesky, and former Enron president Jeffrey Skilling. Insiders, defined as corporate officers and other market participants with non-public information about upcoming decisions or events that could affect a firm's stock price, are generally prohibited from trading in their firm's stock after learning of significant confidential corporate developments. But in Canada, due to lax enforcement, insiders freely trade on their confidential information. The insider advantage is evident in the weeks before a publicly announced firm acquisition, an event that generally leads to a boost in the share price of the target firm. In Canada, the target's share price increases steadily in the weeks *before* the public announcement of the acquisition, revealing that privileged investors are purchasing shares based on inside information about the pending acquisition.[111] The contrast with US markets is striking: the acquisition is kept secret until the public announcement of the acquisition, at which point the target firm's stock price jumps (Figure 4.1).

[110] Morck and Yeung 2009, 155.
[111] Morck 2010, 9–10.

The costs of Canada's regulatory weaknesses are borne by issuing firms and investors alike.[112] Investors, whether domestic or foreign, have less confidence in the integrity of the market than they would have with a stronger regulatory system and are therefore willing to pay less per share. Stock price movements may represent the gyrations of any developed stock market, or they might reflect the machinations of market insiders trading on proprietary information. Firms that issue stock ultimately bear the cost of Canada's regulatory system, not just in payments to provincial regulators and attorneys but also in lower valuations. Weak regulatory enforcement compromises the value of any traded contract representing an ownership stake in a firm. A Bank of Canada study found that Canadian-listed firms traded at a discount to comparable US-listed firms over the 1991–2000 period after controlling for accounting differences and other confounding variables. The average Canadian firm traded at a multiple of book value (measured as assets minus liabilities) that was 8 percent lower than its US-listed counterparts, despite having a 1.5 percent higher return on equity.[113] Not surprisingly, some Canadian firms choose to undertake initial public offerings on US stock markets because of higher expected valuations, even though doing so entails substantial cross-border regulatory and transaction costs.[114] Others will simply rely on banks for their financing.

The inefficiencies inherent in Canada's securities markets are evident in basic indicators of market maturity. Stock market turnover, for example, is a straightforward metric of the liquidity of a market: a mature market is one in which stocks are actively bought and sold. As Hail and Leuz note in an article on the equity cost of capital in forty countries, "Effective securities regulation binds firms to provide disclosures in good and bad times, which reduces information asymmetries and increases liquidity in secondary markets."[115] Figure 4.2 depicts stock market size, measured as the value of total shares traded as a percent of GDP, for Canada and the United States since 1975. The contrast between the highly developed US market and the underdeveloped Canadian market is clear throughout the entire time series.

The growth in derivatives trading has been similarly modest, with Canada considered only a minor player in a highly competitive global

[112] See Kitching 2009, 4.
[113] King and Segal 2008, 250.
[114] Morck and Yeung 2009, 157–60.
[115] Hail and Leuz 2006, 501–2.

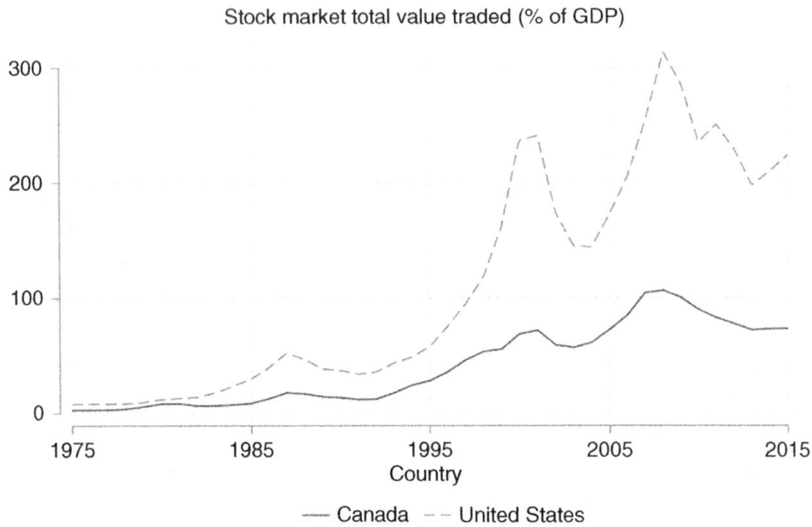

FIGURE 4.2. Stock market development, Canada vs. United States, 1975–2015.
Source: World Bank, Global Financial Development Database.

market. As of 2010, the notional amount of outstanding derivatives worldwide was US$615 trillion, with Canada representing only 2 percent (US$12.4 trillion) of the market.[116] The costs and weaknesses in the Canadian stock markets are in part responsible for the sluggish growth in derivatives, as a large segment of this market consists of equity-linked derivatives – that is, contracts whose value depends on the value of an underlying stock or set of stocks. Other reasons for the shallow market for derivatives are the lack of standardized products across the provinces and the relative scarcity of financial engineers and specialized firms dedicated to devising the latest financial instruments.

Canada's securities market is not sophisticated by standard indicators, but it is not small based on market capitalization. In fact, Canada has the eighth largest stock market in the world, with a total market capitalization of US$1.5 trillion in 2015.[117] Yet this figure is misleading because global markets fall off quickly in terms of size and depth. Canada ranks well behind Japan, Hong Kong, France, and the United Kingdom, and just

[116] OTC Derivatives Working Group, "Reform of the Over-the-Counter (OTC) Derivatives Markets in Canada," October 26, 2010, 5. See also Bell and Hindmoor 2015.

[117] Data from World Federation of Exchanges online database.

slightly ahead of India and Korea. Moreover, a handful of large commercial banks accounts for a large proportion of Canada's market capitalization. Just three banks – the Royal Bank of Canada, Toronto-Dominion, and Bank of Nova Scotia – account for approximately US$290 billion of outstanding shares, or nearly 20 percent of the total stock market.

RE-EVALUATING CANADIAN BANK STABILITY

Canada has experienced current account deficits in most years since 1960 (see Figure 4.3). During the early 1990s, deficits hovered around 4 percent of GDP – comparable to U.S. current account deficits in the early 2000s – while in recent years deficits have ranged between 2.5 and 3.5 percent of GDP.[118] As our discussion in Chapter 3 summarizes, sustained current account deficits and their countervailing capital inflows are one of the key determinants of banking crises throughout the world. Foreign funds in sufficient quantities have a troublesome habit of amplifying risk in the banking system, leading to asset bubbles

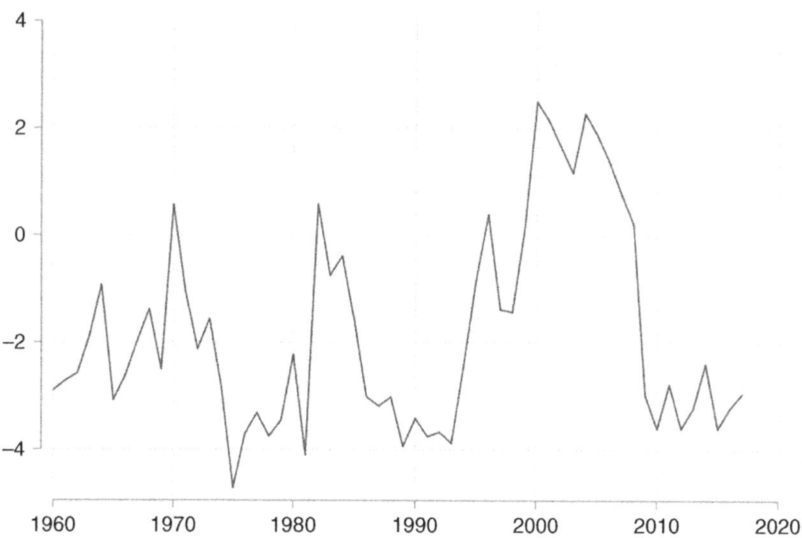

FIGURE 4.3. Canada's current account (% GDP), 1960–2018. *Source:* World Bank, Open Data.

[118] Data from World Bank World Development Indicators.

and other misallocations of capital. When a bubble bursts due to any number of triggers, such as a loan default by a major firm or a single bank failure, then the entire banking system can collapse. However, as Canada's financial history clearly demonstrates, foreign capital has not been destabilizing for the country. The overall financial system has consistently channeled foreign capital safely and productively.

The simplest measure of a bank's risk profile is its leverage ratio, calculated as the value of its outstanding loans as a percentage of its total shareholder equity. If capital inflows prompted banks to take on more risk in their lending portfolios, such behavior would manifest in a correlation between current account deficits and leverage. But as shown in Figure 4.4, no relationship is evident for Canada. There is a modest increase in leverage between 2007 and 2008 at the outset of the global financial crisis, but otherwise the trend is quite stable over the past 20 years. To return to the metaphor in Chapter 3, traditional banking has served as a financial levee against consistent large-scale foreign capital inflows.

The relatively flat trend in the leverage ratio over time suggests that banks have not taken on additional risk in their traditional lending portfolios. Our argument suggests a reason: banks have not felt competitive pressure from the non-bank financial system to change their typical way of doing business. Given the relatively high costs of issuing securities,

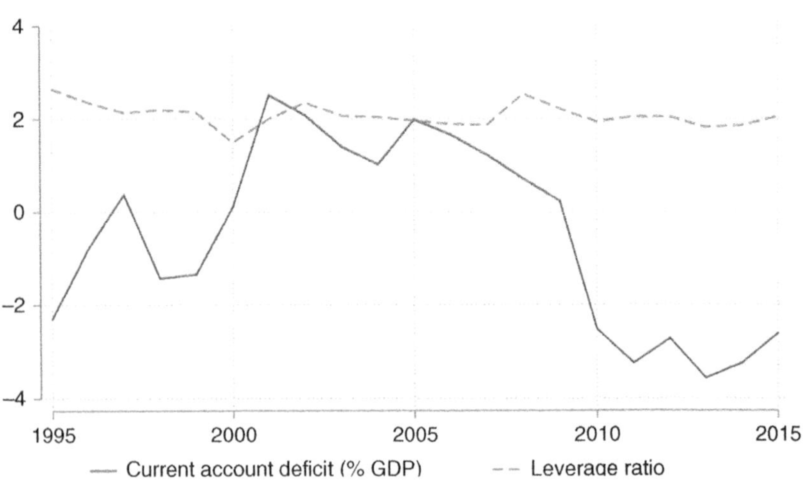

FIGURE 4.4. Capital inflows vs. bank leverage, Canada, 1995–2017. *Source:* World Bank Open Data and OECD iLibrary.

corporations are on the margin more likely to rely on loans for financing. Banks therefore have little reason to extend loans to riskier clients or involve themselves in riskier behaviors to maintain their client bases. The profitability of banks is in fact quite high, with annual return on equity of approximately 20 percent in the years before the financial crisis.[119]

Like most industrialized countries, Canada has a universal banking system in which banks are permitted to engage in a wide range of financial activities, including investment banking and derivatives origination and trading. In 1987, a revision to the Bank Act allowed banks to own and operate securities dealers. Just a year later, all five of the major banks had securities arms: four of them acquired existing brokerage firms, while Toronto Dominion created a securities affiliate from scratch.[120] Some banks dabbled for a short time in high-risk markets, such as collateralized debt obligations and other asset-backed securities, but quickly scaled down their business in these areas after finding the risks too excessive.[121] As a result, interest income from loans rather than trading activity or investment banking has remained banks' dominant source of revenue. And unlike US banks, Canadian banks fund their lending primarily from deposits rather than issuing short-term securities.

We are not the first scholars to highlight Canada's relatively low exposure to market-based activities.[122] However, to our knowledge we are the first to emphasize that the roots of Canada's banking conservatism lie in political decisions regarding securities market development from the 1800s and early 1900s. More than a century of fragmentation, relatively weak regulation, and serious inefficiencies have dulled the influence of securities markets on bank behavior. Today, Canadian banks are rarely considered dynamic or innovative, but they are routinely considered to be among the most stable in the world.

CONCLUSION

A commonly repeated claim in US economic history is that securities markets emerged and flourished because the fragmented banking system was hamstrung in its ability to provide sufficient capital for industrialization.[123] Curiously, in this story the demand for capital is not powerful

[119] Leblond 2013, 203.
[120] Bordo, Redish, and Rockoff 2015, 231.
[121] Bell and Hindmoor 2015, 270–2.
[122] See, e.g., Hardie et al. 2013; Leblond 2013.
[123] Bordo, Redish, and Rockoff 2015.

enough to cause policymakers to change the regulatory environment for banks, such as mandating national chartering and permitting nationwide branching, but powerful enough to trigger a string of legislative initiatives to harmonize securities markets, create a national regulator, and enforce stringent disclosure and anti-fraud protections for investors. In short, the literature suggests that politics stymies the banking industry, but the need for capital obliterates any political resistance to securities market development.

In contrast, the narratives in this chapter suggest that the demand for capital cannot fully explain the character of the markets that have arisen since the 1800s. The Canadian government had an opportunity to emulate the United States in the 1930s by creating a national securities regulator and harmonizing the rules across the provinces, but it chose instead to reaffirm the regional governance of capital markets. The constitutions of the two countries are in fact similarly vague on the regulation of securities, but they unequivocally place the "regulation of trade" under federal auspices.[124] The US government invoked this power to place securities regulation in the hands of the Federal Trade Commission in 1933 and created a separate securities regulator the following year, but Canada made no similar effort. This decision is not readily attributable to complacency about the ability of banks to provide sufficient capital for all of Canada's development needs. Firms in the natural resource sector, especially in highly speculative areas like mining and oil exploration, were eager to facilitate the flow of societal savings into securities to support their extractive endeavors. Even conservative companies with more predictable revenue streams, like railroads and breweries, benefited from direct financing in the early 1900s, bypassing traditional loans from banks. Instead, the absence of a legislative push toward market harmonization in the 1930s stemmed from political pressures from disparate interest groups. Mining interests in the west feared that national regulation would crimp the steady flow of speculative capital and thwart their prospecting efforts and ultimately their profitability. Ontario, with its dominant stock market and mix of industries, was content to maintain its own regulatory sovereignty and not bend to the civil law influences of neighboring Quebec or the risk-acceptant norms of western exchanges. The outcome – continued fragmentation in securities markets – was attributable to the wide variation in the risk profiles of the industries that required capital, not to weak demand for capital

[124] Puri 2009, 1690.

itself. Today the dominance of provincial regulators renders securities markets far less efficient than those in many of the country's peers.[125]

Bankers, financiers, and policymakers could not fully anticipate the implications of their decisions for the future of Canada's financial markets. The origin of the first blue-sky law provides a useful lesson. A bank commissioner in Kansas, eager to protect his turf from competition from securities markets, pushed forward a set of rules that enforced a modicum of honesty in the process of issuing stock. His effort to *deter* the development of securities markets inadvertently *facilitated* their development by mitigating the asymmetric information that leads to market failures. Blue-sky laws and their successors helped to push out the fraudsters and flimflammers (at least some of them), enhance the disclosure of financial information, and improve investor trust.

Canada's relatively underdeveloped securities markets are an overlooked backdrop to its famed history of bank stability. This chapter has brought these markets front and center in the analysis of bank behavior. Despite decades of persistent current account deficits, Canadian banks have held fast to their conservative lending practices and have avoided many of the risky interactions with securities markets that have befallen banks in more market-based economies.

[125] Krippner 2011 makes a similar argument about the policy decisions that inadvertently facilitated the financialization of the US economy in the 1980s and 1990s.

5

Finanzplatz Deutschland

German Bank Stability and Its Decline

Banking stability has long been a hallmark of Germany's economy. This image has been historically embodied by the solid stone façades of Germany's largest banks (now replaced by the glass-and-steel Frankfurt skyline), as well as the stereotypical image of the conservative German banker, clad in his well-tailored dark suit and gazing sternly at the camera through wire-rimmed glasses. Ever since the rise to international prominence of German banking empires, such as the Fuggers, Welsers, and Rothschilds, in the sixteenth to eighteenth centuries, German bankers have had a reputation for prudence, competence, and stability. Until recently, this reputation was largely deserved: with the exception of the interwar era/Great Depression and the notable failure in 1974 of Herstatt Bank – a small private bank that highlighted problems of settlement risk in global finance – the German banking system has been remarkably resilient throughout modern history.

That is, until recently. Over the last fifteen years, the German banking system has been hit by one problem after another, with several of its largest financial institutions failing or requiring large-scale public bailouts. In the wake of the subprime mortgage crisis, two of the Landesbanken (LB) – Germany's publicly owned regional banks that serve as both wholesale banks to local savings banks and the major source of financing to the *Mittelstand*, Germany's famed small- and midsize manufacturing firms – failed. WestLB, the Landesbank of North Rhine-Westphalia, was broken up in 2012, after years of bailouts that are projected to ultimately cost German taxpayers €18 billion.[1] In 2007, Sachsen LB was taken over by Landesbank Baden-Württemberg (LBBW), after massive losses due to exposure to Irish and US mortgage markets left German taxpayers with a bill exceeding €400 billion.[2] The subprime crisis also led to the merger of two of Germany's major commercial banks in 2008, when Commerzbank announced a takeover of Dresdner Bank. The combined bank subsequently declared billions of losses and twice accepted bailout funds from the German government.[3]

Most recently, Deutsche Bank (DB) – the largest bank in Germany, with assets valued at roughly one-half the size of the entire German economy – has found itself in dire straits following a series of financial scandals, fines from both the US and British governments, and sharp declines in its profitability and stock price.[4] In mid-2016, DB failed the US Federal Reserve's stress tests, and the IMF subsequently speculated that it represented "the most important net contributor to systemic risks in the global banking system."[5] Questions still remain about DB's long-term solvency and whether it will survive in its current form in the years ahead.[6]

In short, financial instability has become, over the last decade, nearly as frequent and serious an economic and political issue in Frankfurt and Berlin as it has long been in New York, London, and Washington DC. In this chapter, we aim to explain both the long-term pattern of financial stability in Germany, as well as the factors contributing to its decline in the twenty-first century. As in our earlier study of Canada, we focus on the political decisions that shaped the development of the German banking and securities markets. We begin with a historical narrative of the development of the German financial system, highlighting Germany's unique "three-pillar" banking system, which emerged in the wake of German unification in the nineteenth century and served as the bedrock of German financial stability through the 1970s. We then discuss the early development and historical evolution of German securities markets in the 1870–1945 era.

[1] Matthias Inverardi, "Germany Waves Goodbye to WestLB as Bank Broken Up," *Reuters*, July 1, 2012.

[2] Derek Scally, "Sachsen LB Losses Expose Directors' 'Cluelessness,'" *The Irish Times*, November 13, 2012.

[3] Christoph Pauly, "Germany's Tricky Commerzbank Merger," *Bloomberg*, April 17, 2009.

[4] Jill Treanor, "Deutsche Bank: How Did a Beast of the Banking World Get into This Mess? " *The Guardian*, September 27, 2016.

[5] See IMF Country Report No. 16/191, available at www.imf.org/external/pubs/ft/scr/2016 /cr16191.pdf.

[6] Jack Ewing, "Germany's Troubled Banking Giants Decide Against Merger," *The New York Times*, April 25, 2019.

Our narrative highlights how political developments and policy decisions in the aftermath of two major financial crises – the Panic of 1873 and the crisis of 1931 – arrested the development of German securities markets and led to the establishment of the heavily bank-centric system widely associated with German finance today. The Panic of 1873 triggered a backlash against financial capital, culminating in a series of laws – most importantly, the Stock Exchange Act of 1896 (*Börsengesetz*) – restricting stock market activity and arresting the development German securities markets, which had until then grown rapidly alongside German commercial banking in the mid-nineteenth century. This backlash occurred as part of the broader rise of nationalism, anti-Semitism, and protectionism that emerged as the dominant political theme in Germany in the decades between unification in 1870 and the onset of World War I in 1914.

Although German stock markets partially recovered during the interwar era, the financial crisis of 1931 and the rise of the Nazis to power in 1933 firmly cemented the dominance of commercial banking and the subordinate role of securities markets in German finance. From 1933 onward, the Nazi regime imposed a series of new laws sharply restricting financial capitalism and arresting both the interwar recovery and future development of German securities markets. These laws, which would become the basis for financial regulation in the postwar Federal Republic, shaped German finance throughout the postwar era, well into the 1990s. Thus, as in our case study of Canada, our analysis in this chapter highlights how political and economic development in the pre–World War II period had long-term effects on the structure of Germany's financial system. In both cases, the relative structure of banking and securities markets in place by World War II remained in place through the Bretton Woods era and into the current period of modern globalization.

In contrast to Canada, however, Germany's financial system did eventually undergo a modern-day shift toward more developed securities markets in the 1990s. This transformation, known as Finanzplatz Deutschland, was triggered by the combination of the globalization in finance, the completion of the European Union's single market, and domestic political developments in the post–Bretton Woods era that resulted in a series of laws leading to the emergence of large and centralized national securities markets in Germany. We demonstrate how German banks, operating in this new environment, alongside larger-scale securities markets, have taken on greater risk over the last three decades and have become deeply enmeshed in new securities-related activities. From a financial system that broadly resembled Canada's in both structure and stability, Germany's has become much more similar to that of the United States and the United Kingdom: more heavily focused on securities markets than in the past and far more prone to banking instability. Thus, while Germany, relative to the United States and the United Kingdom, remains far more of a bank-based financial system, this is less true than in the past, and future prospects for German financial stability are less clear than in previous decades.

THE ORIGINS AND DEVELOPMENT OF THE GERMAN FINANCIAL SYSTEM

Why were German banks so stable relative to those in the United States and elsewhere for so long? Why has that changed in recent years? As in Canada, our story begins before Germany was Germany. The modern German financial system emerged in parallel with the rise and consolidation of Germany as a unified nation-state in the mid-nineteenth century. Prior to German industrialization and unification, private banks dominated the financial system in the various territorial entities that would eventually become the German Reich in 1871. These family-owned banks, most notably those of the Rothschilds in Frankfurt and the Welsers and Fuggers in Augsburg, financed the development of German textile manufacturing and the building of the German railway system.[7]

From the sixteenth century onward, Frankfurt emerged as the leading financial center in the German states. Politically, Frankfurt was one of the most important cities of the Holy Roman Empire. From its earliest days as the site of Charlemagne's imperial assembly in 794, Frankfurt became the home of the Imperial Diet and the most frequent site of elections for German kings in the tenth and eleventh centuries.[8] From 1562 to 1792, all German kings and emperors were elected in Frankfurt. Economically, Frankfurt played a central role in the German economy, first in the thirteenth and fourteenth centuries as the site of one of the major medieval trade fairs, and subsequently as a hub of long-distance trade, given its location at the intersection of the major north-south and east-west medieval trade routes through Europe: the river route linking the upper Main (Nuremberg, Bamberg, Würzburg) to the central Rhineland (Mainz) and the overland route linking Italy and the Mediterranean – via Switzerland and the St. Gotthard Pass through the Alps – to the Rhineland and on to the major commercial cities of

[7] Tilly 1997b, 230.
[8] Holtfrerich 1999, 30.

northern and eastern Germany (Hamburg, Bremen, Leipzig, Berlin).[9] Frankfurt's ascendance as Germany's leading financial center accelerated following the influx of Dutch and French merchants and bankers in the late 1500s, who were driven from Antwerp and France during the Counter-Reformation.[10]

By the 1600s, Frankfurt had become the major trading and financial hub of German Europe. Martin Luther famously and pejoratively labeled it "the hole through which all the gold and silver flows out of Germany".[11] Frankfurt's merchants established the first German stock exchange (*Börse*) in 1585, as an exchange for converting currencies of the many political units in the German empire.[12] By the late 1700s, the Frankfurt Börse had become a main location in Europe for the trading of sovereign bonds: the Bethmann banking family placed the first issue in 1779, for the German emperor in Vienna. While the first common stock share – for the Austrian National Bank – in Germany was traded in 1820 in Frankfurt, its exchange remained predominantly focused on sovereign bonds until the 1850s.[13] Thus, German financial markets originated primarily to serve the needs for currency exchange and sovereign debt, rather than for the purpose of providing capital to private firms.

GERMAN BANKING IN THE NINETEENTH CENTURY: THE EMERGENCE OF THE THREE-PILLAR SYSTEM

Germany's modern-day, large commercial banks, the primary source of capital to industrial firms, first emerged between the 1850s and 1870s, in conjunction with trade integration, political unification, and the country's rapid industrialization. Prior to the 1850s, industrial finance had been provided primarily by the major German private banks, which were the chief source of capital for the rapidly growing rail and textile industries that were the primary German industrial sectors prior to the rise of the coal, chemicals, and steel sectors in the latter half of the nineteenth century.[14] The first major joint-stock banks were incorporated in the 1850s, including the Disconto-Gesellschaft (1851), the Darmstädter Bank für Handel und Industrie, 1853, and the Berliner Handelsgesellschaft (Berlin, 1853). These were followed by a

[9] Ibid., 39.
[10] Ibid., 11.
[11] Luther (2015).
[12] See www.deutsche-boerse-cash-market.com/dbcm-en/about-us/our-approach/history-of-the-frankfurt-stock-exchange.
[13] Ibid.
[14] Detzer et al. 2013, 17; Tilly 1997b, 230.

second wave: the Deutsche Bank (1870), the Commerz- und Disconto-Bank (1870), the Deutsche Nationalbank (1871), and the Dresdner Bank (1872).[15] As Gerschenkron describes in his classic 1962 study, these banks' deep involvement in lending, underwriting, and investing their own capital played a central role in fueling Germany's late industrialization and its ability to rapidly emerge – along with the United States – as the main challenger to British industrial dominance in the nineteenth century.[16]

These large commercial banks "operated from the start as industrial banks, taking deposits, extending loans, underwriting new issues on the stock market, and engaging in trade finance."[17] As Germany became a major global industrial power in the 1880s and 1890s, the large banks were the dominant source of financial capital necessary for its mining, metal, chemical, and engineering firms to develop into world-class industrial powerhouses.[18] Blackbourn notes that "reinvested profits, reserves, and share issues hardly covered the high investment requirements of German industry. The role of banks was therefore decisive, much more so than it had been in the first phase of industrialization up to the 1870s."[19] The banks financed these long-term industrial loans through a combination of shorter-term loans and time deposits, along with the issuing of securities on capital markets and the extensive use of the Reichsbank's "virtually unlimited discount facilities."[20]

As Germany rose to industrial supremacy in Europe, the big banks became central to the entire country's economy and the centerpiece of the German financial system. By 1913, the three largest enterprises by balance sheets were banks, and seventeen of the twenty-five largest enterprises in Germany were banks.[21] In this period, the ties between industry and banking also deepened beyond traditional borrower-lender relationships. The big banks frequently converted loans into ownership shares if borrowers faced financial difficulties, which increasingly led the banks to acquire large ownership stakes in – and seats on the corporate boards of – major German industrial firms.[22] Hilferding famously coined the term "finance capital" to describe this combination

[15] Detzer et al. 2013, 34.
[16] Gerschenkron 1962.
[17] Story and Walter 1997, 166.
[18] Blackbourn 2003.
[19] Ibid., 244.
[20] Detzer et al. 2017, 19.
[21] Feldenkirchen 1991, 116.
[22] Detzer et al. 2013, 35.

of financial and industrial capital.[23] Although subsequent scholars have argued that industrial firms enjoyed greater independence from the large banks than believed earlier, they nevertheless agree that the connection between Germany's big banks and its largest industrial companies were a defining feature of the German economy during the rapid industrialization following unification.[24]

Thus, by the early twentieth century Germany's commercial banking sector looked very similar to Canada's, with a small number of large, universal banks dominating lending to the country's major industrial corporations. These banks focused on financing large firms in Germany's heavy industries, such as mining, metals, and chemicals, and they provided a universal range of services, from short- and long-term commercial lending to underwriting and other investment banking services.[25] This piece of Germany's financial market structure is the main reason why the country has long been held up the canonical example of a predominantly bank-based financial system.[26] According to this typology, large German banks, lending directly to Germany's major corporations (and in many cases, taking direct equity stakes in them as well), created an environment in which "patient capital" provides German industrial firms with a steady stream of finance and enables them to invest in long-term, strategic goals that have made Germany's manufacturing sector the envy of the world.[27]

Unlike in Canada, however, a commercial banking sector dominated by a few large, private banks is only one part of the story of German banking. Whereas in Canada, the large banks had developed national branching networks shortly after Confederation and became the dominant lenders to all sectors of the economy, Germany's banking system developed differently, with three separate "pillars" of institutions serving different functions and sets of customers in economy. In this three-pillar system, Germany's large private banks comprised the first pillar. They focused almost exclusively on financing large industrial projects, neglecting the household, agricultural, and small business sectors.[28] Instead, these other sectors' financial needs were served by two further pillars of financial institutions: (1) government-sponsored local savings

[23] Hilferding 1910.

[24] Deeg 1999, 77–9; Tilly 1997a, 280.

[25] Detzer et al. 2013, 35.

[26] Allen and Gale 2000; Hall and Soskice 2001.

[27] Kirsten Wever and Christopher Allen, "Is Germany a Model for Managers?" *Harvard Business Review*, September–October, 1992.

[28] Detzer et al. 2013, 36.

banks (Sparkassen) and regional cooperative banks (Landesbanken), and (2) small private credit cooperatives.

The second pillar in the German banking system consisted of the savings banks (Sparkassen) and regional banks (Landesbanken) established by local and state governments in the nineteenth century. The Sparkassen were established by municipal (city/county) governments and became the primary source of finance and financial services for local artisans and households.[29] The first savings bank was founded in Goettingen in 1801; by 1900, there were 2,700 Sparkassen nationwide, with one-third of the population holding accounts. Detzer et al. (2013) notes that "the money that was saved this way was used primarily to finance housing and public investment in utilities and infrastructure."[30] Moreover, because the activities of the Sparkassen were restricted to specific local areas, they were a key mechanism for ensuring that private credit "was distributed through the country" to individuals and groups not served by the large commercial lenders.[31] Alongside the local Sparkassen, the regional Landesbanken were established by the German states to act both as central banks for the Sparkassen and to promote economic development in Germany's regions as sources of finance to craftsmen and farmers not served by the large commercial banks.[32] The first Landesbank, the Westfälische Provinzialhilfskasse, was established in Münster in 1832. By the turn of the century, the savings banks provided roughly one-quarter of total credit in Germany – roughly equal to the amount of credit provided by the large commercial banks.[33]

The third pillar of the German banking system – the private cooperative banks – also emerged in the 1800s to serve the financial needs of farmers and craftsmen. These began as credit union–style loan associations, before the 1889 Cooperative Law allowed the cooperatives to offer current account credits to their members.[34] The first urban cooperative bank was established in Darmstadt in 1862, while the first rural cooperative, Raiffeisenbank, was set up in 1864.[35] The number of cooperatives grew into the dozens by the turn of the century, and cooperative

[29] Ibid.
[30] Ibid.
[31] Ibid.
[32] Ibid.; International Monetary Fund 2011.
[33] Deutsche Sparkassen und Giroverband (DSGV) 2010, 7.
[34] Detzer et al. 2013, 37.
[35] Deutsche Sparkassen und Giroverband (DSGV) 2010, 1.

lending comprised 8 percent of total credit in Germany by 1910.[36] The cooperative banks established their own regional associations "to refinance loans and circulate credit among themselves."[37]

By the onset of World War I, Germany's banking system had taken on the broad contours of this three-pillar banking system, with the large private banks, the savings and Landesbanken, and the cooperative banks each performing a specific set of functions in the banking system. In a sense, this system was something of a hybrid between the Canadian and American banking systems. Like Canada, industrial lending in Germany was dominated by a small number of private commercial banks. Like the United States, however, consumer, agricultural, and small business banking was mostly provided by the other two pillars, consisting of thousands of local and regional savings and cooperative banks. Because the savings and cooperative banks were government-sponsored and "not driven primarily by the search for profit,"[38] this high level of fragmentation never resulted in the widespread bank failures and unit-banking panics seen in the United States in the late nineteenth and early twentieth centuries. Moreover, developments in the pre-WWI and interwar years offset this fragmentation. By 1913, both the savings and cooperative banks had established large branching networks, in marked contrast to the US banking system, where restrictions on interstate branching persisted well into the second half of the twentieth century.[39] In addition, the savings and cooperative banks also established regional and national clearing systems in the 1910s.[40] The most prominent of these was the *Deutsche Girozentrale* (DGZ, German Sparkasse Clearinghouse), established in Berlin in 1918, as the central clearing bank for the Sparkassen.[41] Within each region, the Landesbanken assumed full control of clearing between the Sparkassen by the 1930s.[42] As a result, the number of savings and cooperative banks in Germany remained large; these numerous German banks were linked together into national networks by the interwar period. As Deeg describes, these regional and national clearing institutions "created a sector-internal capital market that benefited the banks and their clients."[43]

[36] Ibid., 7.
[37] Detzer et al. 2013, 37.
[38] Ibid., 20.
[39] Ibid., 37.
[40] Deeg 2003, 98; Faust 1977, 556.
[41] Detzer et al. 2013, 38.
[42] Ibid., 39.
[43] Deeg 2003, 98.

German Securities Markets in the Nineteenth Century

While the three-pillar banking system was the centerpiece of German finance, securities markets nonetheless played an increasingly important role as the nineteenth century progressed. Although the Frankfurt exchange had developed in the 1500s as a market for sovereign debt, modern commercial stock exchanges emerged throughout Germany in the nineteenth century. By 1900, there were twenty-three exchanges, located in Germany's major commercial cities (Hamburg, Frankfurt), the capitals of the German states (e.g., Berlin, Munich, and Dresden), and cities in the northwestern industrial heartland (Hanover in Lower Saxony; Essen and Düsseldorf in North Rhine-Westphalia).[44] Frankfurt retained its role as the country's main international financial center for the trading of sovereign bonds and international railway stocks, while the other regional exchanges specialized on the basis of geography and function.[45] For example, the Essen and Düsseldorf exchanges listed shares of the coal mines of the Ruhr valley, while the Augsburg and Dresden exchanges were dominated by the industrial firms of Bavaria and Saxony, respectively.[46] In contrast, the exchanges at Munich, Stuttgart, and Dresden were created primarily as sites for the issuing of state bonds for the governments of Bavaria, Württemberg, and Saxony.[47] Thus, the nineteenth century exchanges exhibited a substantial degree of regional specialization, as well as specialization in the main type of securities issued and traded.

Political Unification and the Shift of German Finance to Berlin

While Frankfurt retained its position as Germany's primary international financial center into the early 1800s, the center of gravity in German finance gradually shifted toward Berlin over the century, as Prussia rose to economic and political dominance in the German-speaking world after the Napoleonic Wars. Prussia played the leading role in accelerating economic integration in Germany from 1818 onward, when it abolished internal customs duties and began seeking free trade agreements with the neighboring German states. In 1834, the *Zollverein* – the customs union of German states – was founded with eighteen members, including Prussia as its largest state. By 1867, all German states except for

[44] Burhop and Lehmann-Hasemeyer 2016, 433.

[45] Gommel 1992; Marx 1913.

[46] Gommel 1992; Marx 1913.

[47] Burhop and Lehmann-Hasemeyer 2016, 433.

Austria, Hamburg, and Bremen (the latter two of which joined in 1888) had joined the Zollverein.[48] Politically, Prussia wrestled with Austria throughout the nineteenth century for hegemony over German-speaking Europe. Following the defeat of Napoleon and the Congress of Vienna in 1814–15, the German Confederation (*Deutscher Bund*) was founded, linking thirty-nine states in a loose confederation, with the Austrian Habsburg emperor as the president. In 1866, Prussia defeated Austria in the Austro-Prussian War, annexed several German states (including Frankfurt), and organized a new northern German confederation (*Norddeutscher Bund*) that excluded Austria.[49] These developments led directly to the creation of the unified German Reich in 1871, with Berlin as its capital city and the Prussian Hohenzollern monarch, Kaiser Wilhelm I, as emperor.

Banking and securities market developments in Germany mirrored these political developments. With the founding of the Reichsbank, the imperial central bank, in 1876, and the subsequent development of the German money market, Berlin fully cemented its role as the main financial center.[50] Between 1871 and 1898, the largest banks in Germany's other major cities (Darmstadt, Frankfurt, Dresden, Cologne, Hamburg) all opened branches in Berlin, centralizing banking activity in the political capital.[51] This development fueled a reciprocal relationship, as the largest Berlin banks moved to increase their activities in Germany's other major cities. As Riesser describes in his 1911 report to the US Congress on the role of German banks in the country's economic development, "The continued concentration of the banking business in Berlin, which has already led a number of provincial institutions to establish branches in Berlin, seemed to make it necessary that our connections with the provinces be strengthened."[52] A similar centralization of activity in the German capital occurred in securities markets. Although Frankfurt retained its role as the country's main sovereign bond trading exchange, Berlin's stock exchange quickly became the primary market for the securities of large industrial firms.

The geographic centralization of banking and securities activity in Berlin led to a massive increase in the size and consolidation of German

[48] Henderson 1939.

[49] See https://blogs.loc.gov/law/2017/04/150-year-anniversary-of-the-adoption-of-the-constitution-of-the-north-german-confederation/.

[50] Gommel 1992, 191–2; Marx 1913.

[51] Riesser 1911, 654.

[52] Ibid., 655.

commercial banking. From 1870 to 1908, the 13 largest German banks absorbed 164 private banks and 60 other banks; over the same period, the total capital of the big banks in Germany increased by a factor of two to ten.[53] Not surprisingly, this consolidation of the commercial banking sector further fueled the extension of the big banks into regional banking markets around the country: "such absorptions were often prompted, outwardly, by the desire of the banks to gain a firm footing, a wide circle of customers and business relations for contemplated branches by the acquisition of flourishing private banking firms at the localities in question."[54]

Similar patterns emerged in German securities markets, as stock market activity grew rapidly and concentrated increasingly in Berlin. The big banks themselves were a key driving force behind these trends. As joint-stock universal banks, they issued their own securities and increasingly, in the years after German unification, listed the shares of their investment banking customers primarily on the Berlin exchange.[55] As a result, Berlin's stock exchange grew rapidly in the decade after German unification and surpassed Frankfurt as the country's primary securities market. By the mid-1880s, market turnover in Berlin was seven times larger than in Frankfurt.[56] While several regional exchanges remained important for certain types of firms and securities – notably, Frankfurt for sovereign bonds, Augsburg and Munich for Bavarian industrial firms, Hamburg for firms from northwest Germany and Scandinavia, and Essen and Hanover for the coal producers of the Ruhr valley – Berlin dominated German securities markets, just as it became the center of German commercial banking.

ARRESTED DEVELOPMENT: THE POLITICS OF GERMAN SECURITIES MARKETS, 1870–1945

As in Canada, the development of Germany's financial system cannot be separated from the broader patterns of economic and political development in Germany during the latter half of the nineteenth century. The economic upheaval of the Panic of 1873 and the Long Depression of 1873–1896 were formative events in German domestic politics.[57]

[53] Ibid., 657–9.
[54] Ibid., 659.
[55] Burhop and Lehmann-Hasemeyer 2016, 433.
[56] Ibid.; Gommel 1992, 191–2.
[57] Frieden 2007.

In much the same way that the global financial crisis and economic stagnation of the last decade has contributed to rising populist nationalism on both sides of the Atlantic, the Panic of 1873 and subsequent depression had similar political effects in nineteenth-century Germany. The economic events reshaped the German political landscape, bringing to power a new conservative coalition that embraced protectionism, nationalism, anti-Semitism, and broad-based opposition to all aspects of globalization and finance, including stock markets and international capital. This coalition of agrarian and industrial conservatives – the famed "marriage of iron and rye" – first organized in support of tariffs in the wake of the Panic of 1873.[58] But it also came to see financial capitalism and securities markets, in the 1880s and 1890s, as dire threats to German unity, stability, and national identity. Inevitably, given Jewish dominance in nineteenth-century German finance, conservative opposition to finance and capitalism became inextricably linked to rising anti-Semitism. As we detail below, finance in general, and stock markets in particular, came to be seen in this period as existential threats to both the German economy and German society, and the Jews' prominence in finance made them easy scapegoats for the economic ills of the Panic of 1873 and Long Depression.

Ultimately, these developments led to a series of laws, culminating in the 1896 Stock Exchange Law (Börsengesetz), that severely restricted the development of German securities markets for the remainder of the pre-1914 era. Although German securities markets did partially recover in the interwar era, the 1931 financial crisis and subsequent rise of the Nazi regime led to a further deepening of restrictions on German securities markets. These Nazi-era laws would subsequently become the basis for German financial regulation in the postwar Federal Republic. As a result, the dominant features of German finance in the pre-1945 era – bank dominance and a subordinate role for securities markets – persisted in Germany throughout the postwar era well into the 1980s.

The Panic of 1873 and the Political Backlash against Securities Markets

The Panic of 1873 began as a series of stock market crashes in Vienna, Berlin, and New York from May to September 1873, but rapidly became a transatlantic financial crisis wreaking having on financial markets,

[58] Schonhardt-Bailey 1998.

banks, and the real economies of Europe and the United States. Most immediately, the panic began with the Vienna stock market crash on May 9, 1873. The Berlin stock exchange crashed in September, at the same time that the panic hit New York with the famous collapse of the prominent Philadelphia bank and brokerage house Jay Cooke and Co., after failed speculation in Northern Pacific rail bonds.[59]

As with all major financial crises, the Panic of 1873 was the result of a variety of factors, including widespread speculation in rail and other stocks, US inflation in the decade following the Civil War, and the influx of capital into Germany as a result of French war indemnities from the Franco-Prussian War.[60] Among this panoply of causes, however, Germany's decision to adopt the gold standard and cease minting the silver thaler in 1871 stands out as a critical factor. Adopting the gold standard meant that a country was adopting a fixed exchange rate in terms of gold (with paper currency notes backed by gold reserves) and committed to the free convertibility of domestic currency and gold.[61] Because silver would no longer be used as foreign exchange or as reserves to back paper currency, joining the gold standard reduced both the domestic money supply and demand for silver. As a result, this policy shift triggered a global crash in silver prices and hit the United States especially hard, since silver mines in the American West were the world's largest producers and the resulting silver glut placed downward pressure on the dollar. The United States responded by passing the Coinage Act of 1873, which ended bimetallism and shifted the United States to a de facto gold standard as well; in 1875, the United States formally adopted the gold standard through the Specie Payment Resumption Act.[62] This demonetization of silver and shift to the gold standard by both Germany and the United States triggered a sharp decline in the money supply and available credit and played a key role in piercing the speculative bubble in railroad and other stocks on both sides of the Atlantic.

The Panic of 1873 abruptly ended the broad-based economic boom that Germany had enjoyed in the 1860s and through the initial years of unification. As part of this boom, Germany's stock markets had developed rapidly; from 1870 to 1873, the country experienced a surge in the establishment of new companies and stock listings. In Prussia, 1,000

[59] Kindleberger 1990, 316.
[60] Brustein 2003, 210.
[61] Eichengreen 1996.
[62] Ibid.; Frieden 2007.

new companies were founded in this period, particularly in construction, banking, and railways.[63] Inevitably, however, the boom became a bubble that "degenerated into a wild orgy of speculation...there was a frantic rush to buy shares, land and houses, in the hope of making a quick profit from a rise in price. Gambling on the stock exchange and the property market became a national pastime."[64] Within a year of the Berlin stock market crash, over sixty banks and a hundred industrial firms had failed in Germany.[65] In short order, the panic and financial crash became a real economic crisis and a prolonged recession. As Henderson notes, "All over Germany firms collapsed, credit was unobtainable, and business was stagnant.... Throughout the country, prices fell, sales dropped, wages were reduced, and unemployment rose. It was not until 1876 that German industrial output had recovered to the level of 1872."[66]

The Panic of 1873 and the subsequent Long Depression mobilized political coalitions throughout Europe and North America around populist nationalism and opposition to free trade and international finance. Germany was no exception. Indeed, the political consequences of the panic and depression in Germany from the 1870s through World War I were massive. One key development was the formation of the forerunners to the modern German Social and Christian Democratic parties. In 1875, the Social Democratic Party held its initial party congress at Gotha, and the German Conservative Party formed in 1876, as the party of the Evangelical Church of Prussia and the Junkers, the landowning elite of Prussia east of the Elbe River.[67] With the exception of the Nazi regime in 1933–45, these two parties would become the backbone of German politics in the postwar era.

A second, more immediately important development was the rise to power of a conservative nationalist coalition in the new German Reich.[68] From 1871 to 1878, Otto von Bismarck had governed as prime minister of Prussia and *Reichskanzler* (imperial chancellor) with the support of a majority coalition of pro-free trade, anti-Catholic liberal parties, primarily the National Liberal Party (NLP), along with the German People's Party, Liberals, and Progressives.[69] Despite the economic damage of the

[63] Henderson 1975, 164.
[64] Ibid.
[65] Zucker 1975, 135.
[66] Henderson 1975, 170.
[67] Berghahn 1993, 206.
[68] Steinberg 2011.
[69] Lehmann 2010; Nipperdey 1992, 326.

1873 panic, the NLP remained the largest party in the 1877 Reichstag elections, with 128 seats (32.2 percent of the vote), and the pro-free trade parties retained a small majority (51.8 percent). However, as Kindleberger (1990) notes, "One tragic aspect of the German depression from 1873 to 1879 is that it turned German public opinion against liberalism."[70] In the 1878 German national election, the liberal parties lost approximately 11 percent of the vote and a conservative majority emerged, comprising the new Conservative Party, the Free Conservatives, and the Center Party, the centrist pro-Catholic party.

This newly dominant political coalition comprised those domestic interests in Germany hit hardest by the financial crash and depression. Its members and parties increasingly viewed free trade, the classical gold standard, and financial capitalism as the root causes of their economic problems and, by extension, the problems of Germany as a whole.[71] Trade protection became the first policy issue around which the newly ascendant conservative coalition organized. In what is now renowned as the "marriage of iron and rye," German farmers and industrialists allied to lobby for protective tariffs.[72] This coalition was an "alliance between the … big landowners of trans-Elbia and the big industrialists of Rhineland-Westphalia, Saar-Lorraine, and Upper Silesia."[73] Iron and steel producers, in particular, had expanded rapidly in the 1850–70 period and now faced falling prices and overcapacity in the wake of the panic and depression.[74] Between 1873 and 1879, iron consumption in Germany fell by 30 percent, and prices fell by 50 to 60 percent.[75] In 1876, Germany heavy industry, led by major iron and steel firms, formed the *Zentralverband deutscher Industrieller* (Central Association of German Industrialists) a trade association whose primary purpose was to lobby for increased tariffs.[76]

At the same time, the crash and depression also hit rural Germany and small business hard, stoking the already rising urban-rural tensions in the country. The Junker landowners in Prussia had long supported free trade, as they exported grain to England and Scandinavia.[77]

[70] Kindleberger 1990, 318.
[71] Blackbourn 1984; Kitchen 1978.
[72] Schonhardt-Bailey 1998.
[73] Pflanze 2014, 10; Schonhardt-Bailey 1998.
[74] Schonhardt-Bailey 1998, 293.
[75] Zucker 1975, 135.
[76] Barkin 1970, 34; Kindleberger 1973, 134; Zucker 1975, 136.
[77] Zucker 1975, 136.

By 1878, however, Prussian agriculture faced rising competition from more efficient producers in Russia and the United States.[78] Prior to the depression, agriculture had lobbied for a reduction in iron duties, given its desire to purchase farm machinery at the lowest possible prices.[79] By 1878, however, the agrarian conservatives sought common cause with heavy industry, leading to the combined protectionist policies benefiting both German industrialists and the Junker agricultural elite.[80] They, too, formed a new association, the Union of Tax and Economic Reformers, which soon began coordinating demands for tariffs with the industrial *Zentralverband* in the Reichstag, under the auspices of a new political group known as the Free Economic Association.[81]

The protectionist coalition emerged victorious with the Tariff Act of 1879. The marriage of iron and rye represented a sharp policy reversal for Bismarck and a marked shift in the coalition politics of Germany. Since unification, Bismarck, though himself a Prussian conservative, had aligned with the National Liberals as partners in both free trade and the *Kulturkampf* against Catholicism and the Center Party.[82] Free trade had been a key Prussian policy goal ever since the Congress of Vienna. Prussia and its Junker nobility had spearheaded the creation of the Zollverein, and Bismarck himself had worked to incorporate a most favored nation clause into the 1871 Treaty of Versailles ending the Franco-Prussian War.[83] From 1879 until World War I, with the exception of a brief interlude from 1891 to 1894 under Chancellor Leo von Caprivi, German politics was dominated by this new protectionist coalition.

While the conservative iron and rye coalition first coalesced around trade, it was united by a broader conservative and nationalist backlash against the sweeping economic and political changes shaping Germany in the late nineteenth century. Two further components of this backlash were rising anti-Semitism and increased opposition to financial capitalism. Given the prominence of Jewish bankers in the German financial industry, these two components inevitably became intertwined in the political debate in the wake of the Panic of 1873. Dating to the founding

[78] Schonhardt-Bailey 1998.
[79] Zucker 1975, 134.
[80] Ibid., 142.
[81] Ibid., 141.
[82] Mayer 1998, 19.
[83] Barkin 1970, 33.

of the Rothschilds' banking empire in the 1700s, Jews played a prominent role in German finance. Jewish bankers were partners and founders of several of the *Grossbanken*, including Deutsche Bank (Ludwig Bamberger and Hermann Marcuse), Dresdner Bank (Eugen Guttmann), and Darmstädter Bank (Abraham Oppenheim), and the banking elite in every large city in nineteenth-century Germany included Jewish bankers: "the Rothschilds ... in Frankfurt, Salomon Heine and Moritz Warburg in Hamburg, the Mendelssohns and Bleichroeders in Berlin, and Abraham Oppenheim in Cologne."[84] As Brustein notes, Jews' involvement in the financial sector and commerce was massively disproportionate to their share of the population: "By the end of the nineteenth century, Jewish prominence in German banking, industry, and commerce was staggering... while Jews comprised only one percent of the total German population, they accounted for nearly 18 percent of bank owners and directors in the German Reich and 33 percent in Berlin."[85]

Jewish families were among the wealthiest in Germany in the early 1900s. In 1908, there were twenty-nine German families with fortunes greater than 50 million marks; nine were Jewish, including the Rothschilds, who ranked second with a fortune of 310 million marks.[86] In Prussia, there were 200 millionaires in 1908; 55 of them were Jews, and 33 of these amassed their fortunes in finance and banking.[87] More broadly, Germany's Jewish population was disproportionately upper and middle class – overrepresented in professions such as medicine, law, journalism, and commerce – and underrepresented in agriculture and industrial labor. Jews comprised less than one-tenth of 1 percent of Germans employed in agriculture, forest, and mining.

As Brustein notes, "This occupational imbalance did not go unnoticed by the purveyors of German anti-Semitism."[88] Indeed, as the economic slump continued, the Jews became easy scapegoats for the evils that speculation, unfettered financial capital, and stock markets had wrought on German society. During the boom years before the panic, Friedrich Engels wrote that "stock exchange swindling has dragged all the ruling classes into the whirlpool of speculation.... Ministers, generals, princes, and counts deal in shares with the cunningness stock

[84] Brustein 2003, 205.
[85] Ibid., 207–8; see also Wistrich 1982, 61.
[86] Brustein 2003, 209.
[87] Ibid.; Steinberg 2011, 235–6.
[88] Brustein 2003, 210.

exchange Jews and the state recognizes their equality by conferring titles wholesale upon these stock exchange Jews."[89] In the wake of the panic, the journalist Otto Glagau published a series of articles in the journal *Gartenlaube* (1874–6) and a subsequent book (1878), in which he explicitly linked Jews and the ills of financial capitalism. In the most famous of these, *Der Börsen- und Gründungsschwindel in Berlin* ("The Stock Market and Founding-Era Swindle in Berlin"), Glagau pinned the blame for all of Germany's ills on the evils of "Manchesterism" – unfettered capitalism and trade openness – and the "liberal" coalition behind the *Kulturkampf* that Otto von Bismarck had previously assembled:

> The "liberal" legislators in our parliaments are chiefly Manchester people, and they work, in conjunction with the "liberal" press, mainly in the interests of capital and the stock market. The Manchester-friendly legislation has caused a splendid bankruptcy … Manchester-style economic policy has benefited only a small minority, primarily financiers and speculators; it has inflicted deep wounds on the people. The stock market and founding-era swindle has reduced our national assets by billions, produced general ill humor and bitterness, and supplied Social Democracy with droves of new followers.[90]

In Glagau's mind, the Jews were the source of this "Manchesterism," and they posed a direct threat to the German people and society. He aimed his sights directly at the Berlin-based Jewish bankers whom he blamed for the panic, along with the prominent Jewish leaders of the National Liberal Party, Ludwig Bamberger and Eduard Lasker, who were leading advocates of German adoption of the gold standard and sponsors of the 1869 Public Company Act that had liberalized the establishment of limited liability corporations and fueled the speculative boom on German stock markets:

> Jewry is applied Manchesterism in the extreme. It knows nothing any more but trade, and of that merely haggling and usury. It does not work but makes others work for it, it haggles and speculates with the manual and mental products of others. Its center is the stock exchange. … As an alien tribe it fastens itself to the German people and sucks their marrow. The social question is essentially the Jewish question; everything else is a swindle.[91]

Glagau's views, while extreme and ominous in their foreshadowing of what was to come in the Nazi era, illustrate an important broader trend in German politics and society in the 1870–1914 period: Germany's

[89] Quoted in Henderson 1975, 164.
[90] Glagau 1876, 2.
[91] Quoted in Stoetzler 2009, 218.

financial and economic problems in the wake of the Panic of 1873 and the Long Depression came to be seen as inextricably linked with the rising prominence and wealth of its Jews. Rising anti-capitalism and anti-Semitism strongly influenced the decision of the moderate Center Party – traditionally the party of small business, Catholic Germany, and rural peasants – to ally with the Conservative and Agrarian parties and support protectionism, instead of with the left-wing, labor-oriented parties (the SPD and Communists) which might have better served the economic interests of its core constituents.[92] Anti-Semitic articles soon appeared in *Germania*, the Center Party's main newspaper, unfavorably contrasting Jews' prominent role in German finance against their lack of participation in the "productive strata" of German industry.[93] Thus, even within the mainstream political parties of the time, opposition to financial capitalism and anti-Semitism were viewed as two sides of the same coin. For an increasingly large segment of the German population, Jews became scapegoats for all that was wrong in the world, and Judaism, finance, trade, and globalization all became synonymous with one another as a single existential threat to German society:

> The "Semite," emancipated and overrepresented in business, professions, and progressive politics, became the perfect symbol of the disturbingly modern. He was associated with liberal capitalism or "Manchesterism," with finance or "mobile" capital and its fraudulent speculation, with money-power and materialism divorced from a sense of moral responsibility.[94]

Thus, along with opposition to free trade, opposition to financial capitalism – fueled in part by rising nationalism and anti-Semitism – was a second key issue around which the conservative iron and rye coalition mobilized in the wake of the Panic of 1873. This led to a series of laws and policies that fundamentally altered the trajectory of German financial development by restricting activity on German stock markets and taxing securities transactions. In 1884, a new company law limited the permissible activities on stock exchanges and tightened the requirements for incorporation.[95] In 1885, the *Reichstag* passed a bill imposing a new stamp tax on stock transfers, the stock certificates that provincial bankers, who served as intermediaries between local customers and bankers on Germany's major stock exchanges, delivered to their customers once

[92] Steinberg 2011, 421.
[93] Winkler 2006, 206.
[94] Steinberg 2011, 308.
[95] Burhop and Lehmann-Hasemeyer 2016, 18; Fohlin 2007.

transactions were completed. This new tax raised the cost of business for small bankers and brokerages, on top of commissions and fees from both the provincial banker and the central exchange banker. The "direct effect was that, in order to save expense, the customers of the provincial bankers, in spite of all effort on the latter's part, began to deal directly with the central banker or with the branches established in the district by the great banks."[96] The 1885 law also restricted investor access to the Berlin stock exchange to owners of firms and companies registered in Berlin, which imposed a further barrier to the expansion of the exchange and securities trading more broadly in German finance.[97]

The 1896 Stock Exchange Law

The push within Germany to restrict and regulate securities markets gained steam in the 1890s, following the Baring crisis – the November 1890 sovereign debt crisis in Argentina that nearly brought down Baring Brothers and Company, the world's largest and second-oldest merchant bank, based in London. Although German banks were not directly exposed to Barings, a number of firms had substantial exposure in Argentina and echoes of the instability of 1873 once again stoked fears of global finance and financial capitalism.[98] Closer to home, another series of speculative panics roiled Berlin's stock markets and stoked fears about "plungers" and commodity speculators.[99] Most famous of these was the Ritter and Blumenfeld scandal, in which a group of speculators unsuccessfully attempted to corner the Berlin commodity market in wheat through coordinated activities with provincial bankers and bribery of railway officials aimed at slowing down wheat shipments into the capital. The subsequent bank run bankrupted two prominent private banks (Hirschfeld and Wolf) and resulted in prison sentences for two officials of the Rhine-Westphalian bank.[100] When several additional brokerages failed in a subsequent stock market slump, the political momentum for government action accelerated. The Stock Exchange Enquiry Commission (*Börsen-Enquête-Kommission*) conducted extensive hearings and issued a report in 1893. In 1894, the Imperial Stamp Act doubled the tax on stock transfers that had been imposed in 1885,

[96] Riesser 1911, 619.
[97] Monnet and Quintin 2005, 9.
[98] Friend 1908, 370.
[99] Coffee 2001, 56; Friend 1908, 371.
[100] Friend 1908, 371.

in an effort to further reign in speculation. The tax was raised again in 1890, to triple the pre-1894 rate.[101]

In 1896, the Agrarian Party proposed a new stock exchange law (Börsengesetz). The Agrarians saw grain and commodity speculation as a direct threat to rural German interests and the underlying cause of the plight of rural Germans during the Long Depression. More broadly, as noted above, the Agrarians and the broader conservative/nationalist coalition saw this as an opportunity to "tackle the real evils of the age: capitalism and liberalism, urbanization and Social Democracy, and international Jewry."[102] Here, again, financial capitalism and anti-Semitism were combined by the ruling conservative political coalition into a single policy issue.

The Börsengesetz bill passed on June 22, 1896, with the support of the Center, Conservative, and Agrarian Parties over the staunch opposition of the Liberals and the SPD. At the time, the 1896 law was seen as "the most elaborate attempt ever to regulate speculative markets" (Emery 1898, 286). It was the first case of direct government restriction of specific activities on German securities markets.[103] The law restricted and taxed a variety of securities-related activities, which raised the cost of trading and selling securities and ultimately cemented the dominance of Germany's large banks in corporate finance and investment banking.[104] The law restricted trading in foreign securities and prohibited futures trading in mining and industrial securities and futures trading in grains.[105] It also tightened the rules for listing stocks on exchanges, which raised the cost of brokerage services and drove many private bankers and smaller houses out of business.[106] Given their larger capital reserves, the big banks were better able to absorb these costs. The 1896 law also increased reporting requirements for public stock offerings and extended the stricter entrance requirements that the Berlin exchange had adopted in the 1880s to all German stock exchanges.[107] Finally, the law required "speculators" to register their stock exchange transactions publicly; as Coffee notes, "Failure to do so could lead speculative contracts to be declared null and void as gambling transactions."[108]

[101] Coffee 2001, 56.
[102] Berghahn 2005, 214.
[103] Gehrig and Fohlin 2006.
[104] Wallich 1905, 208.
[105] Riesser 1911, 622; United States Senate 1914, 815.
[106] Plochmann 1908, 742.
[107] Burhop and Lehmann-Hasemeyer 2016, 19.
[108] Coffee 2001, 57.

In 1900, a further increase in the tax on the certificates of foreign bonds, along with a new tax on the issue and transfer of mining stocks, placed smaller brokers and banks at a further competitive disadvantage against the large Berlin-based banks. At the same time, an additional tax in 1900 on the "compensatory transactions" of the big bankers increased the cost of providing stock brokerage services even for the large banks, increasing their incentives to engage in more traditional commercial lending.[109]

These restrictions and taxes on stock trading and exchanges, culminating in the 1896 Börsengesetz, marked a key inflection point altering the trajectory of German financial development. Until the 1890s, both banking and securities markets had developed rapidly in the newly unified and industrializing German Reich. As universal banks, Germany's large private banks (the *Grossbanken*) engaged in both commercial lending and investment banking activities, and they occupied privileged places of access on the Frankfurt and Berlin exchanges. Absent the new restrictions and taxes on trading and stock exchange–related activities of the 1880s and 1890s, one might have expected both banking and securities markets in Germany to continue developing apace. The new transfer taxes, however, incentivized the major banks to move their stock trading off of the stock exchanges and put smaller brokerages at a competitive disadvantage. In order to avoid the new transfer taxes, the Grossbanken increasingly purchased large blocks of individual stocks and began to execute individual customer orders internally, paying tax only on the net balance of shares purchased.[110] Smaller brokerage houses, by contrast, could not afford to make such large block purchases and increasingly lost business to the big banks.[111] In addition, this "internalization" of stock transfers within the large banks reduced trading volume on the exchanges themselves and accelerated the already-substantial share ownership of Germany's major industrial firms in the hands of the Grossbanken.[112] Finally, the new disclosure requirements for speculators also reduced trading volume on the exchanges by discouraging smaller investors from participating, thereby further increasing the competitive advantage and position of the Grossbanken. By the onset of World War II, the Grossbanken controlled the lion's share of

109 Riesser 1911, 619–20.
110 Coffee 2001, 57.
111 Riesser 1911, 620.
112 Coffee 2001, 57.

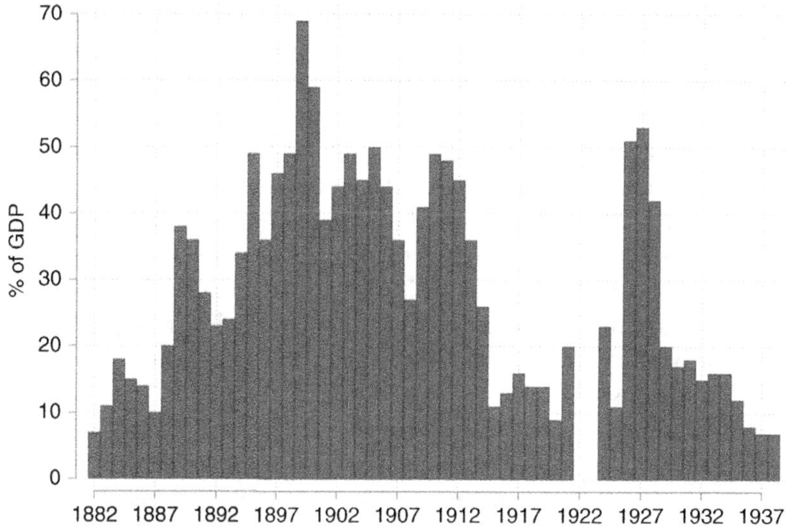

FIGURE 5.1. Annual trading volume, Berlin stock exchange clearing house, percent of GDP, 1882–1938. Reproduced from Burhop and Lehmann-Hasemeyer (2016); data from annual reports of the Bank des Berliner Kassenverein.

underwriting in German securities markets, as smaller brokerages and traders exited the exchanges and found themselves at an increasing competitive disadvantage.

While these new taxes and restrictions on stock trading and exchanges accelerated the concentration of investment banking and trading activities in the hands of the largest commercial banks, their most important effect was to arrest the development of German securities markets for the remainder of the pre-1914 era. From 1896 to 1914, securities market development in Germany stalled and overall trading volume plummeted sharply (Figure 5.1). With the exception of a brief resurgence in the Weimar era between the end of hyperinflation in 1924 and the onset of the Great Depression in 1929, stock trading and securities markets, both in terms of overall volume and their importance relative to bank lending in German finance, did not return to the levels they had attained by 1896 until the reforms of the Finanzplatz Deutschland period in the 1990s. Thus, while the 1896 reforms were the product of the economic and political upheaval caused by the Panic of 1873 and the Long Depression, they had long-term effects that fundamentally altered the trajectory of financial development in Germany for the next century.

In addition to arresting the development of German stock exchanges, the 1896 Börsengesetz and related laws further accelerated the trend toward greater banking concentration and locked in the dominance of traditional commercial lending relative to securities transactions. By the 1890s, this process was already well underway, driven by the combination of commercial and investment banking in the large Berlin-based banks, along with these banks' movement into provincial banking from 1870 onward through the establishment of local branches, agencies, and deposit offices throughout Germany. The financial crises of 1873 and 1900 also contributed to this process, as the major banks took over smaller banks through a process of "liquidation" and consolidation.[113]

Even before the adoption of the Börsengesetz, Germany's large banks had already enjoyed a comparative advantage against smaller private banks and brokerage houses, by virtue of the liberal discount window lending provided by the Reichsbank since its founding in 1876 (and, earlier, by the Bank of Prussia).[114] The availability of this lending facility encouraged German banks to finance their industrial clients through debt rather than equity and fueled the close bank-industry ties that remain the hallmark of Germany's economy.[115] As Coffee notes, "Secure in the knowledge that they could rediscount their loans to corporate clients with the Reichsbank, the major German private banks could 'lend to the hilt,' undeterred by the fear of illiquidity."[116] This situation contrasted sharply with developments in both the United States – where the Federal Reserve was not established until 1913 – and the United Kingdom, where the Bank of England was far less willing to provide similar discount window credit to the British banking sector.[117]

Riesser (1911) notes that experts had warned since the mid-1880s that the effect of the taxes and regulations of securities transactions would be "to [further] monopolize the banking business in the hands of a few concerns."[118] These warnings proved to be prescient. By 1905, there

113 Riesser 1911, 636–7, 651–2.
114 Tilly 1986, 144.
115 Coffee 2001, 55; Tilly 1986, 145.
116 Coffee 2001, 55.
117 Ibid.; Tilly 1986, 145.
118 Riesser 1911, 618.

were only five large banks with more than 100 million marks in capital, and these banks' assets totaled about half of all private banks' assets in Germany.[119] By 1913, Germany's three largest corporations were banks, as were seventeen of the twenty five largest enterprises in the country. As Tilly notes, these levels of bank size and concentration were unique to Germany and the defining feature of its financial system.[120] This bank concentration was matched, on the borrower side, by the consolidation and cartelization of German heavy industry, marked most notably in the 1890s by the formation of coal and pig iron syndicates in the Rhine-Westphalia region.[121]

By World War I, the broad contours of Germany's classic bank-dominated financial system had taken shape, with substantial restrictions on securities activities, a system dominated by traditional commercial lending, a division of labor between the three pillars of German banking, and close ties between the large private banks and German industrial firms, driven by the consolidation of market power in the hands of a handful of large lenders and a small number of large borrowers/producers. What our analysis illustrates is that this outcome was far from inevitable or even obvious in the early nineteenth century. Up to the Panic of 1873, the trajectory of financial development suggested that Germany might be on the path toward developing large and deep securities markets alongside its traditional banking pillars. Instead, major policy decisions in the wake of the Panic of 1873 and the Long Depression – most notably, the 1896 Börsengesetz – arrested the nascent development of German securities markets. These policies emerged as part of the broader domestic coalition politics of the time, with the conservative political coalition that first organized as the "marriage of iron and rye" in opposition to free trade and globalization also setting its sights on rolling back the increasing financialization of the German economy. Thus, in contrast to Canada – where the relative absence of "affirmative acts of policy design" resulted in Canadian securities markets remaining fragmented and underdeveloped – the German case is one in which government policy choices directly contributed to the persistent underdevelopment of securities markets in the nineteenth century.[122]

[119] Tilly 1986, 113.
[120] Ibid.
[121] Riesser 1911, 614.
[122] Jacobs and Teles 2007, 158–9.

The Interwar Era: The 1931 Financial Crisis and Nazi Repression of Securities Markets

The economic and political turmoil in Germany during the interwar era is widely known.[123] The economic instability of the Weimar hyperinflation (1921–4), followed by the onset and global spread of the Great Depression (1929–33), left the German economy and financial system in tatters. At the depths of the Depression, in 1932, German industrial production was only 61 percent of its 1929 level and unemployment exceeded 30 percent.[124] Although Germany's banks weathered the shocks from the Depression's onset in the United States and a series of attacks on Germany's gold standard peg in 1929–30, the financial system collapsed in 1931 following the July failure of Darmstädter- und Nationalbank (Danat-Bank) and Dresdner Bank, the country's second and third largest commercial banks.[125]

The 1931 crisis was both a currency and banking crisis, and in many respects, it represents a perfect storm of events: Germany's long-running reparations saga from 1919 to 1931, the 1929 stock market crash in the United States that sparked the Great Depression, the subsequent cycle of currency crises and banking panics in the wake of the 1931 failure of Austria's Credit-Anstalt bank, and the persistent budgetary problems and political weakness of the Weimar government.[126] Although scholars continue to debate the relative importance of these domestic and international factors in triggering the 1931 crisis,[127] there is substantial evidence that these political and global macroeconomic factors were more important than specific bank-centric factors such as risky lending or leverage. Rather, German banks' problems stemmed primarily from difficulties in accessing funds from foreign banks or the Reichsbank.[128] Ferguson and Temin (2001) go so far as to argue that the failure of Danat-Bank and other German financial institutions would likely have been avoided entirely had Germany "gone off gold by devaluing or imposing capital controls."[129] Thus, the 1931 crisis appears to have been triggered by a series of factors related to

[123] See, e.g., Feldman 1993; Frieden 2007; James 1986; Weitz 2013.
[124] James 1984, 68.
[125] Burhop and Lehmann-Hasemeyer 2016, 31.
[126] Eichengreen 1996; Frieden 2007.
[127] See, e.g., Eichengreen 1996; James 1984; Kindleberger 1973; Temin 2008.
[128] Balderston 1991.
[129] Ferguson and Temin 2001, 40.

global macroeconomic conditions and the problems of the interwar gold standard, rather than structural weakness in the German financial system.

As with the Panic of 1873, the 1931 crisis had enormous economic and political consequences in Germany.[130] One key consequence was the further acceleration of concentration and consolidation in the first pillar of German banking – the large, private commercial banks – that had been a central trend in German finance since unification in the 1870s. In the wake of the 1931 crisis, Danat and Dresdner Banks were merged and 91 percent nationalized, leaving Germany with only three major private commercial banks: Deutsche Bank, Commerzbank, and Dresdner. The Weimar government had also taken large stakes in Deutsche (35 percent) and Commerz (69 percent) during the crisis. These state shares were re-privatized in 1937, leaving Germany with a "Big Three" of private commercial banks.

Alongside the Big Thee commercial banks, the second and third pillars of German banking – the savings and cooperative banks – continued to grow rapidly during the interwar years, with their deposit base increasing at nearly twice the rate of that of the big banks between 1933 and 1938 (68 percent and 62 percent, respectively, compared to 39 percent for large bank deposits).[131] The savings banks had also been hit by the 1931 crisis due to their extensive lending to the city and county governments that had established them in the nineteenth century. In order to prevent such bank-government exposure in the future, the Weimar federal government granted the Sparkassen legal autonomy in 1931. This new legislation also mandated that only publicly owned savings banks would be permitted to call themselves Sparkassen.[132] This restriction on entry into the savings bank market inhibited future competition from private firms in the household lending sector and ensured that the deposit base of the savings banks would be used primarily for loans to local governments.

The most salient and enduring financial legacy of the 1931 crisis, however, was the further restriction of German securities markets.[133] As discussed in the previous section, the 1896 Börsengesetz and related laws led to a sharp decline in the size and scope of German stock exchanges and securities markets in the two decades prior to World War I and a further collapse in activity during the 1914–18 conflict (Figure 5.1).

[130] Data in this paragraph are from Balderston 1991, 597.
[131] Detzer et al. 2013, 39.
[132] Ibid.
[133] Burhop and Lehmann-Hasemeyer 2016.

In spite of these legal restrictions on securities activities, German equity markets had nonetheless begun to approach prewar levels in market capitalization and the number of listed companies by the mid-1920s. This was due in large part to the overall improvement in the state of the German economy following the end of hyperinflation in 1924, the first reduction in German war reparations under the Dawes Plan, and the French military withdrawal from the Ruhr valley, Germany's major coal and steel producing region, in 1925. At the same time, some scholars have argued that this growth in German stock markets was also partly driven by Weimar investors' beliefs that "shares could act as a hedge against inflation and hyperinflation."[134]

The 1931 financial crisis brought this nascent recovery in German securities markets to an abrupt halt. In July 1931, the government closed all German stock exchanges following the bankruptcy of Danat and Dresdner banks, the country's second- and third-largest institutions. The exchanges reopened briefly before closing a second time in September 1931, as the government fought to stabilize the Reichsmark following Britain's departure from the gold standard. The exchanges remained shuttered until April 1932.[135]

Adolf Hitler's ascendancy to power in January 1933 was the final nail in the coffin. The collapse of the Weimar Republic and rise of the Nazi regime ensured that German securities markets would not recover from the damage of the 1931 crisis. Under the Nazis, a new series of laws and restrictions reversed the Weimar-era recovery of securities markets and further cemented the dominance of banking in the German financial system. These new laws and regulations imposed even more stringent restrictions on stock markets and securities underwriting than the 1896 Börsengesetz and related legislation in the wake of the Panic of 1873. Moreover, as the basis for the legal and regulatory structure of postwar German finance in the Federal Republic, the Nazi-era securities and banking laws would have a long-term impact on the trajectory of German financial development.

For Hitler and the Nazi regime, private financial markets existed solely to serve the state's political and military requirements.[136] The allocation of capital was not something to be left to private bankers and financial markets; rather, the government needed to take an active role through the use of "numerous regulations and interventions in market, in order

[134] Ibid., 15; see also Henning 1992, 219, 225–8; Mosley and Singer 2008.

[135] Beer 1999, 225; Burhop and Lehmann-Hasemeyer 2016, 31.

[136] Nathan 1944, 5.

to further rearmament and autarky as far as possible."[137] Furthermore, the Nazis "regarded finance as an activity dominated to an unwelcome extent by 'Jewish' interests and as a largely unproductive activity that failed to contribute to national wealth."[138] In short, a financial market structure dominated by Jews, focused on speculation and profit, and ensuring independent, private centers of wealth and influence over the economy was utterly anathema to the basic economic and political goals of the National Socialist Party.

In his 1944 study of Nazi war financing and banking, Otto Nathan aptly described how direct control and regulation of banking and finance was a central element of the Nazis' political strategy:

> Instead of leaving to interest rates and the deposit-generating decisions of the banking system the determination of the volume of funds available for short- and long-term use, the German government saw to it that the central bank and other credit institutions provided whatever funds were considered necessary. Instead of permitting the market mechanism to set interest rates, the government fixed them in terms of its politico-military requirements. Instead of depending on the mechanism of the market for the allocation of funds, the government used special devices to syphon accumulated funds into desired channels. Direct controls made new private investment through the capital market either completely impossible or subject to government approval.[139]

For the Nazis, the goal of banks and the financial system was not to generate private profits or to channel capital to its most efficient uses, but rather to direct resources to those sectors and purposes deemed most essential to the government's military and political efforts. Consequently, "the banking and credit system, like so many other parts of the economy, was made an aide-de-camp, a servant of the military master."[140]

Reorienting the German financial sector to this goal required extensive Nazi regulation and intervention, including the adoption of foreign exchange controls and the empowerment of the Reichsbank to determine the total volume and purposes of credit in the economy.[141] Under the German Credit Act (*Kreditwesengesetz*) of December 5, 1934, the Nazi government also assumed full jurisdiction over all credit institutions not already owned by the government; this gave government officials full control over interest rates, commissions, and fees set by German banks.

137 Buchheim and Scherner 2006, 390.
138 Burhop and Lehmann-Hasemeyer 2016, 34–5.
139 Nathan 1944, 5.
140 Ibid., 8.
141 Ibid., 6.

Thus, while the Nazis formally left the large commercial banks as de jure private institutions, the Credit Act represented a de facto nationalization of their activities.[142]

Nazi regulation and restriction of securities markets was even more stringent. This was due, at least in part, to the fact that securities markets, unlike concentrated commercial banking, implied a diffusion of control among many shareholders that was incompatible with Hitler's authoritarianism. While the government could exert near-total control over the lending activities and operations of the large commercial banks through laws like the Credit Act, exercising similar control over capital markets was more challenging. Nonetheless, the Nazis did their best to direct securities markets toward their political goals in much the same way. The government reduced the number of stock exchanges from twenty-one to nine and centralized supervision by removing state regulatory authority.[143] Between 1933 and 1935, the government imposed new regulations requiring all issues of securities to be approved by the Ministry of Finance, Ministry of Economics, and the Reichsbank.[144]

In addition, as a way to direct German capital toward military rearmament, the Nazis passed legislation in 1934–5 requiring all public companies with rising profits or "a return on equity of in excess of six percent" to invest these "excess profits" in government bonds.[145] Companies in this position retained ownership of the bonds but management of them was entrusted to a government agency, the Golddiskontbank (Gold Discount Bank).[146] After three years, when this legislation expired, these profits were to be returned to shareholders in either cash or securities; however, the law was extended in 1937 and modified again in 1941 to keep these profits in the hands of the government.[147] In order to avoid these penalties, over 40 percent of German public companies transformed into private enterprises over the 1933–8 period.[148]

The Nazi government imposed an additional series of wealth and capital gains taxes that further contributed to the decline in securities markets.[149] In October 1934, it doubled the wealth tax on stock shares

[142] Ibid., 15–16.

[143] See www.deutsche-boerse-cash-market.com/dbcm-en/about-us/our-approach/history-of-the-frankfurt-stock-exchange.

[144] Burhop and Lehmann-Hasemeyer 2016, 31; Spoerer 1996, 165.

[145] Burhop and Lehmann-Hasemeyer 2016, 31.

[146] Beer 1999, 293–5; Nathan 1944, 21.

[147] Nathan 1944, 21.

[148] Beer 1999, 295; Burhop and Lehmann-Hasemeyer 2016, 32; Mertens 2007, 106.

[149] Burhop and Lehmann-Hasemeyer 2016, 32; Hof 2008, 133–4.

from 0.5 percent to 1 percent of market value and lengthened the minimum period to hold securities to avoid speculation taxes from three months to one year. The government also removed the capital gains tax exemption for corporate securities, leaving only government bonds exempt.[150] In December 1934, the government tightened admissions requirements to stock exchanges, raising the minimum nominal value of a new stock issue on the Berlin exchange from 500,000 to 1,500,000 marks.[151]

These Nazi-era restrictions of stock market and equity activity culminated in the 1937 *Aktiengesetz* (Stock Corporation Act), which drastically curtailed the rights of stock shareholders and granted the government authority to dissolve public companies "deemed to endanger the national welfare" without the need to compensate shareholders.[152] The law also eliminated shareholders' voting rights on dividend policy and the dismissal of directors, and it imposed a tenfold increase in the amount of capital required for new private companies to incorporate.[153]

Collectively, these new laws, restrictions, and taxes on securities market activity during the Nazi era had "long-lasting adverse repercussions" on the development of German securities markets.[154] Whereas prospects for the recovery and continued development of German securities marked once again appeared bright at the height of the 1920s, these hopes were dashed by the onset of World War II in 1939. As in the 1890s, the dual combination of financial crisis and active government policies arrested the growth of securities markets and locked in the dominance of commercial banking as the primary source of industrial financing. Unlike in the nineteenth century, however, this time there would be no turning back the clock as in the Weimar era. Instead, the combined shocks of the 1931 financial crisis and the Nazi's rise to power in 1933 arrested the development of German securities market and ensured they would remain small and subservient to banking even in the postwar era. This time, the effects would last for decades.

150 Beer 1999, 301; Burhop and Lehmann-Hasemeyer 2016, 33.

151 Nathan 1944, 21.

152 Mertens 2007, 101.

153 Burhop and Lehmann-Hasemeyer 2016, 34; Mertens 2007, 96.

154 Burhop and Lehmann-Hasemeyer 2016, 30.

POSTWAR GERMAN FINANCE: BANK DOMINANCE, SUBORDINATE SECURITIES MARKETS, PERSISTENT STABILITY

World War II and the collapse of the Nazi regime left the Germany economy and financial system in turmoil.[155] Under the postwar occupation, the heads of the Big Three private banks were deposed and convicted of war crimes, and the Allied government broke the Big Three into ten regional institutions.[156] However, following the establishment of the Federal Republic in 1949, the German financial system was quickly reconstituted in its prewar format. The "Big Bank Act" of 1953 partially consolidated the ten regional banks; by 1958, the process was complete, and Deutsche Bank, Dresdner Bank, and Commerzbank once again assumed their dominant roles in German industrial finance. At the same time, the continued operation of the 1937 Aktiengesetz continued to limit the development of securities markets in the postwar German financial system.[157]

Despite the shocks of Weimar-era hyperinflation, the 1931 banking crisis, and World War II, the overarching themes of German finance were the persistence of the three-pillar banking system and the continued dominance of banking over securities. By the late 1950s, the status quo ante in German banking had been restored, with a handful of large commercial banks dominating industrial lending and the savings and cooperative banks dominating lending to households, the agricultural sector, and the Mittelstand of small and midsize manufacturers. The large banks continued to dominate lending to manufacturing, providing 60 percent of credit to the sector through the 1970s and financing 80 percent of German trade transactions during the country's export-led growth boom in the postwar era.[158] Moreover, the close bank-firm ties continued to extend beyond lending to include bank ownership stakes of major German enterprises, including voting rights on corporate boards. In the 1960s, German banks held a majority of shares in German public companies, and representatives of the large, private commercial banks held the position of chairman of the board in a majority of these firms.[159] These deep and extensive bank-firm ties illustrate why Germany has long been portrayed as the archetypical bank-based economy by both financial systems scholars in economics and varieties of capitalism scholars in political science.[160]

155 See Judt 2006.
156 Detzer et al. 2017, 39.
157 Ritschl 2005.
158 Detzer et al. 2013, 39; Story and Walter 1997; Tilly 1996, fig. J2.
159 Edwards 1996, 112–5.
160 See Allen and Gale 2000; Hall and Soskice 2001.

Although the three pillars of German banking persisted into the postwar era of the Federal Republic, the lines between them began to grow fuzzier, especially with respect to the provision of credit to large German industrial firms. Indeed, one of the most salient features of postwar German banking has been the secular decline in the big banks' market share in the provision of industrial credit, as banks from the other pillars have moved into the sector. In 1950, the large commercial banks held 19.1 percent of total assets; by 1988, this share had fallen to only 8.9 percent. In contrast, the Landesbanken and savings banks steadily increased their share, from 10.8 percent and 20 percent.[161]

The major implication of this shift was that the big banks now faced greater competition – primarily from the Landesbanken – in lending to Germany's large industrial corporations. While the big banks remained preeminent in this sector, they no longer enjoyed de facto monopoly power. By 1975, four of the ten largest banks in Germany were Landesbanken. The cooperative banks also joined the fray. In 1976, the federal government removed the legal limits on the size of the cooperative banks' central organization, the *Deutsche Genossenschaftsbank* (DB Bank), and it promptly joined the Landesbanken as a large-scale competitor for the big banks' core business of industrial lending.[162] The big banks responded, with only mixed success, to move themselves into the savings and cooperative banks' core business of lending to the Mittelstand, Germany's small and midsize businesses. Even today, the savings and cooperative banks continue to provide more than 65 percent of lending to the Mittelstand and more than 40 percent of all credit to German companies and households.[163] Likewise, the big banks have established national branching networks to compete with the savings banks for the household lending business, but again have met with relatively limited success.[164]

In sum, while the barriers between the three pillars blurred from the 1970s onward, the basic structure of German banking that emerged prior to World War II remains today, with large private banks, saving banks, and cooperative banks each playing a major role in the German financial system. While mortgage banks and foreign banks emerged as larger players from the 1970s onward, they have remained small relative to the three main banking pillars.

[161] Edwards 1996, 100.

[162] Deeg 2003, 54–5.

[163] *Economist*, November 10, 2012.

[164] Deeg 2003, 116–21; Detzer et al. 2013, 41.

Securities Markets: A Secondary Role in Postwar German Finance

The second key feature of postwar German finance was the continued subordinate role of securities markets. The key policy decisions of the 1890s and 1930s, discussed above, had an enduring legacy, arresting the development of German securities markets and locking in a financial system dominated by commercial banking well into the post–Bretton Woods period. Indeed, as Story and Walter wrote in the 1990s, "a central feature of German stock exchanges is their diminutive size."[165] In 1857, only 203 joint stock firms existed in the German confederation.[166] By 1873, there were 441 companies listed on the Berlin stock exchange.[167] Over a century later, in 1982, there were only 450 joint stock companies ("AB" corporations) listed on German stock exchanges, compared with over 300,000 private, limited liability companies ("GmbH" firms).[168] German corporate investment in the early 1980s was still financed overwhelmingly from internal profits (61 percent) and bank borrowing (18 percent), with only a paltry 2.4 percent generated from the issue of new stock shares.[169] Similarly, only 17 percent of private German households owned shares in public companies in 1998, compared with nearly 50 percent in the United States.[170]

While the Frankfurt and Berlin exchanges hosted active trading in debt securities and commodities from the 1950s onward, corporate stock trading was limited in the postwar decades and German securities markets never developed into "serious rivals to the London or Paris exchanges prior to German unification."[171] Relative to almost every other industrialized country – and especially in comparison to the United States, United Kingdom, and even Canada – Germany securities markets remained, until the 1980s, of limited size and importance in the German economy. In comparison to London or New York, Frankfurt barely registered as a major financial center in the world economy until the 1990s. Frankfurt was Germany's oldest and largest exchange, and home to the major commercial banks, the major Landesbanken, and the DG bank, the central bank of the Sparkassen. Yet, despite its long and storied history, Frankfurt remained small, with less than half of all

165 Story and Walter 1997, 172.
166 Monnet and Quintin 2005, 8.
167 Burhop and Lehmann-Hasemeyer 2016, 3.
168 Story and Walter 1997, 172.
169 Ibid., 174.
170 Guiso, Haliassos, and Jappelli 2002.
171 Coffee 2001, 52.

trading (44 percent of turnover) by the 1980s. Moreover, a significant portion of securities activity in Germany took place off the exchanges; the banks themselves controlled a substantial portion of securities trading through their own private, free market, which they ran via telephone and direct interaction with clients, and which was entirely unregulated by the state agencies.[172] Corporate bond trading remained overwhelmingly weighted toward government securities, with German commercial paper markets remaining effectively nonexistent well into the 1980s.[173]

As in Canada, the fragmentation of financial regulation has been a key factor in limiting the development of German securities markets.[174] This, too, is a legacy of the pre-WWII era. In the Weimar Republic, there were twenty-one stock exchanges that the Nazis consolidated into nine in the 1930s. Nonetheless, the major Nazi-era securities law, the 1934 Credit Law (*Kreditwesengesetz*), "strengthened regional stock exchanges at the expense of Berlin, and charged the states with the supervision of markets."[175] This state-level structure was re-established after World War II under the new Federal Republic. Eight stock exchanges remained in operation in the postwar era: Frankfurt, Berlin, Munich, Stuttgart, Düsseldorf, Hanover, Bremen, and Hamburg. These exchanges continued to lack a coordinated clearance and settlement system, and supervisory authority remained distributed at the regional level with power vested in the economy ministries of the German states. While relations between the state securities regulators were governed by formal treaties – and while an umbrella association, the *Arbeitsgemeinschaft der deutschen Wertpapierbörsen* (Association of German Stock Exchanges), was established in 1952 to facilitate cooperation between the regional stock exchanges – in reality very little cooperation occurred and the association had no permanent staff or real regulatory authority.[176] German tax law in the postwar era further reinforced the dominance of bank-centric finance. Until 2002, the short-term (up to one year) capital gains tax was 50 percent, creating a strong disincentive for firms and investors to participate in German stock markets.[177] Other accounting and tax laws, including high corporate tax rates and accelerated depreciation schedules, also create disincentives for

[172] Story and Walter 1997, 176.

[173] www.bankofengland.co.uk/-/media/boe/files/quarterly-bulletin/1987/commercial-paper-markets-an-international-survey.

[174] On fragmentation of markets in the German political economy, see Streeck 1997.

[175] Story and Walter 1997, 176.

[176] Ibid.

[177] Detzer et al. 2013, 79.

German firms to participate in securities markets by encouraging them to utilize internally generated funds and enabling them to offset the cost of borrowing from German banks.[178]

German finance in the postwar era reflected the long-term impact of these regulatory institutions and laws. The close connections between commercial banks, major industrial firms, and politicians, long present in the pre-1914 and interwar eras, deepened further in the four decades from the founding of the Federal Republic to the collapse of the Berlin Wall. Leading bankers from the Big Three banks served as advisors to German chancellors throughout the postwar era, while the savings and cooperative banks remained a major source of financing for state and local governments, respectively. These close ties between German banks and industrial firms impeded the development of securities markets into the 1970s and early 1980s.[179] With the Big Three banks continuing to dominate lending to large German enterprises, and Germany's Mittelstand – the small and midsize firms at the heart of its industrial economy – remaining almost exclusively private, the number of firms listed on German stock exchanges remained limited, and the large banks continued to dominate as the largest shareholders of those companies that were publicly listed. The large banks' central place as major shareholders and seat-holders on corporate boards also meant that hostile takeovers in Germany were rare, since it was difficult for outside actors to acquire controlling stakes in German corporations and German law (the Equity Law of 1966) empowered owners and managers to protect companies from takeover by active minorities.[180]

Ultimately, as Story and Walter (1997) describe, securities markets remained of secondary importance in German finance well into the late twentieth century:

> Germany is not a nation of shareholders. It is an industrial state run by managers and owners. Only a fraction of total savings reach the equity market. Most privately owned shares are held by the banks, which advise their owners on how to vote at annual general meetings. Share turnover is limited, and dividend payouts are low. Shareholders in effect are invited to observe their investment gain in value in the longer term, rather than to take their profit and then decide what to do with them. Everything in the German institutional and legal environment for shares promotes shareholder patience.[181]

[178] Story and Walter 1997.
[179] See Streeck 1997.
[180] Mayer and Alexander 1990; Story and Walter 1997.
[181] Story and Walter 1997, 174.

Just as the German banking system shares a key similarity with Canada's – a small number of large, private commercial banks dominating corporate finance – so, too, both countries have quite underdeveloped securities markets relative to the United States, United Kingdom, and other industrialized countries. Like Canada, Germany remained an overwhelmingly bank-centric financial system, with fragmented and underdeveloped securities markets, well into the 1980s.

Persistent Stability: The Absence of Systemic Banking Crises in Germany, 1871–2008

Along with the notable continuity of its three-pillar structure and the persistent subordination of securities markets, the most striking feature of Germany's financial system since World War II has been its persistent stability. With the exception of the 1931–3 banking crisis, Germany did not experience a systemic banking crisis between its unification in 1871 and the onset of the global financial crisis in 2008. This remarkable run of stability actually extends back further: in the entire post-Napoleonic era through unification under Bismarck, Germany experienced only a handful of minor episodes of banking instability, in sharp contrast to the near-constant banking crises in the United States during the nineteenth century and the periodic episodes of major crisis in the UK.[182] Even the Panic of 1873, while a major economic and political crisis that led to a number of bank failures, was a stock market crisis that did not become a systemic banking crisis.

Germany did experience several individual bank failures in 1973–5 in the wake of the collapse of the Bretton Woods system and the global recession that corresponded with the first oil shock. However, none of these failures rose to the level of a systemic banking crisis. The most notable of these failures was the collapse of the small, private Bankhaus Herstatt, which failed after landing on the wrong side of several large speculative bets on foreign exchange trading. This failure alerted German and international authorities to cross-border settlement risk and eventually led to the establishment of the Basel Committee on Banking Supervision and the Basel I capital adequacy accord.[183] Nonetheless, these individual failures did not spark a broader banking crisis in the German financial system, and they are notable primarily for being the exceptions that prove the rule. Indeed, what is most remarkable about the postwar German

[182] Tilly 2009.

[183] See Kapstein 1994; Oatley and Nabors 1998; Singer 2004, 2007.

banking system is that its stability and resilience persisted in the face of multiple changes: the blurring of lines between the traditional banking pillars, the return of international capital mobility in the 1970s and 1980s, and deepening European economic integration in the 1980s and 1990s. In contrast to the United States and the United Kingdom, where banking crises became a regular feature of the post–Bretton Woods era, Germany's banking system mirrored Canada's in remaining stable throughout latter half of the twentieth century.

FINANZPLATZ DEUTSCHLAND: THE DEVELOPMENT OF GERMAN SECURITIES MARKETS, 1985–2000

If one ended the story of Germany's financial development in 1980, it would be remarkably similar to that of Canada: a system dominated by a small number of large universal banks, with small and fragmented securities markets and persistent financial stability. Here, however, the road diverges, as Germany's financial system has taken a different route over the last three decades, with strikingly different results. In contrast to Canada, Germany's financial system experienced a third critical transition in the 1990s that resulted in a modern-day shift toward more developed German securities markets. This transformation, triggered by the combination of the globalization in finance, the completion of the European Union's single market, and domestic political developments in the post–Bretton Woods era, resulted in a series of laws creating larger and more centralized national securities markets in Germany, alongside its traditional three-pillar banking system. As we explain here in the remainder of this chapter, these developments have transformed the German financial system into something more closely resembling the American or British system – a development that, unfortunately, has brought with it a level of banking crises and financial instability previously unseen in German history.

This modern transformation of the German financial system occurred in response to a set of domestic and international shocks that fundamentally altered the competitive landscape. Domestically, Germany's big banks faced increasing competition from both the Landesbanken and the Sparkassen during the first thirty years of the postwar era for their bread-and-butter business of providing credit to large German industrial firms. At the same time, the 1970s oil shocks and the subsequent recessions of 1974–5 and 1979–82 led to sharp declines in industrial investment and demand for loans from Germany's big banks.[184] As the 1980s

[184] Detzer et al. 2013.

progressed, lower interest rates, falling oil prices, and the depreciation of the deutsche mark against the dollar left Germany with large trade surpluses and German corporations with substantial export-driven profits. This further reduced their dependence on financing from Germany's large banks and left the banks searching for places to invest overseas.

Globally, rising international capital mobility and the completion of the European single market in the 1980s and 1990s meant that German banks also faced increasing competition from foreign banks, since German firms could now access capital from foreign banks and securities markets.[185] The most serious threat came from London, where the United Kingdom's "Big Bang" in 1986, under Margaret Thatcher, transformed London into Europe's preeminent financial center and a challenger to New York for global dominance.[186] But US markets also were a strong attraction for German firms, especially in the wake of the "Volcker shock" in 1979–82, when US Federal Reserve Chairman Paul Volcker raised short-term interest rates from 9.5 percent to more than 16 percent in May 1981, in an attempt to bring inflation under control.[187] In addition to triggering a recession throughout the industrialized world and precipitating the Latin American debt crisis, the Volcker shock led to large-scale capital outflows from Europe to the United States, with German private funds comprising a larger share.[188]

This combination of domestic and international shocks left both Germany's big banks scrambling for a response. As noted earlier, the banks' first effort was to try to compete against the savings and cooperative banks for the lending business of the Mittelstand, but this proved largely unsuccessful. The big banks also moved some of their operations overseas, to take advantage of the possibilities offered in London and New York, including deeper private bond markets, computerized trading, and the availability of new instruments such as options and futures. Most notably, Deutsche Bank relocated its investment services operations to London in 1984, in order to take advantage of "the preeminence of the London market in the domain of corporate finance and money management."[189] This ability to take advantage of capital

[185] Like other industrialized countries in this period, Germany abolished its last capital controls in 1981 (Detzer et al. 2013, 21).

[186] Vogel 1998.

[187] Boughton 2001, 319.

[188] "Germany as a world Financier," *FT*, January 15, 1989.

[189] Alfred Herrhausen (Deutsche Bank), quoted in Story and Walter 1997, quoting *Financial Times*, November 28, 1984.

mobility and overseas opportunities was a two-way street; however, just as German banks began to enter British and American markets, American, Japanese, and French banks likewise became players in the German market, especially after 1984, when the Bundesbank sought to stem capital outflows to the United States by allowing foreign subsidiaries to lead-manage deutsche mark-denominated bond issues for foreign borrowers.[190] By 1990, 272 foreign banks were operating in Germany, comprising 5 percent of total assets.[191] The negotiation of the Single European Act in 1986, and the prospect of the completion of the single market by 1992, further exacerbated German banks' concerns about losing their core commercial banking business at home.

Faced with these domestic and international challenges to their long-standing business model of commercial lending to large-scale German industrial firms, the big banks engaged in a concerted effort to promote the development of centralized, national securities markets in Germany. Their hope was that, even as their traditional core business declined, they could achieve a dominant position in investment banking and securities-related activities in Germany. Through a combination of market liberalization, financial product innovation, and centralization of Germany's fragmented regional stock markets, the big banks hoped to establish Frankfurt as a financial center (Finanzplatz Deutschland) to rival London and New York – one in which they, rather than British and American banks such as J. P. Morgan and Barclays, would occupy the dominant position.[192]

The Frankfurt Coalition and the Impetus for Reform

To pursue this goal, the Big Three private banks, along with the DG bank – which by the late 1980s had joined them as a major player in lending to Germany's large corporations – organized into what became known as the "Frankfurt Coalition."[193] The group started informally in the mid-1980s, with a focus on convincing the German government to establish an electronic trading platform that would link Germany's eight regional stock exchanges. These banks were joined by the state government of Hesse, which stood to gain substantially from the development of Frankfurt as a major

[190] Story and Walter 1997.

[191] "Mehr Marktorientierung der Bankenaufsicht Gefordert," *Handelsblatt*, January 24, 1991 (quoted in Story and Walter 1997).

[192] Deeg 1999.

[193] Deeg 2003, 180; Deeg 2005, 180.

international financial center.[194] Larger non-financial firms, which were no longer as dependent on bank loans from the Big Three for external financing, also lent their support.[195] Not surprisingly, the smaller regional banks and the governments of the other Länder opposed any efforts to centralize market power in Frankfurt/Hesse, fearing that the Landesbanken and larger companies that comprised the major buy- and sell-side players on the regional stock exchanges would eventually be forced to move their business to Frankfurt.[196]

The Frankfurt Coalition soon gained support from both the Bundesbank and the federal government in its efforts. While the banks' main interest in advocating Finanzplatz Deutschland lay in profit and market share, the Bundesbank and Kohl government saw the opportunity and need for establishing Frankfurt as a counterbalance to London and Paris, in light of deepening European financial and monetary integration. In June 1989, Karl Otto Pöhl, president of the Bundesbank, gave a speech in Frankfurt lamenting the "unsatisfactory state of affairs," in which trading of German securities took place primarily in London, and Germany lacked a central, major financial center to rival both London and Paris.[197] Pöhl believed that the impending completion of the single European market would inevitably result in the creation of "some financial centers of gravity" within the European Union, and he worried that a future European central bank – if and when the European single currency was established – could only be located in a "high performance European financial center."[198] In light of this, Pöhl bluntly stated that Germany's best and only option was to transform Frankfurt into an international financial center on par with London and Paris, even if this meant that Germany's other regional securities markets would be disadvantaged by this: "What is not traded in Frankfurt goes off to London or Paris, not to other German stock market centers. Frankfurt is the only city that has any chance at all of being a serious prospect as an international center. It is here that the necessary basic conditions must be met, and met quickly."[199]

The federal government joined the Bundesbank in embracing the Frankfurt Coalition's goals. Its primary international concern was that Germany would be unable to play an effective leadership role

[194] Deeg 2005, 180; Lütz 2002.

[195] Deeg 1999, 88.

[196] Coleman 1996.

[197] Ibid, 141. In the late 1990s, it was estimated that 5–25 percent of German stock turnover took place in London, rather than in Frankfurt or on the German regional exchanges (Deeg 1999, 92).

[198] Coleman 1996, 141.

[199] Ibid.

in the emerging regulatory bodies governing European and global finance – such as the Basel Committee on Banking Supervision and the International Organization of Securities Commissions (IOSCO) – as long as Germany's securities markets and regulatory bodies remained highly fragmented at the subnational level.[200] If the rules of international finance were left to the Americans, British, and others to design, German banks might be put at a competitive disadvantage and the German economy left in a weaker position in the coming decades.[201] At the same time, however, the government had strong domestic financial reasons for supporting the development of securities markets. In the wake of the fall of the Berlin Wall and German unification in 1989–90, Helmut Kohl saw securities market reform – especially the development of money markets, which the Bundesbank strongly opposed – as a way to access German savings to finance reconstruction and reunification.[202]

The Frankfurt Coalition's efforts, combined with the support of both the Bundesbank and the Kohl government, led directly to the first set of reforms to German securities markets. In June 1989, the Bundestag passed the first Financial Market Promotion Law (*Finanzmarktförderungsgesetz*, FFG I), which allowed stock quotes to be made on German exchanges in foreign currency, established a computerized trading exchange (the *Deutsche Terminbörse*, DTB), and abolished the capital transfer and stock exchange turnover taxes, which were believed to be a key factor in "diverting equity business to London and Luxembourg." A related 1989 amendment of the Stock Exchange Law (Börsengesetz) permitted the trading of options and futures contracts, and led to the opening of the *Terminbörse* (German Options and Futures Exchange).[203] The banks also announced the privatization of the Frankfurt stock exchange in July 1990, as a precursor to transforming Frankfurt into the premier national exchange.[204]

Finanzplatz Deutschland Emerges

The impetus for reform accelerated in early 1992, when Theo Waigel, the German finance minister, formally launched the government's Finanzplatz

[200] Deeg 2005, 180.
[201] Lütz 2002.
[202] Story and Walter 1997.
[203] Konoe 2010, 88.
[204] Story and Walter 1997.

Deutschland ("Finance Center Germany") campaign.[205] This led to a series of laws that rapidly and radically transformed the structure and regulation of securities markets in Germany. In 1993, the Frankfurt stock exchange was formally privatized and incorporated into a new German Exchange Company (*Deutsche Börse AG*, DBAG), which was jointly owned by the big banks and the regional stock exchanges and brokers, with each exchange/broker group holding a 10 percent stake.[206] The new company was headed by Rolf Breuer, head of Deutsche Bank's capital markets group.

In 1994, a second Financial Market Promotion Law (FFG II) established a Federal Securities Supervisory Office (*Bundesaufsichtsamt für den Wertpapierhandel*, BaWe) modeled after the US Securities and Exchange Commission, permitted money market funds, and altered the Stock Corporation Act to enable companies to price shares as low as DM 5, in the hopes of deepening stock markets by attracting small investors.[207] FFG II also harmonized German securities and corporate governance laws with EU directives. Subsequent regulatory changes in 1997, issued by the Federal Banking Supervisory Office (*Bundesaufsichtsamt für das Kreditwesen*, BAKred), made it easier for banks to avoid the standard 8 percent capital requirements when underwriting certain asset-backed securities.[208] A further wave of reforms in the late 1990s and early 2000s legalized share buybacks and hedge funds, abolished capital gains taxes for corporations, and reformed German corporate governance to encourage the breakup of the classic cross-holding relationship between German banks and industrial firms.[209]

As a result of these reforms, German securities markets – and the relative balance between banking and securities in the German financial system – changed markedly. Frankfurt became Germany's central, national securities market, and the reforms "triggered the big banks' aggressive move into investment banking activities."[210] In the 1990s, German stock markets substantially increased in market capitalization and trading volume (Figures 5.2 and 5.3). By the turn of the century, the German financial system had evolved significantly from the archetypical

205 Christopher Parties, "Germany Plans Shake-up of Stock Markets," *Financial Times*, January 17, 1992.
206 Konoe 2010, 89.
207 Deeg 2005, 180; Story and Walter 1997.
208 Konoe 2010, 92.
209 Deeg 2005; Detzer et al. 2013.
210 Detzer and Hein 2014, 2.

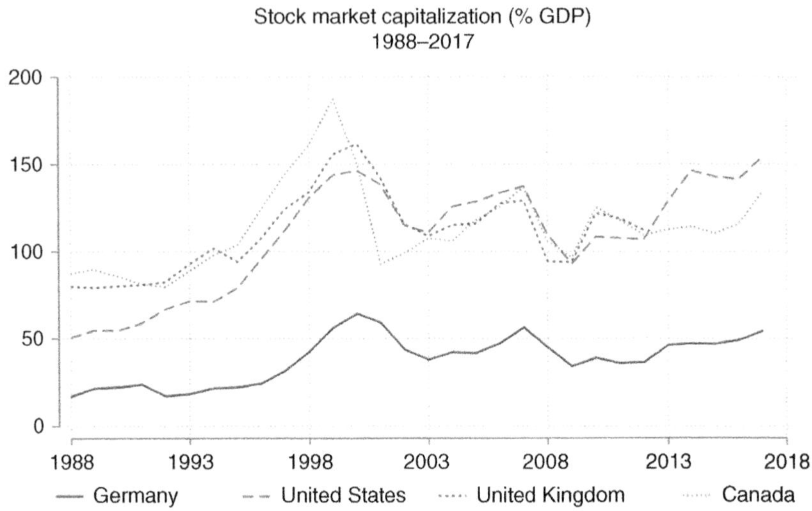

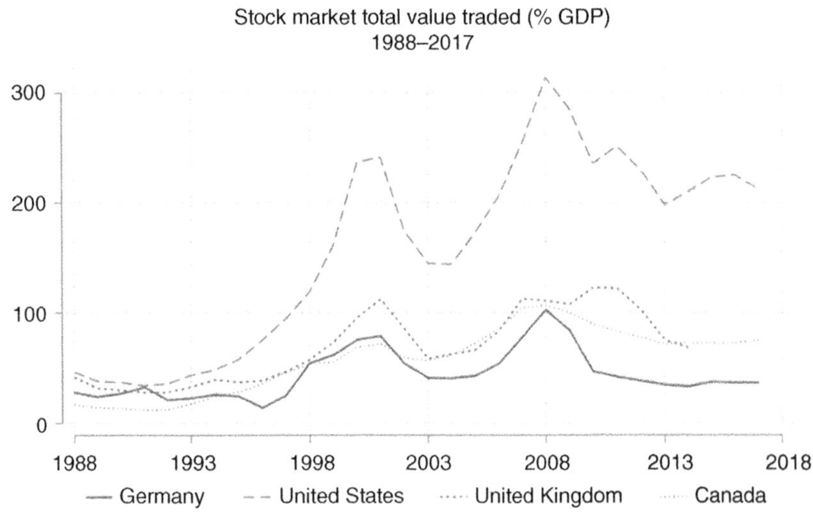

FIGURES 5.2 AND 5.3. Stock market capitalization and volume, Germany and others, 1988–2017. *Source:* World Bank, Global Financial Development Database.

bank-based system described in the Varieties of Capitalism literature into a system that looked much more similar to the Anglo-American model of a modern financialized economy.

Although the German system today continues to lag far behind the United States and United Kingdom, as well as Canada, on these metrics, the growth of securities markets since 1990 represents a third critical period in the history of the country's financial development. In this new environment, German financial firms, large corporations, and investors have all significantly changed their behavior.[211] Germany's large commercial banks have shifted a greater share of their operations into investment banking activities, moving away from their classic bread-and-butter business of lending to German industrial firms and taking large ownership stakes in their clients. This was fueled, in part, by aggressive expansion into investment banking through mergers and acquisitions. Deutsche Bank acquired the British investment bank Morgan Grenfell in 1989 and the US-based Bankers Trust in 1997, while Commerzbank acquired British-based Kleinwort Benson in 1995.[212] By 1999, Deutsche, Dresdner, and Commerzbank ranked first, third, and fourth, respectively, among large European banks in the share of total capital allocated to investment banking relative to commercial operations.[213] Between 1990 and 2001, securities portfolios became a substantially larger share of German banks' balance sheets (rising from 11.6 percent in 1990 to 18.5 percent in 2001).[214] From 1989 to 2009, bank loans to GDP in Germany increased by approximately 50 percent, from 80 percent of GDP to 120 percent; over the same period, banks' holdings of securities more than tripled, from approximately 20 percent of GDP to nearly 70 percent. By 2000, the ratio of banks' non-interest income to interest income had risen to an all-time high of 86 percent (Figures 5.4 and 5.5).[215]

Likewise, German industrial firms have also turned increasingly toward stock exchanges to access capital, in contrast to the traditional bank-based model. Over the course of the 1990s, equity shares surpassed bank loans as German non-bank corporations' largest source of liabilities and new equity.[216] At the same time, both the Big Three private banks

[211] Deeg 2005, 182; see also Hardie et al. 2013.
[212] Hackethal 2003, 7.
[213] Ibid.
[214] Weber 2002, 9.
[215] Hackethal 2003, 9.
[216] Detzer et al. 2013, 61.

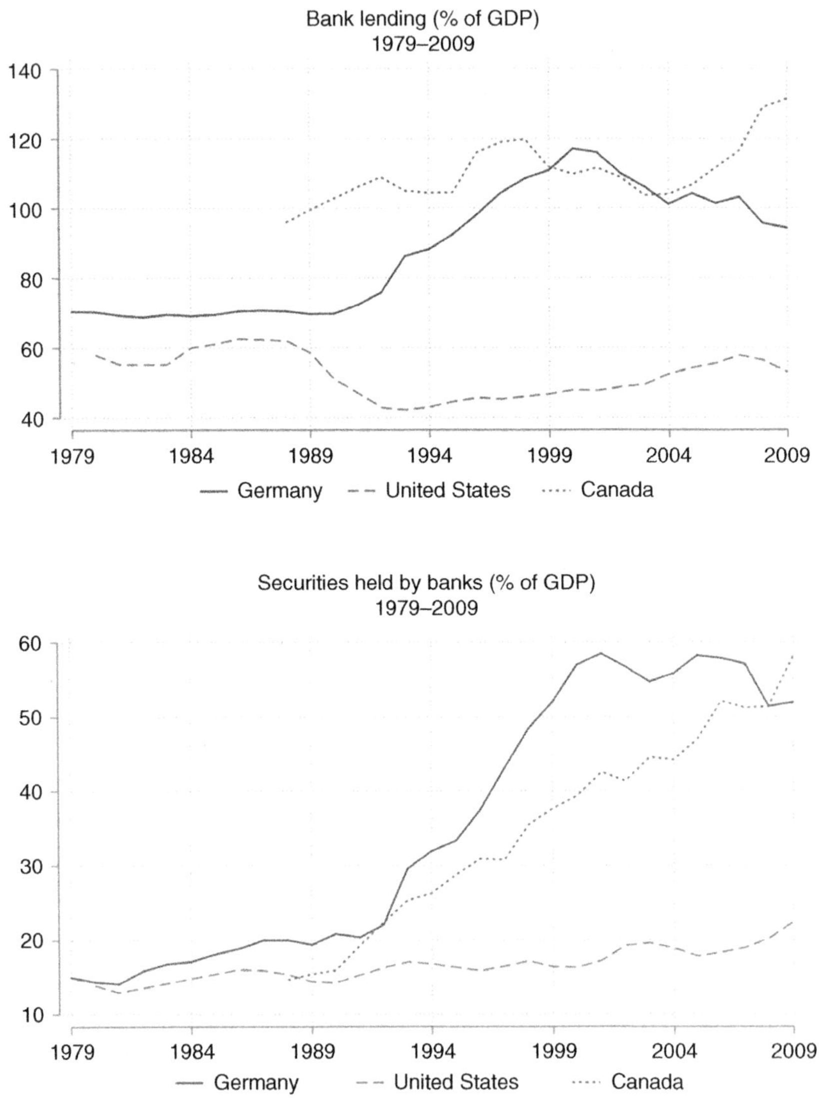

FIGURES 5.4 AND 5.5. Bank loans/GDP and securities held by banks/GDP, Germany, 1979–2009. *Source:* OECD iLibrary.

and the major Landesbanken have also moved away from the traditional position of taking large stakes in private German firms and direct roles in corporate governance. In 1974, banks held 20 percent of the supervisory board seats in the 100 largest German corporations; by 1993, this had fallen to 6.3 percent, and it fell to 5.6 percent by 2005.[217] Consequently, the classic "relationship banking" model, with its "mutual emphasis on a long-term relationship between a firm and its main bank(s)" has now been partially "replaced by more market-based, transaction-oriented exchanges."[218] German finance still remains far more focused on traditional commercial banking than the United States or the United Kingdom. But the gap between these two types of financial systems has narrowed considerably in the modern era of Finanzplatz Deutschland.

RE-EVALUATING GERMAN BANKING STABILITY

While the stereotypical image of the well-tailored, bespectacled German banker endures, the twenty-first century German financial system bears only a partial resemblance to that of the past. The changes implemented in the period of Finanzplatz Deutschland, between the mid-1980s and the early 2000s, have transformed Germany in important ways into an Anglo-American style financial system, in which securities markets and new financial instruments play a significantly greater role than they did historically. To be sure, Germany's securities markets remain small relative to those in the United States and United Kingdom, and the legacy of the classic bank-based system persists in Germany's high bank credit/GDP ratios and its large number of private corporations. Nonetheless, the twenty-first-century German financial system – in marked contrast to the postwar era until the late 1980s – is now one in which banks compete intensively alongside securities markets for firms' business. Where it once stood apart in marked contrast to the American and British financial systems, Germany now looks like a "catch-up" version of those systems itself, rather than one built on clearly differentiated foundations.

In addition, the German financial system no longer bears a close resemblance to Canada's. Although the three pillars of German banking continue to exist, the lines between them – and, in particular, the divisions between the Big Three private banks and the Landesbanken – have blurred considerably. Many of the Landesbanken have purchased private banks,

[217] Dittmann, Maug, and Schneider 2009.
[218] Deeg 2005, 182.

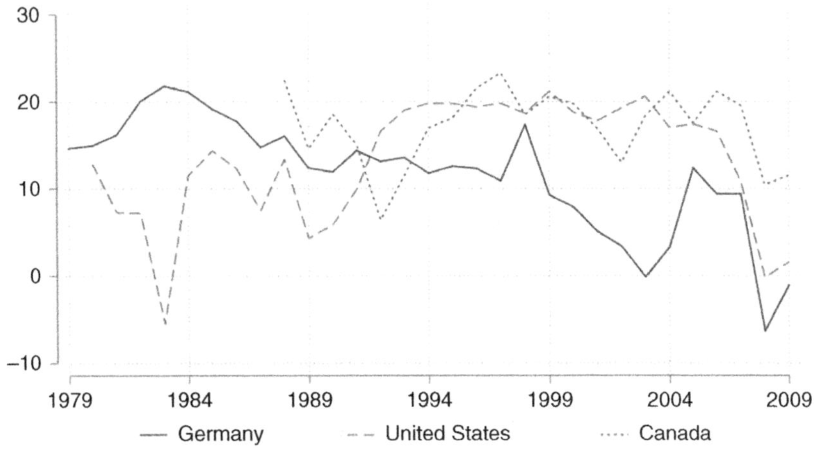

FIGURE 5.6. Return on pretax equity of the banking sector, Germany and others, 1979–2009. *Source:* OECD iLibrary.

and the clear delineations between the Canadian side of German banking (a small number of large commercial banks dominating major industrial lending) and the American side (a large number of small savings and cooperative banks dominating consumer/small business lending) have become blurred over time. More importantly for financial stability, however, is the fact that German securities markets no longer look like those in Canada: decentralized, poorly linked, and unsophisticated. Instead, as a result of the reforms of the 1990s and early 2000s, Germany now has a centralized, national securities market in Frankfurt, a single national financial regulator, and sophisticated financial markets that – while not yet at the level of those in the United States or United Kingdom – can no longer be characterized as underdeveloped or highly fragmented.

It should come as little surprise, at this point in the book, for us to note that German banks' behavior has changed significantly in this new environment. Faced with greater competition in their core domestic markets, German banks have experienced persistent decline and low levels of profitability and return on equity since the 1990s. German banks' returns now rank with Japan among the lowest in the OECD (see Figure 5.6).

As the IMF noted in 2011, these low returns were a key factor in leading the large private banks to "take on increased leverage and invest heavily abroad in search for higher returns" in the years prior to the 2008 global crisis.[219] Indeed, as Figure 5.7 illustrates, German banks'

[219] International Monetary Fund 2011, 17.

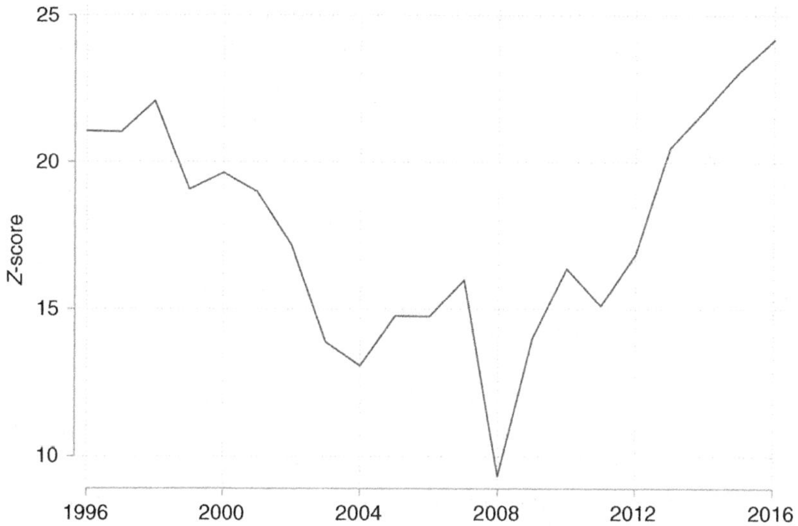

FIGURE 5.7. Asset-weighted national Z-score, Germany, 1996–2016. *Source:* St. Louis Federal Reserve FRED (World Bank/BankScope data.)

Z-scores declined sharply in the decade between the rise of Finanzplatz Deutschland and the onset of the 2008 crisis.

To recall, the Z-score captures the probability of default of a country's banking system, calculated as the weighted average of the riskiness of individual bank's balance sheets. Banks' individual Z-scores are ratios measuring their return on assets (ROA) plus the equity/assets ratio over the standard deviation of ROA.[220] Lower values indicate higher likelihood of default. Thus, as Figure 5.7 illustrates, German banks' behavior – as measured by the riskiness of their balance sheets – changed markedly in the decade prior to the global crisis, at precisely the same time that securities market became larger and more prominent in the German financial system.

The consequence of these changes in German banking have become clear in the last decade. Banking crises have become a serious and persistent problem in Germany, in marked contrast to the past century and a half of German financial history. Indeed, as noted at the outset of this chapter, German banking crises have closely mirrored those in the United States and United Kingdom, in frequency, severity, and causes,

[220] World Bank, Bank Z-Score for Germany [DDSI01DEA645NWDB], retrieved from FRED, Federal Reserve Bank of St. Louis; https://fred.stlouisfed.org/series/DDSI01DEA645NWDB, August 13, 2018.

in the last decade. From 2008 to 2011, Germany, like the United States and United Kingdom, experienced a systemic banking crisis, based on the World Bank's classification. During the crisis, both Germany's large private banks (such as Deutsche Bank) and the Landesbanken were massively exposed to subprime mortgages and toxic assets, leaving German state and federal authorities to intervene with hundreds of billions of dollars of aid.[221] Similarly, German banks joined their French counterparts in investing massive sums in PIIGS countries (i.e., Portugal, Ireland, Italy, Greece, and Spain) hit hardest by the Eurozone crisis in 2010–17.

The Landesbanken, in particular, were the most visible culprits. Between 2001 and 2005, the LB loaned money to riskier German companies, at lower rates, than other banks in Germany, and they led the way among German banks into large-scale investing in corporate debt and asset-backed securities.[222] This was driven, in part, by incentives created in 2001, when the European Commission and the German government agreed to abolish formal government guarantees of debt issued by publicly owned banks, including the Landesbanken, from July 2005 onward.[223] This ruling, which found that government guarantees of LB debt violated Article 87(1) of the Treaty on European Union, came in response to years of pressure from Germany's private banks, which had long complained that these guarantees constituted state aid and an unfair competitive advantage.[224]

In the wake of the Commission's ruling, the Landesbanken rushed to issue massive amounts of new government-guaranteed debt before 2005. Between 2001 and the onset of the global financial crisis in 2008, the Landesbanken issued a staggering total of approximately €450 billion in new bonds.[225] Yet this new influx of capital stemming from changes in European and German government regulation and guarantees is only one part of the story. The other, equally important part, was the new competitive environment of Finanzplatz Deutschland in which the LB were operating. Absent greater competition from deeper securities markets and private commercial banks, the LB might have channeled this windfall of new capital into its core businesses of relatively safe commercial

[221] International Monetary Fund 2011.

[222] Laura Noon, "The Landesbanken: Inside Germany's Trillion Euro Blind Spot," *Reuters*, September 17, 2013.

[223] Puri, Rocholl, and Steffen 2011, 558.

[224] Grossman 2006, 338–41.

[225] By comparison, from 1998 to 2001, the Landesbanken collectively issued only approximately $15 billion in bonds. Fischer et al. 2014, 37.

lending and providing services and capital to the savings banks and their respective German state governments. Instead, the Landesbanken funneled this money into two new and far-riskier activities: increased lending to lower-quality borrowers and massive investment in the surging global market for corporate and asset-backed securities.

On the lending side, the LB moved aggressively into new lending to lower-quality firms. Between 2001 and 2008, the quality of LB borrowers declined significantly, in excess of the overall decline in borrower quality occurring among German banks in this period.[226] Drawing on data from 1997 to 2008, covering 1,578 loans to German firms by the LB and other banks, Fischer et al. find that the average Z-score of firms borrowing from the LB declined by nearly 25 percent more relative to borrowers from non-*LB* in the 2001–8 period.[227] On the securities side, the LB funneled massive new capital into investment in asset-backed securities. By 2006, the Landesbanken guaranteed 8.4 percent of the $1 trillion securities market in global asset-backed commercial paper (ABCP), the major source of short-term operating cash for large corporations worldwide.[228] While the ABCP market doubled in size globally from 2000 to 2006, growth in LB ABCP exceeded this level by a further 50 percent.[229] At the same time, the LB placed a large share of this new capital into structured investment vehicles (SIVs) – off-balance sheet accounts that invested heavily into the mortgage-backed securities at the heart of the 2008 global financial crisis. By 2006, the LB had €97 billion in exposure to ABCP and SIVs, with Sachsen LB (€25 Billion) and West LB (€34 billion) leading the way.

As noted at the outset of the chapter, these two Landesbanken were the ones that failed spectacularly in 2008, and which were eventually merged into Landesbank Baden-Württemberg (LBBW) after losing billions of dollars investing in Irish and American subprime securities.[230] Faced with the prospect of massive losses throughout the banking system, the German government created a new €480 billion fund, the Special Fund for Financial Stability (*Soffin*) in October 2008.[231] Its purpose was to provide both direct emergency liquidity assistance and government

[226] Fischer et al. 2014.

[227] Ibid., 13, 40.

[228] Ibid., 21–2; Laura Noon, "The Landesbanken: Inside Germany's Trillion Euro Blind Spot." *Reuters*, September 17, 2013.

[229] Fischer et al. 2014, 23–4.

[230] Matthias Inverardi, "Germany Waves Goodbye to WestLB as Bank Broken Up," *Reuters*, July 1, 2012; and Derek Scally, "Sachsen LB Losses Expose Directors' 'Cluelessness,'" *The Irish Times*, November 13, 2012.

[231] "Germany's Faltering Bank Bailout Program," *Spiegel Online*, December 23, 2008.

guarantees that would help banks access liquidity in private markets.[232] Soffin soon found itself on the hook for a wide range of rescue packages, including a combined €18 billion in bailouts and more than €15 billion in government guarantees as "risk shields" against future losses for four of the Landesbanken: WestLB, Sachsen LB, BayernLB (Bavaria), and HSH Nordbank (Hamburg).[233] Ultimately, WestLB was broken up in July 2012, with €40 billion of its assets sold to Halaba (the Landesbank Hessen-Thüringen) and more than €150 billion in assets wound down through a "bad bank," the *Erste Abwicklungsanstalt* (EAA).[234]

Within months of establishing Soffin, the German government also was forced to use it to provide emergency financing to the second-largest commercial bank in the country, Commerzbank. In August 2008, Commerzbank announced a €9.8 billion takeover of Dresdner Bank, the country's third largest institution.[235] Allianz, Germany's largest insurance company, had previously purchased Dresdner in 2001 for €24 billion "in pursuit of the failed strategy of creating a ... one-stop shop offering the full array of financial products, including insurance, retail banking, investment banking, and asset management."[236] However, after years of heavy losses by Dresdner Kleinwort Benson, Dresdner's investment banking arm, Dresdner's value had sharply plummeted. As the German magazine *Der Spiegel* noted, "Dresdner Bank is regarded as a 'poison pill,' which may yet have huge hidden losses lurking in its portfolio, for example at its investment banking unit Dresdner Kleinwort."[237] This warning proved prescient. Only months later, in January 2009, the newly combined Commerzbank announced that it would receive €10 billion in bailout funds from Soffin to help it cover the massive losses still on the books from Dresdner's pre-merger balance sheet.[238] This number would eventually rise to €16.2 billion.[239] In return, the

[232] Ibid.

[233] "TIMELINE-German Landesbanken's Bailout and Restructuring So Far," *Reuters*, September 17, 2013.

[234] Matthias Inverardi, "Germany Waves Goodbye to WestLB as Bank Broken Up," *Reuters*, July 1, 2012.

[235] David Jolly, "Commerzbank Paying Allianz €9.8 Billion for Dresdner Bank," *The New York Times*, August 31, 2008.

[236] Andreas Nolting, "German Banking Gets Boost from Mega-Merger," *Spiegel Online*, September 1, 2008.

[237] Ibid.

[238] "Commerzbank Bailout Deal to Be 'A Painful Birth,'" *Spiegel Online*, January 9, 2009.

[239] "Government Must Learn from Mistakes in Commerzbank Bailout," *Spiegel Online*, April 7, 2011.

German government received a 25 percent stake in *Commerzbank*, plus one share, which gave it partial veto power over company decisions.[240] Ultimately, the German government would inject nearly €30 billion into the German banking system by 2012.[241]

Although Commerzbank began repaying €14.3 billion of its bailout in 2011, problems in the German banking system persisted. Chief among these was the saga of Deutsche Bank, which had rapidly evolved from Germany's largest and most traditional commercial bank into an "Anglo-American investment bank" from the late 1980s onward.[242] During this period, Deutsche Bank engaged in a myriad of legal and illegal activities involving subprime mortgage securities, complex derivatives, and the manipulation of LIBOR, the London interbank offer rate that is the benchmark rate for global interbank lending.[243] From 1994 to 2007, the bank's earnings composition shifted from nearly all commercial bank lending to more than 70 percent from investment-related activities.[244] The consequences for Deutsche Bank's stability were clear: core capital declined from 10 percent in the early 2000s to less than 9 percent by 2007.[245] At the same time, the bank's traditional commercial lending has also contributed to its losses. In September 2011, Deutsche Bank sold off $160 million in bad loans made through its Deutsche Postbank subsidiary.[246] In June 2018, the company offloaded $1 billion in non-performing loans to shipping companies.[247] At the time of writing, reports of billions of dollars of non-performing loans from Deutsche Bank to Donald Trump and Jared Kushner also raised questions about the stability of the bank's traditional commercial lending portfolio.[248]

[240] "Commerzbank Bailout Deal to Be 'A Painful Birth,'" *Spiegel Online*, January 9, 2009.

[241] "Government Must Learn from Mistakes in Commerzbank Bailout," *Spiegel Online*, April 7, 2011.

[242] Ullrich Fichtner, Hauke Goos, and Martin Hesse. "How a Pillar of German Banking Lost Its Way," *Spiegel Online*, October 28, 2016.

[243] Ibid.

[244] Ibid.

[245] Ibid.

[246] Louise Bowman, "Germany: Europe's Bad-Debt Goliath," *Euromoney*, October 31, 2012.

[247] Arno Schuetze, "Deutsche Bank Sells $1 Billion Non-Performing Ship Loan Portfolio," *Reuters*, June 14, 2018.

[248] Allan Smith, "Trump's Long and Winding History with Deutsche Bank," *Business Insider*, December 8, 2017.

Questions still remain about DB's long-term solvency and whether the German government will provide it with bailout funds, despite public denials by Angela Merkel and other government officials.[249]

In sum, German banking has undergone a massive transformation in the era of Finanzplatz Deutschland. Both through riskier commercial lending and more extensive direct participation in trading, underwriting, and other investment banking activities, German banks' behavior in the last two decades has been markedly different from that in the pre-1990s world in which securities markets were fragmented, underdeveloped, and largely an afterthought in the German financial system. As a result, Germany now finds itself confronting the persistent specter of banking crises, and the future of German banking and the stability of the German financial system remain unclear in ways that would have seemed unthinkable even thirty years ago. As we finish writing this book, Deutsche Bank and Commerzbank – Germany's two largest commercial banks – have just cancelled talks on a potential merger after weeks of discussions.[250] Among the core sticking points of these negotiations were the massive stock of debt securities on Commerzbank's balance sheet (including nearly €10 billion in Spanish and Italian sovereign bonds) and the deep losses and problems over the last decade in Deutsche Bank's investment banking business.[251] Despite widespread reporting that the German government strongly favored the DB/Commerz merger, in order to create a large and stable "national champion" to finance German export industries and compete against international banking powerhouses from the United States and China, it is not at all clear that the merger would have accomplished this goal or enhanced financial stability in Germany.[252] Indeed, the securities-related balance sheet problems of Deutsche and Commerz highlight the stark new reality of German banking in the twenty-first century: the old world of German finance – dominated by its three banking pillars, limited securities markets, and long history of financial stability – is gone, most likely forever. In its

[249] Evelyn Cheng, "Don't Look for a Bailout of Deutsche Bank Anytime Soon," CNBC, September 27, 2016.

[250] Jack Ewing, "Germany's Troubled Banking Giants Decide Against a Merger," *The New York Times*, April 25, 2019.

[251] Olaf Storbeck and Stephen Morris, "The Hurdles in a Deutsche Bank and Commerzbank Merger," *Financial Times*, March 18, 2019.

[252] "Germany's Two Top Banks Launch Merger Talks to Create National Champion," *Business Standard*, March 17, 2019; and Jack Ewing, "Do Two Troubled Banks Make One Good One? Germany May Find Out," *The New York Times*, February 25, 2019.

place is a new system, in which banks compete alongside and participate in Germany's larger, more centralized securities markets and banking crises have become a central feature, rather than a rare exception, of German finance.

CONCLUSION

A widely repeated claim about Germany is that it has a quintessentially bank-based financial system, in contrast to more market-based systems like those of the United States and United Kingdom. In this system, the story generally goes, banks and industrial firms have close relationships and deep ties, which result in patient capital and allow banks to behave more prudently and act with longer time horizons than in market-based systems. As we have documented in this chapter, this distinction overlooks the substantial changes in German finance over the last thirty years, and in doing so misses an important element explaining both the stability of German banking over the long run and the substantial spike in instability in the twenty-first century. The narrative here illustrates that German banks remained remarkably stable from Germany's unification in 1870 into the post–Bretton Woods era, despite changes in the competitive landscape of German banking, the return of international capital mobility, and the political upheavals of the interwar and Nazi eras.

After more than five decades without a systemic banking crisis, financial instability returned to Germany only after the government moved to create national, centralized stock markets and liberalize securities regulation in the 1990s. Unlike Canadian banks, which have held fast to their conservative lending practices up to the present day, German banks have changed their behavior markedly in this new modern era of Finanzplatz Deutschland, with unfortunately predictable, adverse results for financial stability. While many aspects of Germany's classic bank-based financial system remain, the modern German financial system has grown increasingly similar to more market-based systems. Unfortunately, as this chapter illustrates, importing key elements of Anglo-American, market-based finance has had the side effect of importing similar levels of banking instability. Like the United States and United Kingdom, Germany has now spent the better part of a decade dealing with the after effects of serious financial instability. In our view, this is directly related to the structural change in German finance, as securities markets have come to play an increasingly prominent role in the allocation of capital.

As German finance has become more Anglo and less Canadian, the stereotype of the boring, conservative, stable German banker has begun to fade into historical memory. Nowadays, one is more likely to find a new German banking stereotype in the financial press: the large bank frequently in need of government or EU bailout financing or perpetually teetering on the edge of insolvency.[253] At least part of this change, we have argued here, can be attributed to the relative decline of the traditional bank-centric model of German finance and the rapid development of securities markets. As German banks have faced greater competition from securities markets, as well as become more deeply involved in the business of those markets themselves, they have lost a good measure of their conservative, stable bias that had made Germany a paragon of financial stability for nearly seventy years.

What lies ahead for German banking, securities markets, and financial stability? Given the number of major events currently unfolding in Germany and the European Union – banking union and other financial regulatory reforms in the wake of the Eurozone crisis, the looming threat of Brexit and the possible relocation of many London-based banks and investment firms to Frankfurt, and the still-uncertain future of Deutsche Bank – the future remains unclear. One could imagine further consolidation in the German banking sector in the coming years, along with a further blurring of the lines between the classic three pillars of German banking. One could also imagine more cross-border consolidation among major banks in the European Union, as banking union and the Single Supervisory Mechanism create incentives for French, Dutch, German, and other countries' banks to join forces. In any case, what does seem clear is that Germany is unlikely to roll back the clock and reverse the changes of the Finanzplatz Deutschland era, which have created larger-scale, more centralized national securities markets in the country. Unfortunately, this means that Germany is also unlikely to be able to put the genie of financial instability back into the bottle. Put simply, Germany's financial system has become less Canadian and more American, for better or for worse. Whether the benefits outweigh the costs in the years ahead remains to be seen.

[253] See, e.g., Desmond Lachman, "Deutsche Bank's Long Shadow," *U.S. News and World Report*, October 5, 2016.

6

Policy Responses

What to Do (and Not to Do) about Financial Instability

> The peculiar essence of our financial system is an unprecedented trust between man and man; and when that trust is much weakened by hidden causes, a small accident may greatly hurt it, and a great accident for a moment may almost destroy it.
>
> Walter Bagehot (1873), *Lombard Street: A Description of the Money Market*, pp. 158–9.

Trust is ubiquitous in the financial system. Banks trust that customers will repay their loans. Depositors trust that banks will manage their money carefully. And banks trust other banks to provide liquidity and to remain standing day after day. But as Walter Bagehot – arguably the most prominent scholar of banking in modern history – noted in his famed account of London's 1866 financial panic, trust in the financial system can erode from "hidden causes."[1] When trust is weakened, even seemingly small accidents – like the collapse of London bank Overend, Gurney, and Company, which triggered the panic – can cause systemic financial crises.

This book has attempted to bring to light the hidden – or at least overlooked – causes of banking crises in the industrialized world since the 1970s. Our sleuthing led us to identify two sets of triggers. The first, a country's recent history of capital inflows, sets the stage for potential distortions in the financial system. The extent of a country's capital inflows has emerged as a consistent correlate of banking crises across countries and time, even going back hundreds of years.[2] Countries that

[1] Bagehot 1873, 159.

[2] Reinhart and Rogoff 2009b.

run persistent current account deficits (because they import more goods and services than they export) face a heightened risk of various kinds of mischief, including rising asset prices, frenzied borrowing by companies and individuals, and a painful correction if the capital inflows should stop suddenly.

The second variable, the structure of a country's financial system, is not a trigger per se, given that it changes only slowly over time. Banks often sit alongside other financial institutions, including stock and bond markets, which provide alternative sources of financing for borrowers and alternative investments for savers. We argue that the variation in the relative prominence of banks versus securities markets helps to determine whether capital inflows are channeled safely and productively through the national economy, or whether they instead cause banks to take on excessive risks and increase the likelihood of a financial crisis.

As social scientists, we concern ourselves with probabilities: Will a certain mix of foreign capital and domestic financial structure increase or decrease the likelihood of financial instability? We cannot predict the precise moment that a bank will collapse, nor can we provide assurances that a banking system is unequivocally stable. Instead, we show the conditions under which banking crises are more or less likely. Our findings suggest that the combination of substantial inflows of foreign capital and a prominent securities market makes Walter Bagehot's "small accidents" more likely to grow into great accidents with deleterious consequences for the national economy.

Political decisions are fundamental in understanding financial stability across countries and time. A nation's financial structure reflects the accretion of government decisions about bank charters, securities market rules, prudential regulations, and consumer safety protections. Government policy can, over time, encourage thriving securities markets, or it can stymie these markets in response to interest group pressures or other political reasons. Our case studies of Canada and Germany demonstrate how seemingly innocuous political decisions about financial rules and territorial boundaries can accumulate over many years and solidify a country's financial market structure for generations. Indeed, in the realm of financial stability, politics must be understood over the long term. Political leaders with different ideologies can come and go without leaving financial devastation in their wake – and in fact we found no evidence that the likelihood of banking crises varies as a function of the current government's partisan leaning. Instead, political decisions shape markets over the long haul by either solidifying the prominence of traditional banks or allowing room for securities markets to mature.

In our study of Canada, we argued that the country's remarkable history of bank stability was attributable in part to its equally remarkable fragmented and underdeveloped stock markets. The Canadian Constitution granted the national government the sole authority to regulate the banking industry, but authority over stock markets was relegated to the provinces. During the economic crisis of the early 1930s, while the US government seized the opportunity to create a national securities regulator and to minimize the role of state regulatory agencies, Canada made few changes to its regulatory system. The government took no steps to create a national regulator, instead reaffirming the authority of the provinces to supervise their stock exchanges in accordance with their particular needs. To this day, Canada is the only industrialized country without a national securities regulator. We argue that the country's underdeveloped securities markets have had a salutary effect on its banks. We explored the causes and consequences of recent foreign capital inflows and demonstrate that banks have been successful in channeling foreign capital to borrowers without taking on undue risk.

Like Canada, Germany has had a long history of bank stability, but it has recently taken a dangerous turn. Our Germany case study highlighted how policy decisions in the aftermath of two major financial crises – the Panic of 1873 and the crisis of 1931 – arrested the development of German securities markets and solidified a heavily bank-centric financial system. Our historical narrative illustrated how interest-group and party politics, rising nationalism and anti-Semitism in the late nineteenth century, and the Nazis' ascendance to power in the 1930s, all conspired to hobble the development of German stock markets prior to World War II, allowing banks to engage in long-term conservative lending with "patient capital" throughout the postwar era until the 1980s. In recent years, however, financial competitors from within Germany and from the European Union have prompted the large German banks to seek alternative sources of revenue. Deutsche Bank, Commerzbank, and the other large banks have become champions of *Finanzplatz Deutschland*, a single large securities market designed to compete with more established markets in New York and London. As this market has developed, the conservative bias of the large banks has eroded, and many required emergency bailouts in the early twenty-first century.

GLOBAL IMBALANCES: SHOULD WE WORRY?

Scholarship in the 1980s and 1990s highlighted the dangers of excessive capital inflows for emerging-market countries such as Chile, Argentina, and Mexico, each of which experienced major financial crises in the 1970s and 1980s. For these countries, foreign capital emboldened profligate politicians and overwhelmed the capacity of poorly regulated banking systems to make productive investments. Later in the century, a wave of capital inflows into the Asian "tiger" economies prompted a lending boom to the real estate sector as banks converted their borrowed dollars into domestic currency loans to developers. The default of a Thai bank in 1997 led to a massive reversal of capital flows, prompting bank failures and government interventions in Thailand, Indonesia, Malaysia, and other countries in the region. With a litany of crises in Latin America and Asia to analyze, scholars largely agreed that capital inflows that meet an underdeveloped and poorly regulated financial system place a country at great risk for a crisis.

More recently, the Great Recession generated interest among policymakers and scholars in the economic and political consequences of global capital flows for mature economies like the United States. Ben Bernanke, who conducted research on international macroeconomics before becoming chair of the Federal Reserve Board in 2006, argued that the advanced economies were the unwitting beneficiaries – or victims – of a "global saving glut."[3] Emerging-market countries, still reeling from their recent episodes of financial instability, had begun to run large and prolonged current account surpluses in the early twenty-first century. This strategy, which included maintaining undervalued exchange rates and encouraging strong domestic saving rates, resulted in the steady export of capital from the emerging markets to the United States and western Europe.[4] Bernanke argued that these inflows pushed interest rates down to dangerous levels and incentivized banks and other financial institutions to devise higher-yielding investments to satisfy investors' demands.

Bernanke's arguments, and those of many of his contemporaries, suggested that sustained capital inflows were dangerous even for mature and ostensibly well-regulated financial systems. Richard Portes, a

[3] Bernanke 2011.

[4] See Manger and Sattler 2014.

leading advocate of the global imbalance view of financial instability, articulated the argument as follows:

> The global imbalances that have built up in the past decade permitted and indeed stimulated the dysfunctional aspects of financial markets and instruments that are now troubling us. They brought low interest rates, the search for yield, and an excessive volume of financial intermediation, which even the sophisticated American and British financial systems could not handle responsibly.[5]

As this concise summary makes clear, the causal chain linking imbalances to crises runs from current account deficits to large capital inflows to distortions in the allocation of capital. In this stylized view, current account deficits in the United States, United Kingdom, and elsewhere were financed with large capital inflows from surplus countries that ended up being intermediated poorly by the domestic financial system.

Chinn and Frieden (2011) tell a similar story that positions the United States in 2008 in the same category as Mexico in 1982 or Thailand in 1997. In each case, capital inflows flooded the domestic financial system, stimulated an economic boom and a flurry of spending, and ultimately culminated in a devastating crash.

What does this book have to say about the global imbalances story? On the one hand, the centrality of capital inflows in our empirical analyses suggests that international macroeconomic considerations are undoubtedly important in understanding the causes of crises. On the other, we note several problems with the global imbalances view. The first problem is fundamentally about research design. There are far more cases of large capital inflows, asset bubbles, and macroeconomic imbalances that *do not* result in banking crises than cases that do. When scholars identify a banking crisis and then note the status of the country's current account in the preceding years, they have no causal leverage for determining whether capital inflows were a culprit or a benign bystander. Social scientists refer to this research design as selecting on the dependent variable, a label with decidedly derisive overtones. By focusing only on crises, an analyst could miss the fact that a supposedly troublesome variable is also present in countries with stable financial systems. For example, while the United States ran a large current account deficit in the years before 2008, so did Australia and New Zealand, whose banks remained remarkably stable. Moreover, persistent current account deficits have been the norm in the United States for decades, even during

[5] Portes 2009, 2.

periods of financial stability. Foreign capital helped to fuel the dot-com bubble in the late 1990s, but even when the bubble burst in 2001–2 – wiping out more than $5 trillion in stock market capitalization – there was no subsequent banking crisis.

A second problem with the global imbalances view is that capital does not always flow from surplus to deficit countries. In the case of the United States from 2002 to 2007, approximately two-thirds of foreign capital inflows arrived from countries with which the United States was not running large current account deficits, such as the United Kingdom and certain Eurozone countries.[6] Indeed, the primary source of the large US current account deficits prior to the Great Recession – its $300 billion bilateral trade deficit with China – had very little, if anything, to do with either the large influx of foreign capital into the United States in the 2002–7 period, or the collapse of these flows in 2007–9. These facts challenge the excess savings view of the financial crisis, in which capital from surplus countries creates inherent distortions as it flows to vulnerable deficit countries.

Finally, an underlying weakness of arguments that place blame on foreign capital is an implicit assumption that banking systems are fundamentally alike. This book makes clear that national financial systems vary in important ways. Our hypothesis is that banks tend to take on more risk when they face competition from securities markets, and these risks are magnified in the face of capital inflows. Therefore, a national financial system with a large and deep securities market is more likely to experience a banking crisis in the face of capital inflows than a financial system with a relatively underdeveloped securities market. This argument helps to explain why capital inflows are sometimes, but not always, a source of instability for banking systems in the advanced industrialized countries.

Nevertheless, global imbalances are a legitimate cause for concern. They heighten vulnerability to crises, even if their impact on any particular country is contingent on domestic market characteristics. Particularly worrisome is new research that suggests that imbalances reflect an underlying global financial cycle driven largely by US policy. Economist Hélène Rey has persuasively demonstrated that there are large common movements in asset prices, gross capital flows, and bank leverage throughout the world's major economies. US monetary policy is at the heart of the cycle. The Fed's interest rate policy helps shape

[6] Borio and Disyatat 2011; Whelan 2010.

the market's expectations about volatility, which in turn drives capital flows, asset price inflation, and credit creation. The Fed's decisions, in short, might drive the flows of potentially destabilizing capital that lead to banking crises elsewhere in the world.

A recent article by Bauerle Danzman, Winecoff, and Oatley also emphasizes the likelihood of crises using a global systemic lens.[7] These authors argue that when the United States is a net importer of foreign capital, the rest of the world system struggles to attract foreign investment – which is no blessing for economies seeking productive capital, but it removes the potentially dangerous trigger of instability. In a sense, the United States siphons away all the fuel, leaving little fire-starting capacity for other countries.

These studies suggest that observers should keep a close eye on global imbalances. Regions that experience sustained waves of capital inflows face heightened vulnerability, although the results for any particular country are likely to vary as a function of domestic market structure.

PROBLEMS WITH ALTERNATIVE DOMESTIC STRUCTURE ARGUMENTS

To be sure, we are not the first scholars to emphasize domestic financial market structure as a key determinant of crises. Yet the existing literature has focused overwhelmingly on the structure of banking sectors, leaving the relationship between banking and securities markets under-theorized and underexplored. For example, Bordo, Redish, and Rockoff (2015) argue that the structure of Canada's banking system has enabled it to avert crises for the last 150 years, in sharp contrast to the United States. They identify unit banking in the United States, resulting from legislated prohibitions against bank branching across state lines until 1994, as the reason why American banking evolved differently from Canadian banking. In contrast, Canada instituted national bank charters at its founding, which led early on to a small number of diversified banks with branches across the provinces. In their view, the concentration and national diversification of Canadian banks have made them stable and less prone to crisis than their US counterparts.

As we discussed in Chapter 4, this story overlooks a central factor explaining Canadian banks' conservative bias and history of stability: weak competitive pressures on banks stemming from Canada's

7 Bauerle Danzman, Winecoff, and Oatley 2017.

underdeveloped securities markets. We argue that Canada's long history of financial stability is not simply the result of the concentrated nature of the Canadian banking system or the structure of Canadian banking regulation. Instead, Canada's banking conservatism and enduring stability are the result of political decisions regarding securities market development from the 1800s and early 1900s. More than a century of fragmentation, relatively weak regulation, and serious inefficiencies have dampened the influence of securities markets on banks' risk taking. While this may help explain why Canadian banks are rarely considered dynamic or innovative, it also explains why they have been among the most stable in the world for the last seven decades.

Similarly, Calomiris and Haber, in their widely publicized study *Fragile by Design* (2014), focus on differences in the structure of banking markets and the rules for allocating credit as key explanations for cross-national variation in banking instability. Their core argument is that banking systems are the outcome of political struggles – what the authors refer to as the "game of bank bargains" – between the government, voters, and interest groups. The authors identify two key variables, regime type and the presence or absence of an agrarian populist coalition, to explain why banking systems vary in structure. Their case studies highlight the variation in banking and bank stability across three democracies (United States, United Kingdom, and Canada) and two countries with long histories of authoritarianism (Mexico, Brazil).

Our argument and evidence in this book suggest that these variations in the structure of banking alone are insufficient for understanding and explaining variation in financial crises across time and space. Once again, as we show in our case study of Canada, there is more to the story of Canadian financial stability than nationally chartered banks and differences in the structure of the banking system on either side of the Canada-US border. We argue that differences in the size and structure of securities markets, and the effects these have on the behavior of banks, should be a central element of any cross-national explanation of variation in the frequency and severity of banking crises.

Our criticism, then, does not pertain to Calomiris and Haber's focus on the political coalitions that give rise to particular financial systems, which in fact reflects our own approach to exploring the political roots of financial instability. Rather, our target is their omission of broader aspects of financial markets. Indeed, their emphasis on agrarian populism as a driver of US bank fragmentation in the nineteenth century could also be used to explain the eventual *absence* of fragmentation in securities markets. In Canada, the natural resource sectors – mining, oil, etc. – resisted the formation of nationally harmonized and tightly regulated securities markets, as we discuss in Chapter 4. In Germany, a series of agrarian populist and nationalist coalitions, starting with the "iron and rye" coalition in the late nineteenth century and continuing into the interwar era with the Nazi regime, actively opposed large-scale securities markets and imposed taxes and regulations explicitly designed to inhibit their development. Our analysis of Germany also suggests that other non-agrarian and non-populist coalitions may also be relevant in shaping financial markets. Germany's large banks, which in the recent past had little interest in seeing a thriving securities market, have now pushed ahead with *Finanzplatz Deutschland* as a means to get a leg up on their smaller bank competitors. In short, coalitional politics are just as relevant for shaping securities markets as for shaping the banking industry. Our case studies suggest that these coalitions are historically contingent on and not easily explained by the variables – liberalism, agrarian populism, and political regime – employed by Calomiris and Haber.

REGULATION: WHAT KIND, AND BY WHOM?

> The obligation of building party walls, in order to prevent the communication of fire, is a violation of natural liberty, exactly of the same kind with the regulations of the banking trade which are here proposed.
>
> Adam Smith, *The Wealth of Nations*, p. 414.

Observers typically do not associate Adam Smith with government regulation. Widely known for his "invisible hand" metaphor, Smith explained how the individual pursuit of self-interest leads to the advancement of society's broader material interest.[8] The metaphor is frequently used by supporters of free-market economics who are skeptical of government interference in any market. However, even Smith understood that banking poses some particularly thorny challenges for societies. In the passage above, Smith's primary concern was the provision and exchange of paper money, which was a particular source of financial instability in his native Scotland in the late 1700s. His comparison of bank regulation to fire walls in a building reflects his understanding of the devastation that can arise when banks collapse, not to mention his advocacy – despite his libertarian bona fides – of the government's necessary role in creating bank regulation.

[8] Smith 2003, 572.

Calls for more or better regulation have become the sine qua non of concluding chapters of many books on banking crises. Our arguments and findings suggest that some of these proposed regulations are more promising than others in reducing the chance of a future banking crisis. Below we evaluate five policy dimensions that are directly relevant for this book.

Should Bank Capital Requirements Be Increased?

Our findings support the recommendation to increase capital requirements for banks, especially large banks whose collapse would be especially problematic for systemic stability. Quite simply, more stringent capital requirements are likely to be the most direct and effective means of guarding against future banking crises. As shown in Chapter 3, bank capital tends to decline in response to the volatile mix of capital inflows and securities markets. Our empirical analysis is not designed to test the direct connection between bank capital and crises, but economists are largely in agreement that bank capital is a buffer against shocks.[9] Moreover, our findings suggest that lower capital buffers and a higher incidence of crises are the result of common triggers.

Capital requirements stipulate that a bank's capital must constitute a certain percentage of the bank's assets. In other words, a minimum fraction of a bank's loans must be funded with unborrowed money – generally money received from shareholders and owners.[10] When bank capital is high relative to assets, the bank is able to absorb losses if borrowers are unable to repay. When capital is low, loan losses can topple the bank.

In a compelling diagnosis of the cause of bank failures, Admati and Hellwig (2013) argue that excessive leverage is the most frequently recurring trigger of crises across time and space. Banks, unlike companies in other sectors, rely on borrowed money to a far greater degree. Nonfinancial companies get most of their money from invested profits or by issuing shares of stock. On average, such equity financing outside of the banking sector is approximately 60 percent, whereas most large, internationally active banks generate less than 5 percent of their funding from shareholders.[11] If, as Admati and Hellwig advocate, banks were required to increase equity financing to 20–30 percent, the benefits for financial

[9] See, e.g., Admati and Hellwig 2013.

[10] Ibid., 6.

[11] Binyamin Appelbaum, "When She Talks, Banks Shudder," *The New York Times*, August 9, 2014.

stability would be substantial and the costs limited. Better capitalized banks would have a lower probability of becoming insolvent, and banks would be less able to become highly leveraged, only to pass on the financial and social costs to governments and society when things went wrong. It is also possible that higher equity requirements would lead banks themselves to reduce their size or break into smaller component companies, thereby accomplishing some of the goals of the proposals described above.

Tightening banks' capital requirements is often politically challenging. Bankers view capital buffers as expensive because they limit the extension of credit and provide a competitive advantage to less stringently regulated foreign banks.[12] Political leaders who are beholden to banks for financial and electoral support will hesitate to impose regulations that are deemed to be burdensome and anti-competitive; even unelected regulators tend to side with bankers' preferences, especially in financial systems in which regulators have lucrative banking jobs waiting for them after they resign from their regulatory posts.

Some analysts are skeptical of banks' resistance to higher capital levels. Martin Wolf, for example, has argued that large increases in equity financing requirements should not be deemed extreme, because current requirements do not take into account the economic and social costs of banking crises. Today's global standards recommend a floor of 7 percent equity financing for internationally active banks, which Wolf notes is "far below levels markets would impose if investors did not continue to expect governments to bail out creditors in a crisis, as historical experience shows."[13] Indeed, he refers to the 7 percent standard as a "capital inadequacy ratio."[14] He, too, joins Admati and Hellwig in calling for a tripling or quadrupling of existing levels:

> [E]quity requirements need to be very much higher, perhaps as high as 20 or 30 per cent, without the risk-weighting. It would then be possible to dispense with the various forms of contingent capital that are far more likely to exacerbate panic in a crisis than assuage it. It is only because we have become used to these extraordinarily fragile structures that this demand seems so outrageous.[15]

If policymakers are serious about addressing systemic risk and ensuring that national banking systems are resilient to shocks and no longer

[12] Singer 2004, 2007.
[13] Martin Wolf, "Basel: The Mouse That Did Not Roar," *The Financial Times*, September 14, 2010.
[14] Ibid.
[15] Ibid.

prone to frequent bank failures and crises, then substantial increases in equity funding requirements for individual banks are necessary.

For bank capital, international standards are a potential solution to the political challenge of implementing tighter regulations, but also a potential hindrance to the sustainability of those regulations. Successive agreements known as the Basel Accords, negotiated by the Basel Committee on Banking Supervision, have attempted to provide a level playing field for banks around the world. However, as depicted in Singer (2007), the original Basel Accord in 1988 was championed by US and British regulators as a sort of political shield: it enabled these regulators to tighten capital requirements and thereby shore up the stability of their respective banking systems without jeopardizing their international competitiveness.[16] With all major banking centers adopting the standard, no regulatory agency needed to fear the political repercussions that would normally come with unilateral tightening of the rules. Banking systems were undoubtedly more stable, and less prone to collapse, after the implementation of the Basel Accord.

However, as the 1990s progressed without serious episodes of instability, support for the Basel Accord's arguably crude requirements began to erode. Regulators created a new standard, Basel II, which allowed banks to determine their own capital levels using internal assessments of loan risk and external assessments by rating agencies.[17] In a sense, Basel II was the antithesis of Basel I in that it provided political cover for all regulators to adopt laxer standards.[18] The lower capital levels permitted under Basel II played an important facilitating role in the global financial crisis of 2007–10.[19]

The lesson from Basel is that international standards serve a purpose for domestic regulators. In times of instability, that purpose may be to make stricter regulations more politically and industrially palatable to the domestic financial system. In good times, as memories of past crises fades, negotiating new international standards provides political cover for regulators to relax their requirements.[20]

[16] On the notion of political cover in the context of international institutions, see Dreher, Sturm, and Vreeland 2009; McDowell 2016.

[17] King and Sinclair 2003; Lavelle 2013, chap. 9.

[18] See Singer 2007, 62–6.

[19] Admati and Hellwig 2013, 96.

[20] On the legitimacy afforded by the Basel Committee's various standards, see Newman and Posner 2018, 48–52. On their credibility and impact, see Wilf 2016. On legitimacy and global governance, see Brassett and Tsingou 2011.

Accountability must therefore fall on domestic regulators, not on international standards-setting bodies.[21] Bank regulators in financial systems with well-developed securities markets should be especially concerned about the sufficiency of capital buffers, especially when the country is running a persistent current account deficit. Just as monetary policymakers have early warning systems that portend the onset of inflation – such as the rise in the price of key commodities – so too should bank regulators pay careful attention to capital inflows, especially in market-based financial systems.

The political challenge is overcoming domestic opposition to stricter capital requirements from the financial sector.[22] This is no small feat, given the powerful lobbying position of banks and the financial industry in most countries.[23] Nonetheless, as more and more countries develop deeper and more liquid securities markets in the years ahead, more stringent national capital regulations and new international standards will become more important than ever before. If the governments of the leading countries in the global financial system do not make this a key policy priority in the coming years, only one thing is certain: there will be more banking crises, at regular intervals, and future analysts will look back across time and wonder why the worst financial crisis since the Great Depression did not lead to regulatory and policy changes that ensured such damage did not occur again.

Should Countries Impose Capital Controls?

The potential dangers of sustained capital inflows raise a simple policy question: Should countries impose capital controls as a prudential measure? Capital controls come in many shapes and sizes, but their main goal is to inhibit the flow of capital for purposes such as buying and selling stocks, bonds, and real estate. During the Bretton Woods era, from the end of World War II to the early 1970s, many countries restricted capital flows for capital account transactions, but these controls soon fell out of favor and become more difficult to enforce.[24] Today

[21] On the other hand, the European states wield less and less power over their respective national banking systems. See Epstein 2017; Mügge 2010.

[22] On the political economy of capital requirements in Europe, see Howarth and Quaglia 2013.

[23] Quaglia 2010.

[24] See Eichengreen 1996, chap. 4; Helleiner 1994, chap. 2.

the wealthy industrialized countries generally maintain open capital accounts, although some have taken steps to limit certain types of international financial transactions.[25]

The arguments and findings in this book offer no specific support for the imposition of capital controls by industrialized country governments. Our empirical analyses suggest that countries are often able to accommodate capital inflows (and outflows) without causing instability in the banking system. Restricting capital account transactions due to fears of banking crises would be like refusing to leave one's house for fear of catching a cold. The benefits of international finance are substantial, even with the periodic crises that unfortunately characterize the modern financial system.[26] Moreover, capital controls have a decidedly mixed record in terms of effectiveness, especially in the contemporary era of financial globalization.[27] The International Monetary Fund has softened its opposition to capital controls for emerging markets, suggesting that they may serve an important purpose in certain circumstances.[28] Yet even for rich, industrialized countries that borrow in their own reserve currencies, the feasibility of permanent, large-scale capital controls seems limited at best and potentially disastrous at worst. The number of actors now dependent on international finance and trade has grown substantially since the 1970s, and capital controls simply do not make sense in an era of cross-border supply chains and globalized production.[29] In this environment, the costs of foregoing the large, long-term benefits of international finance to avoid the relatively small chance of a periodic banking crisis makes little economic or political sense.

Too Big to Fail: Should We Break Up Large Banks?

In 1984, Continental Illinois – then one of the largest banks in the United States – failed after an aggressive lending strategy went sour. Individual depositors were protected by the Federal Deposit Insurance Corporation (FDIC), a body established by the Banking Act of 1933, also known as the Glass-Steagall Act. However, the government took a giant step further to prevent the demise of Continental from having

[25] Chinn and Ito 2008.
[26] Kose et al. 2006; Wolf 2008.
[27] See, e.g., Eichengreen 1996; Neely 1999.
[28] International Monetary Fund 2016.
[29] On the importance of global supply chains in today's economy, see Johns and Wellhausen 2016.

a deleterious impact on the rest of the economy. The FDIC stepped in with a $4.5 billion rescue package, and the Federal Reserve provided ongoing liquidity support.[30] At the time, these responses by the central bank and a key regulator were uncontroversial, but they eventually gave rise to the phenomenon known as "too big to fail."[31] The government had, in effect, created a precedent: if a bank were large enough to create systemic instability in the event of its collapse, then it could expect an emergency bailout if trouble were to arise.

The "moral hazard" of this implicit bailout promise has been the target of much discussion by economists, political scientists, and policymakers, especially in the immediate aftermath of the global financial crisis of 2008–10.[32] More concretely, the concern is that creditors of large, systemically important banks have learned to expect a government-provided safety net, and therefore they become lax in monitoring the banks' activities.[33] Large banks behave accordingly by internalizing the benefits of risk taking but offloading the costs of failure on to taxpayers.[34]

A simple, albeit politically challenging, strategy to address the too-big-to-fail problem is to prevent banks from getting large enough to cause systemic disruption, and to break up banks that have already attained such status. The analyses in this book require us to remain skeptical about such an approach. We find no evidence that bank size and concentration are linked to the incidence of crises. Canada, for example, has had banks that are too-big-to-fail for much of its history, yet it has never experienced a systemic banking crisis. Germany, likewise, has had similarly large and concentrated banks since unification in the nineteenth century, yet it only began to experience frequent banking crises in the last two decades, once securities markets became larger and more sophisticated. Thus, the problem does not appear to be the presence of large banks, but rather the broader structure of the financial system in which they operate.

Our central empirical findings – that banks engage in riskier lending and hold less capital when operating in financial systems with larger securities markets – hold across space and time, independent of the size of banks or the degree of bank concentration. It is notable that the only three OECD countries that have not experienced banking crises

[30] Singer 2007; Sprague 1986; Zweig 1985.
[31] Stern and Feldman 2004, viii–ix.
[32] See, for example, Johnson and Kwak 2011.
[33] Stern and Feldman 2004, 2.
[34] Johnson and Kwak 2011, chap. 6.

since the 1970s have five-bank concentration ratios between 80 and 95 percent of total assets. In other words, in these countries, five or fewer large banks have dominated the financial system for decades without adverse effects on financial stability. Our findings suggest that even a financial system populated entirely by small and midsize banks will be crisis-prone if those banks operate alongside large, well-developed securities markets.[35] In light of these findings, the potential economic costs (in terms of efficiency and economies of scale) of breaking up large banks, as well as the likely political opposition to such policies, may not be worth incurring.

The lack of domestic consensus about whether and how to address the too-big-to-fail issue is mirrored by equally divided opinions about how to address the problem at the international level. As James Bullard, president of the St. Louis Federal Reserve, has noted, there is even less consensus across the industrialized world on this issue than there is domestically in the United States: "Other countries often seem to be less concerned about TBTF as an issue than we are in the U.S. There is sometimes a tendency [in other countries] to view large financial firms as national champions, deserving of protection."[36] Thus, even if the United States were to move forward unilaterally with policies to break up or limit the size of its large banks, it is not clear that other industrialized countries would follow suit. Given the globalized nature of international banking, and the inevitable concerns about competitiveness if American banks were to face size restrictions while Japanese, British, and German banks did not, the political feasibility of these proposals seems limited.[37]

Should We Re-introduce Glass-Steagall?

In addition to creating the FDIC, the Glass-Steagall Act of 1933 notably legislated a separation between commercial and investment banking. For many observers, Glass-Steagall is inextricably linked with these specific provisions. In the words of the act, its goal was to "provide for the

[35] Paul Krugman is similarly skeptical of breaking up large banks, and notes that small bank failures can still have systemic consequences. See Paul Krugman, "Financial Reform 101," *The New York Times*, April 1, 2010.

[36] James Bullard, "The State of the Debate on 'Too Big to Fail,'" Regional Economist, July 2016. Available at www.stlouisfed.org/publications/regional-economist/july-2016/the-state-of-the-debate-on-too-big-to-fail. On "economic patriotism" more generally, see Clift and Woll 2012.

[37] On resistance by France and Germany to ring-fencing of too-big-to-fail banks, see Hardie and Macartney 2016.

safer and more effective use of the assets of banks, to regulate interbank control, to prevent the undue diversion of funds into speculative operations, and for other purposes."[38]

At the height of the Great Depression of the 1930s, bank failures appeared to be connected to stock market volatility. Not dissimilar to the Panic of 1907, banks during this period engaged in stock market speculation, and some banks derived a large share of their revenues from investment banking – that is, underwriting shares of stock. Members of Congress believed that commercial banks, which accepted deposits from individuals and businesses, should no longer be allowed to become "infected" by the risky activities of investment banks.[39] After 1933, commercial banks were no longer permitted to underwrite stock or to own investment banking divisions. Investment banks could engage in these activities but were not permitted to accept deposits from individuals or corporations.

The separation between commercial and investment banks began to erode in the 1980s as banks pushed the limits of what regulators would tolerate, and in 1999 the Gramm-Leach-Bliley Act dismantled any remaining barriers.[40] Today, financial holding companies in the United States are permitted to own commercial banks, investment banks, insurance firms, and other financial services operations.

Given the central role of asset-backed securities in the global crisis of 2008–10, along with the rapid contagion between commercial and investment banks during the crisis, a number of politicians – most notably, Senator Elizabeth Warren of Massachusetts – have vocally called for the re-imposition of Glass-Steagall as the centerpiece of new legislation to prevent future banking crises. As Warren stated in 2015, "That high wall between high-risk trading and boring banking was punched full of holes until in the late 1990s, it was knocked down when Glass-Steagall was eventually repealed," she said. "And not long after that, the worst crash since the 1930s hit the American economy."[41] The implication, plainly stated, is that the primary culprit of the 2008 financial crisis was universal banking, and that separating commercial and investment banking would prevent future crises from striking the US economy.

38 See www.federalreservehistory.org/essays/glass_steagall_act on the Banking Act of 1933.

39 Johnson and Kwak 2011, 34.

40 The text of the act is available at www.federalreservehistory.org/essays/gramm_leach_bliley_act.

41 Kevin Cirilli, "Warren Calls for Return of Glass-Steagall," *The Hill*, July 14, 2015.

To date, Glass-Steagall has not been re-adopted in its full form, and it appears unlikely to become law again in the near future. Nevertheless, a more limited version of this proposal was passed as part of the Dodd-Frank Wall Street Reform and Consumer Protection Act of 2010.[42] Under this so-called Volcker Rule (named after former Federal Reserve Chairman Paul Volcker, who championed its adoption), banks insured by the FDIC are prohibited from trading in stocks, bonds, currencies, and derivatives for their own account.[43] This policy remains controversial, with the largest US financial institutions ardently opposed to it, while progressive politicians such as Warren and former Maryland Governor Martin O'Malley remain supportive.

In our view, the return of Glass-Steagall, like breaking up large banks, is unlikely to enhance financial stability.[44] Once again, as we observe in Canada, Germany, and other countries including Australia and New Zealand, it is possible to have a stable financial system comprised primarily or entirely of large conglomerate financial institutions that engage simultaneously in traditional commercial lending and a range of investment banking activities (underwriting, equity and bond trading, derivatives). Those advocating the return of Glass-Steagall, from our perspective, focus too narrowly on the American experience of the last decade and mistake correlation for causation. It is true that banking crises have become more frequent and severe in the United States since the 1980s – when financial institutions first began to circumvent Glass-Steagall and move into underwriting and insurance – and the Great Recession did follow shortly after the 1999 Gramm-Leach-Bliley Act. Nonetheless, it is not at all clear that the 2008 crisis would have been avoided were Glass-Steagall still in place. Indeed, the first two major financial institutions that failed in the United States in 2008, Bear Stearns and Lehman Brothers, were stand-alone investment banks. Moreover, the continued existence of a barrier between commercial and investment activities would most likely have done little to halt the cross-border banking flows or highly interconnected linkages between banks that lay at the heart of the global crisis. As our research has shown, banks will engage in riskier behavior regardless of whether they themselves are universal banks or stand-alone commercial institutions, simply by virtue of competing alongside well-developed securities markets for business.

[42] See www.federalreservehistory.org/essays/dodd_frank_act.

[43] Ibid.

[44] See Ang and Richardson 1994; Benston 1990; Kroszner and Rajan 1994.

Who Should Regulate?

As political scientists, we are naturally inclined to think about actors and institutions. Regulation does not emerge from the ground, nor does the government per se oversee banking regulation and supervision. Regulation is a delegated responsibility to actors with preferences, incentives, and bureaucratic structures, all of which interact to create tradeoffs and influence decisions.

The agencies responsible for bank regulation often have competing objectives. In some countries, bank regulation is part of the central bank's mandate along with setting and implementing monetary policy. The US Federal Reserve, for example, is the lead regulator for state-chartered banks that are members of the Federal Reserve system, and also supervises bank holding companies. In contrast, Canada bureaucratically separates the functions of bank regulation and monetary policy. The Bank of Canada is solely responsible for monetary policy, whereas an independent agency – the Office of the Superintendent of Financial Institutions – is tasked with regulating banks and other financial institutions.

These seemingly innocuous organizational details can have important influences on policy outcomes, especially if the agency's tasks are in tension with one another. Financial stability and price stability, for example, may respond differently to a central bank's key policy lever, the interest rate. When prices begin to rise, a central bank can raise its key interest rate to dampen inflationary pressures. Higher rates lead to higher borrowing costs for businesses and consumers and therefore generate downward pressure on prices. However, interest rate hikes – especially those that are sudden or large in magnitude – are potentially harmful to banks' profits and could increase the probability of bank failures.[45] The mechanism, in brief, is the change in the difference between the deposit rate and the lending rate. An increase in the deposit rate comes into effect immediately, whereas the lending rate on fixed-rate loans cannot be increased for existing loans. As a result, a monetary policymaker concerned about financial stability would raise interest rates only gradually in reaction to inflationary pressures, thereby allowing banks more time to adjust their lending strategies. On the other hand, a policy of strict price stability would require more aggressive interest rate adjustments.

[45] See Copelovitch and Singer 2008 for a review of the literature.

When political leaders choose to delegate bank regulatory authority to the central bank, they are forcing the central bank to engage in a delicate balancing act between financial stability and price stability. In previous research, we find that countries with so-called regulatory central banks are likely to face higher inflation than countries that separate bank regulation and monetary policy in different agencies.[46] The reason for this outcome is straightforward: regulatory central banks are held publicly accountable in the event of bank failures or sudden drops in bank profitability, and are therefore especially sensitive to short-term bank stability when setting interest rate policy. This sensitivity comes at a cost of greater inflation. In related work, Winecoff (2014) finds that banks have lower capital levels in countries with regulatory central banks because they can count on the central bank to adjust interest rates only gradually, with their stability interests in mind.[47]

Our research and related work on central banks suggest two additional complications. First, central bank independence – the practice of granting central bankers a large degree of autonomy to conduct monetary policy without interference from politicians – has become the norm throughout the industrialized world and many emerging-market countries.[48] In democratic political systems, such independence gives central bankers and regulators an unusual amount of power – or "unelected power," to use former Bank of England Deputy Governor Paul Tucker's words.[49] Expanding a central bank's portfolio to include bank regulation and supervision essentially amplifies the problem of democratic legitimacy. The second, related issue is that the findings of the book suggest that the connection between banking and securities markets is particularly worrisome for financial stability. A logical bureaucratic approach to this problem is to structure a regulatory agency such that banking, securities, and other financial market activities are all under its jurisdiction. A single financial regulator would therefore internalize any externalities from financial activities (e.g., potentially dangerous activities in the securities realm could not be easily dismissed as being outside the regulator's purview) and would presumably have the wherewithal to address emerging sources of risk across the financial landscape. But such a powerful agency, if granted political independence as part of a

[46] Ibid.

[47] Winecoff 2014.

[48] See Bernhard 1998; Bernhard, Broz, and Clark 2002; Bodea and Hicks 2015a, 2015b; McNamara 2002.

[49] Tucker 2018, x–xii.

central bank, could prove to be an "overmighty citizen" whose unelected authority causes tension – philosophical and practical – with democratic politics.[50]

Separating regulatory agencies into silos – one for banking, one for securities, another for insurance and other activities – is an alternative approach, but it too comes with drawbacks and challenges. Of primary concern for this book is the sharing of information between and among markets, and the heightened supervisory attention to banks that are tethered to securities markets through wholesale funding, securitization of mortgages, and overnight lending to securities firms. Supervision becomes more difficult as regulators with functional jurisdictions meet a financial landscape with few boundaries between financial activities. Moreover, the type of supervision that we advocate – known in the industry as "prudential regulation," which includes capital adequacy requirements and other steps to enhance the stability of the entire financial system – is less familiar to securities regulators than bank regulators.[51] As one senior bank regulator in the United States told us, "Bank regulators are like doctors; securities regulators are like cops."[52] In summary, separating regulatory agencies into functional specialties addresses the concern that a single regulator could be too powerful, but it complicates efforts to supervise financial institutions whose activities span the gamut of financial services.

As a policy matter, creating new administrative bodies is often politically easier than dismantling or modifying existing bodies. Following this dictum, the United States created the Financial Stability Oversight Council (FSOC) as part of the Dodd-Frank act of 2010. The FSOC is tasked with monitoring risks to the US financial system and responding to emerging threats. One of its main powers is the ability to designate financial institutions – such as insurance companies, investment firms, and the like – as systemically important and therefore subject to supervision by the Federal Reserve. The FSOC is not an agency per se; rather it is a committee, housed within the Treasury Department, composed of ten voting members including the Treasury secretary, the Fed chairman, and the heads of the Securities and Exchange Commission, the Comptroller of the Currency, the Federal Deposit Insurance Corporation, and several other regulatory bodies.[53] By bringing together regulators from across

50 The term "overmighty citizen" is attributed to Permanent Secretary to the Treasury (UK) Terry Burns in Tucker 2018, ix–xii.

51 See Singer 2007, chap. 5.

52 Interview with retired senior regulator (US), March 3, 2005.

53 See www.treasury.gov/initiatives/fsoc/.

the financial spectrum, the FSOC in principle can identify emerging risks that transcend any single financial activity, such as banking or insurance, and respond appropriately. On the downside, accountability for financial stability is spread across the representatives on the committee, whereas the costs for policy implementation still rest with individual regulators who might have few incentives to shed light on emerging risks in their respective domains.

Our recommendations for "who should regulate" are therefore circumspect. There are important trade-offs involved in every bureaucratic decision. The findings of this book suggest that developments in securities markets can affect risk taking in banking, and therefore regulators from these two areas should maintain regular communication and information sharing. The strategy pursued by the United States of creating a pan-regulatory committee to oversee financial stability might be the most politically viable option for developed countries, especially given the difficulty of altering the mandates of existing regulators or otherwise making substantial bureaucratic changes.

CONCLUDING THOUGHTS

Throughout this book, our focus has been on highlighting the underexplored relationship between banking systems, securities markets, and financial stability. Our argument and evidence suggest that this relationship is the key underlying factor explaining why banking crises occur in some countries, at some times, and not in others. Our findings also highlight what we believe to be a major gap in the existing literature on financial crises, which has largely overlooked the role of deeper, structural factors – and, specifically, the structure of domestic financial systems – in explaining the incidence of financial crises.

Research on financial instability follows a cyclical pattern not unlike financial instability itself. Immediately after a crisis, books and research articles emerge, and then scholars shift their gaze to other areas as the world becomes more financially stable. Our book is, in essence, off-cycle. As of this writing, banking systems are generally stable throughout the world, including in the United States, the United Kingdom, and the emerging-market countries. While we had no intention of timing the completion of this book according to the state of the financial world, our timing is fortuitous in the sense that our contributions will not, and should not, be tethered to any particular crisis.

The cycle of scholarship also follows the trajectory of an auger as it bores a hole into the earth. Early works on crises focus on the visible, granular details on the surface: the identities and preferences of the actors, including bankers, regulators, and politicians; the details of particular investments, instruments, and business strategies; and the immediate consequences of bank failures. A second wave of research delves into the systemic factors that are not specific to any particular crisis, like exposure to the global economy, credit growth, or political partisanship. And finally, research emerges that exposes the deep, longer-term causes of financial instability. We consider this book to represent this latter stage of research. Being at the bottom of an auger's helical bit has some trade-offs, of course. The names and faces that we identify are of policymakers and business leaders from hundreds of years ago, not those of today's actors who are ultimately responsible for recent episodes of instability. However, our deep exploration into financial and political history has allowed us to isolate the policies and institutions that make countries more vulnerable to crises as they contend with the realities of global capital flows.

References

Abiad, Abdul, Enrica Detragiache, and Thierry Tressel. 2008. A New Database of Financial Reforms. IMF Working Paper 08/266.

Accornero, Guya, and Pedro Ramos Pinto. 2015. 'Mild Mannered'? Protest and Mobilisation in Portugal under Austerity, 2010–2013. *West European Politics* 38 (3): 491–515.

Admati, Anat, and Martin Hellwig. 2013. *The Bankers' New Clothes: What's Wrong with Banking and What to Do about It.* Princeton, NJ: Princeton University Press.

Adrian, Tobias, and Hyun Song Shin. 2010. The Changing Nature of Financial Intermediation and the Financial Crisis of 2007–2009. *Annual Review of Economics* 2 (1): 603–18.

Ahlquist, John, Mark S. Copelovitch, and Stefanie Walter. Forthcoming. The Political Consequences of External Economic Shocks: Evidence from Poland (with John Ahlquist and Stefanie Walter). *American Journal of Political Science.*

Allen, Franklin, and Douglas Gale. 2000. *Comparing Financial Systems.* Cambridge, MA: MIT Press.

2009. *Understanding Financial Crises.* Oxford: Oxford University Press.

Alt, James, David Dreyer Lassen, and Joachim Wehner. 2014. It Isn't Just about Greece: Domestic Politics, Transparency and Fiscal Gimmickry in Europe. *British Journal of Political Science* 44 (4): 707–16.

Amri, Puspa D., Greg M. Richey, and Thomas D. Willett. 2016. Capital Surges and Credit Booms: How Tight Is the Relationship? *Open Economies Review* 27 (4): 637–70.

Amri, Puspa D., and Brett Matthew Kocher. 2012. The Political Economy of Financial Sector Supervision and Banking Crises: A Cross-Country Analysis. *European Law Journal* 18 (1): 24–43.

Anand, Anita I., and Andrew J. Green. 2010. Why Is This Taking So Long? The Move Toward a National Securities Regulator. *University of Toronto Law Journal* 60 (2): 663–86.

Ang, James S., and Terry Richardson. 1994. The Underwriting Experience of Commercial Bank Affiliates Prior to the Glass-Steagall Act: A Reexamination of Evidence for Passage of the Act. *Journal of Banking & Finance* 18 (2): 351–95.

Angrist, Joshua D., and Jörn-Steffen Pischke. 2008. *Mostly Harmless Econometrics: An Empiricist's Companion*. Princeton, NJ: Princeton University Press.

Armingeon, Klaus, and Kai Guthmann. 2014. Democracy in Crisis? The Declining Support for National Democracy in European Countries, 2007–2011. *European Journal of Political Research* 53 (3): 423–42.

Armstrong, Christopher. 1997. *Blue Skies and Boiler Rooms: Buying and Selling Securities in Canada, 1870–1940*. Toronto: University of Toronto Press.

1981. *The Politics of Federalism: Ontario's Relations with the Federal Government, 1867–1942*. Toronto: University of Toronto Press.

Baerg, Nicole Rae, and Mark Hallerberg. 2016. Explaining Instability in the Stability and Growth Pact: The Contribution of Member State Power and Euroskepticism to the Euro Crisis. *Comparative Political Studies* 49 (7): 968–1009.

Bagehot, Walter. 1873. *Lombard Street: A Description of the Money Market*. London: Henry S. King & Co.

Balderston, Theo. 1991. German Banking Between the Wars: The Crisis of the Credit Banks. *Business History Review* 65 (3): 554–605.

Barkin, Kenneth D. 1970. *The Controversy over German Industrialization, 1890–1902*. Chicago: University of Chicago Press.

Barnichon, Regis, Christian Matthes, and Alexander Ziegenbein. 2018. *The Financial Crisis at 10: Will We Ever Recover?* FRBSF Economic Letter. Federal Reserve Bank of San Francisco.

Barth, James R., Gerard Caprio, and Ross Levine. 2012. *Guardians of Finance: Making Regulators Work for Us*. Cambridge, MA: MIT Press.

2008. *Rethinking Bank Regulation: Till Angels Govern*. Cambridge: Cambridge University Press.

Bauerle, Danzman, Sarah W. Kindred Winecoff, and Thomas Oatley. 2017. All Crises Are Global: Capital Cycles in an Imbalanced International Political Economy. *International Studies Quarterly* 61 (4): 907–23.

Bechtel, Michael M., Jens Hainmueller, and Yotam Margalit. 2014. Preferences for International Redistribution: The Divide over the Eurozone Bailouts. *American Journal of Political Science* 58 (4): 835–56.

Beck, Nathaniel. 2015. Estimating Grouped Data Models with a Binary Dependent Variable and Fixed Effects: What Are the Issues? Presented at the Society of Political Methodology Annual Meeting, University of Rochester.

Beck, Thorsten, Asli Demirgüç-Kunt, and Ross Levine. 2006. Bank Concentration, Competition, and Crises: First Results. *Journal of Banking & Finance* 30 (5): 1581–603.

Beck, Thorsten, Asli Demirgüç-Kunt, Ross Levine, and Vojislav Maksimovic. 2001. Financial Structure and Economic Development: Firm, Industry, and Country Evidence. In *Financial Structure and Economic Growth*, edited by Asli Demirgüç-Kunt and Ross Levine. Cambridge, MA: MIT Press.

Beer, Joachim. 1999. *Der Funktionswandel der deutschen Wertpapierbörsen in der Zwischenkriegszeit (1924–1939)*. Berlin: Lang.

Bell, Stephen, and Andrew Hindmoor. 2015. *Masters of the Universe, Slaves of the Market*. Cambridge, MA: Harvard University Press.

Bellucci, Paolo. 2014. The Political Consequences of Blame Attribution for the Economic Crisis in the 2013 Italian National Election. *Journal of Elections, Public Opinion and Parties* 24 (2): 243–63.

Benston, George J. 1990. *The Separation of Commercial and Investment Banking: The Glass-Steagall Act Revisited and Reconsidered*. New York: Oxford University Press.

Berghahn, Volker Rolf. 1993. *Germany and the Approach of War in 1914*. 2nd ed. New York: St. Martin's Press.

2005. *Imperial Germany, 1871–1918: Economy, Society, Culture, and Politics*. New York: Berghahn Books.

Bernanke, Ben. 2000. *Essays on the Great Depression*. Princeton, NJ: Princeton University Press.

2011. Global Imbalances: Links to Economic and Financial Stability. Presented at the Banque de France Financial Stability Review Launch Event. Paris, France.

Bernhard, William T. 1998. A Political Explanation of Variations in Central Bank Independence. *American Political Science Review* 92 (2): 311–27.

Bernhard, William T., J. Lawrence Broz, and William Roberts Clark. 2002. The Political Economy of Monetary Institutions. *International Organization* 56 (4): 693–723.

Bernhard, William T., and David Leblang. 2006. *Democratic Processes and Financial Markets: Pricing Politics*. New York: Cambridge University Press.

Binhammer, H. H. 1968. *Money, Banking and the Canadian Financial System*. Toronto: Methuen.

Blackbourn, David. 2003. *History of Germany 1780–1918: The Long Nineteenth Century*. 2nd ed. New York: Wiley-Blackwell.

1984. Peasants and Politics in Germany, 1871–1914. *European History Quarterly* 14 (1): 47–75.

Blinder, Alan S. 2013. *After the Music Stopped: The Financial Crisis, the Response, and the Work Ahead*. New York: Penguin Books.

Blustein, Paul. 2016. *Laid Low: Inside the Crisis That Overwhelmed Europe and the IMF*. Waterloo: CIGI Press.

Bodea, Cristina, and Raymond Hicks. 2015a. International Finance and Central Bank Independence: Institutional Diffusion and the Flow and Cost of Capital. *The Journal of Politics* 77 (1): 268–84.

2015b. Price Stability and Central Bank Independence: Discipline, Credibility, and Democratic Institutions. *International Organization* 69 (1): 35–61.

Bordo, Michael D., Angela Redish, and Hugh Rockoff. 2015. Why Didn't Canada Have a Banking Crisis in 2008 (or in 1930, or 1907, Or...)? *The Economic History Review* 68 (1): 218–43.

Bordo, Michael D., Hugh Rockoff, and Angela Redish. 1994. The US Banking System from a Northern Exposure: Stability versus Efficiency. *The Journal of Economic History* 54 (2): 325–41.

Borio, Claudio. 2014. The International Monetary and Financial System: Its Achilles Heel and What to Do about It. BIS Working Paper 456, Basel.

2003. Towards a Macroprudential Framework for Financial Regulation and Supervision? BIS Working Paper No. 128, Basel.

Borio, Claudio E. V., and Piti Disyatat. 2011. Global Imbalances and the Financial Crisis: Link or No Link? BIS Working Paper 346, Basel, Bank for International Settlements.

Bothwell, Robert, Ian M. Drummond, and John English. 1987. *Canada, 1900–1945*. Toronto: University of Toronto Press.

Boughton, James M. 2001. *Silent Revolution: The International Monetary Fund, 1979–1989*. Washington, DC: International Monetary Fund.

Brassett, James, and Eleni Tsingou. 2011. The Politics of Legitimate Global Governance. *Review of International Political Economy* 18 (1): 1–16.

Breckenridge, Roeliff Morton. 1910. *The History of Banking in Canada*. Washington, DC: Government Printing Office.

de Bromhead, Alan, Barry Eichengreen, and Kevin O'Rourke. 2012. Right-Wing Political Extremism in the Great Depression. *VoxEU*. Available at https://voxeu.org/article/right-wing-political-extremism-great-depression. Accessed August 20, 2018.

Broner, Fernando, Tatiana Didier, Aitor Erce, and Sergio L. Schmukler. 2013. Gross Capital Flows: Dynamics and Crises. *Journal of Monetary Economics* 60 (1): 11333.

Broz, J. Lawrence. 2013. Partisan Financial Cycles. In *Politics in the New Hard Times: The Great Recession in Comparative Perspective*, edited by Miles Kahler and David A. Lake, 75–101. Ithaca, NY: Cornell University Press.

1997. *The International Origins of the Federal Reserve System*. Ithaca, NY: Cornell University Press.

Bruner, Robert F., and Sean D. Carr. 2008. *The Panic of 1907: Lessons Learned from the Market's Perfect Storm*. New York: John Wiley & Sons.

Brustein, William. 2003. *Roots of Hate: Anti-Semitism in Europe Before the Holocaust*. Cambridge: Cambridge University Press.

Buchheim, Christoph, and Jonas Scherner. 2006. The Role of Private Property in the Nazi Economy: The Case of Industry. *The Journal of Economic History* 66 (2): 390–416.

Bulmer, Simon. 2014. Germany and the Eurozone Crisis: Between Hegemony and Domestic Politics. *West European Politics* 37 (6): 1244–63.

Burhop, Carsten, and Sibylle Lehmann-Hasemeyer. 2016. The Berlin Stock Exchange and the Geography of German Stock Markets in 1913. *European Review of Economic History* 20 (4): 429–51.

Butzbach, Olivier, Suzanne J. Konzelmann, and Marc Fovargue-Davies. 2013. Institutional Foundations of the Anglo Saxon Banking Systems: Some Are More Liberal Than Others. In *Banking Systems in the Crisis: The Faces of Liberal Capitalism*, edited by Sue Konzelmann and Marc Fovargue-Davies, 220–50. London: Routledge.

Caballero, Julián A. 2016. Do Surges in International Capital Inflows Influence the Likelihood of Banking Crises? *The Economic Journal* 126 (591): 281–316.

Calomiris, Charles W., and Stephen H. Haber. 2014. *Fragile by Design: The Political Origins of Banking Crises and Scarce Credit*. Princeton, NJ: Princeton University Press.

Calvo, Guillermo. 1998. Capital Flows and Capital-Market Crises: The Simple Economics of Sudden Stops. *Journal of Applied Economics* 1 (1): 35–54.

Carter, David B., and Curtis S. Signorino. 2010. Back to the Future: Modeling Time Dependence in Binary Data. *Political Analysis* 18 (3): 271–92.

Chinn, Menzie D., and Jeffry A. Frieden. 2011. *Lost Decades: The Making of America's Debt Crisis and the Long Recovery*. New York: W. W. Norton & Company.

Chinn, Menzie D., and Hiro Ito. 2008. A New Measure of Financial Openness. *Journal of Comparative Policy Analysis* 10 (3): 309–22.

Chwieroth, Jeffrey M., and Andrew Walter. 2015a. Great Expectations, Veto Players, and the Changing Politics of Banking Crises. LSE Systemic Risk Centre Discussion Paper No. 28, London: London School of Economics.

2015b. Policy Responses to Banking Crises over the Long Run. Paper Presented at the American Political Science Association Annual Conference, San Francisco, CA.

2019. *The Wealth Effect: How the Great Expectations of the Middle Class Have Changed the Politics of Banking Crises*. Cambridge: Cambridge University Press.

Čihák, Martin, Asli Demirgüç-Kunt, Erik Feyen, and Ross Levine. 2012. Benchmarking Financial Systems around the World. World Bank Policy Research Working Paper 6175.

Clark, William Roberts, and Mark Hallerberg. 2000. Mobile Capital, Domestic Institutions, and Electorally Induced Monetary and Fiscal Policy. *American Political Science Review* 94 (2): 323–46.

Clift, Ben, and Cornelia Woll. 2012. Economic Patriotism: Reinventing Control over Open Markets. *Journal of European Public Policy* 19 (3): 307–23.

Coffee, John C. 2001. The Rise of Dispersed Ownership: The Roles of Law and the State in the Separation of Ownership and Control. *The Yale Law Journal* 111 (1): 1–82.

Coleman, William D. 1996. *Financial Services, Globalization and Domestic Policy Change*. London: Palgrave Macmillan.

Copelovitch, Mark, Jeffry Frieden, and Stefanie Walter. 2016. The Political Economy of the Euro Crisis. *Comparative Political Studies* 49 (7): 811–40.

Copelovitch, Mark S., and David Andrew Singer. 2008. Financial Regulation, Monetary Policy, and Inflation in the Industrialized World. *The Journal of Politics* 70 (3): 663–80.

2017. Tipping the (Im)Balance: Capital Inflows, Financial Market Structure, and Banking Crises. *Economics & Politics* 29 (3): 179–208.

Crespo-Tenorio, Adriana, Nathan M. Jensen, and Guillermo Rosas. 2014. Political Liabilities: Surviving Banking Crises. *Comparative Political Studies* 47 (7): 1047–74.

Crow, John W. 2002. *Making Money: An Insider's Perspective on Finance, Politics, and Canada's Central Bank*. Etobicoke: Wiley.

Cruise, David. 1987. *Fleecing the Lamb: The Inside Story of the Vancouver Stock Exchange*. Vancouver: Douglas & McIntyre.

Crystallin, Masyita, Levan Efremidze, Sungsoo Kim, Wahyu Nugroho, Ozan Sula, and Thomas Willett. 2015. How Common Are Capital Flows Surges? How They Are Measured Matters a Lot. *Open Economies Review* 26 (4): 663–82.

Deeg, Richard. 2005. Change from Within: German and Italian Finance in the 1990s. In *Beyond Continuity: Institutional Change in Advanced Political Economies*, edited by Walter Streeck and Kathleen Thelen, 169–202. New York: Oxford University Press.

1999. *Finance Capitalism Unveiled: Banks and the German Political Economy*. Ann Arbor: University of Michigan Press.

2003. On the Development of Universal Banking in Germany. In *The Origins of National Financial Systems: Alexander Gerschenkron Reconsidered*, edited by Douglas J. Forsyth and Daniel Verdier, 85–103. London: Routledge.

DeLean, Tess, and Joseph P. Joyce. 2014. Stock Markets and the Costs of Banking Crises. *Journal of Financial Economic Policy* 6 (4): 342–61.

Demirgüç-Kunt, Asli, and Ross Levine. 2004. *Financial Structure and Economic Growth: A Cross-Country Comparison of Banks, Markets, and Development*. Cambridge, MA: MIT Press.

1996. Stock Market Development and Financial Intermediaries: Stylized Facts. *The World Bank Economic Review* 10 (2): 291–321.

Detzer, Daniel, Nina Dodig, Trevor Evans, Eckhard Hein, and Hansjörg Herr. 2013. Studies in Financial Systems No. 3: The German Financial System. Financialisation, Economy, Society, and Sustainable Development Project, European Commission.

Detzer, Daniel, Nina Dodig, Trevor Evans, Eckhard Hein, Hansjörg Herr, and Franz Josef Prante. 2017. *The German Financial System and the Financial and Economic Crisis*. New York: Springer International Publishing.

Detzer, Daniel, and Eckhard Hein. 2014. Finance-Dominated Capitalism in Germany: Deep Recession and Quick Recovery. Institute for International Political Economy Berlin, Working Paper 39/2014, Berlin School of Economics and Law.

Deutsche Sparkassen und Giroverband (DSGV). 2010. *Fakten, Analysen, Positionen*. Berlin: Finanzgruppe DSGV Zur Geschichte der Sparkassen in Deutschland.

Diamond, Douglas W. 1991. Monitoring and Reputation: The Choice between Bank Loans and Directly Placed Debt. *Journal of Political Economy* 99 (4): 689–721.

Diaz-Alejandro, Carlos. 1985. Good-bye Financial Repression, Hello Financial Crash. *Journal of Development Economics* 19 (1–2): 1–24.

Dinas, Elias, and Lamprini Rori. 2013. The 2012 Greek Parliamentary Elections: Fear and Loathing in the Polls. *West European Politics* 36 (1): 270–82.

Dittmann, Ingolf, Ernst Maug, and Christoph Schneider. 2009. Bankers on the Boards of German Firms: What They Do, What They Are Worth, and Why They Are (Still) There. *Review of Finance* 14 (1): 35–71.

Dreher, Axel, Jan-Egbert Sturm, and James Raymond Vreeland. 2009. Global Horse Trading: IMF Loans for Votes in the United Nations Security Council. *European Economic Review* 53 (7): 742–57.

Drezner, Daniel W., and Kathleen R. McNamara. 2013. International Political Economy, Global Financial Orders and the 2008 Financial Crisis. *Perspectives on Politics* 11 (1): 155–66.

Driscoll, John C., and Aart C. Kraay. 1998. Consistent Covariance Matrix Estimation with Spatially Dependent Panel Data. *The Review of Economics and Statistics* 80 (4): 549–60.

Durham, John George Lambton. 1839. *Report on the Affairs of British North America*. Toronto: Robert Stanton. Available at http://archive.org/details/reportonaffairsooodurh. Accessed June 11, 2018.

Dyson, Kenneth. 2014. *States, Debt, and Power: "Saints" and "Sinners" in European History and Integration*. New York: Oxford University Press.

Easterbrook, William Thomas, and Hugh G. J. Aitken. 1956. *Canadian Economic History*. Toronto: Macmillan.

Edwards, Franklin R. 1996. *The New Finance: Regulation and Financial Stability*. Washington, DC: AEI Press.

Efremidze, Levan, Sungsoo Kim, Ozan Sula, and Thomas D. Willett. 2017. The Relationships among Capital Flow Surges, Reversals and Sudden Stops. *Journal of Financial Economic Policy* 9 (4): 393–413.

Emery, Henry. 1898. The Results of the German Exchange Act of 1896. *Political Science Quarterly* 13 (2): 286–319.

Eichengreen, Barry. 1996. *Globalizing Capital: A History of the International Monetary System*. Princeton, NJ: Princeton University Press.

Epstein, Rachel A. 2017. *Banking on Markets: The Transformation of Bank-State Ties in Europe and Beyond*. Oxford: Oxford University Press.

Faust, Helmut. 1977. *Geschichte der Genossenschaftsbewegung: Ursprung und Aufbruch der Genossenschaftsbewegung in England, Frankreich und Deutschland sowie ihre weitere Entwicklung im deutschen Sprachraum*. Heusenstamm: Knapp.

Feldenkirchen, Wilfried. 1991. Banking and Economic Growth: Banks and Industry in Germany in the Nineteenth Century and Their Changing Relationship during Industrialization. In *German Industry and German Industrialisation: Essays in German Economic and Business History in the Nineteenth and Twentieth Centuries*, edited by W. R. Lee, 106–38. London: Routledge.

Feldman, Gerald D. 1993. *The Great Disorder: Politics, Economics, and Society in the German Inflation, 1914–1924*. New York: Oxford University Press.

Ferguson, Thomas, and Peter Temin. 2001. Made in Germany: The German Currency Crisis of July 1931. MIT Department of Economics Working Paper 01-07.

Fernandez-Albertos, José, and Alexander Kuo. 2016. Economic Hardship and Policy Preferences in the Eurozone Periphery: Evidence from Spain. *Comparative Political Studies* 49 (7): 874–906.

Fernandez-Arias, Eduardo, and Peter J. Montiel. 1996. The Surge in Capital Inflows to Developing Countries: An Analytical Overview. *The World Bank Economic Review* 10 (1): 51–77.

Fischer, Markus, Christa Hainz, Jörg Rocholl, and Sascha Steffen. 2014. Government Guarantees and Bank Risk Taking. ESMT Working Paper No. 14-02, Berlin.

Fohlin, Caroline. 2007. *Finance Capitalism and Germany's Rise to Industrial Power.* Cambridge: Cambridge University Press.

Forbes, Kristin J., and Francis E. Warnock. 2012. Capital Flow Waves: Surges, Stops, Flight, and Retrenchment. *Journal of International Economics* 88 (2): 235–51.

Freixas, Xavier, Luc Laeven, and José-Luis Peydro. 2015. *Systemic Risk, Crises, and Macroprudential Regulation.* Cambridge, MA: MIT Press.

Frieden, Jeffry A. 2007. *Global Capitalism: Its Fall and Rise in the Twentieth Century.* New York: W. W. Norton & Company.

Frieden, Jeffry A., and Stefanie Walter. 2017. Understanding the Political Economy of the Eurozone Crisis. *Annual Review of Political Science* 20: 371–90.

Friedman, Milton, and Anna Schwartz. 1971. *A Monetary History of the United States, 1867–1960.* Princeton, NJ: Princeton University Press.

Friend, Emil. 1908. Stock-Exchange Regulation in Germany. *Journal of Political Economy* 16 (6): 369–74.

Frost, James D. 1982. The "Nationalization" of the Bank of Nova Scotia, 1880–1910. *Acadiensis* 12 (1): 3–38.

Funke, Manuel, Moritz Schularick, and Christoph Trebesch. 2016. Going to Extremes: Politics after Financial Crises, 1870–2014. *European Economic Review* 88: 227–60.

Gandrud, Christopher, and Mícheál O'Keeffe. 2017. Information and Financial Crisis Policy-Making. *Journal of European Public Policy* 24 (3): 386–405.

Garrett, Geoffrey. 1998. *Partisan Politics in the Global Economy.* Cambridge, UK: Cambridge University Press.

Gehrig, Thomas, and Caroline Fohlin. 2006. Trading Costs in Early Securities Markets: The Case of the Berlin Stock Exchange 1880–1910. *Review of Finance* 10 (4): 587–612.

Genovese, Federica, Gerald Schneider, and Pia Wassmann. 2016. The Eurotower Strikes Back: Crises, Adjustments, and Europe's Austerity Protests. *Comparative Political Studies* 49 (7): 939–67.

Gerschenkron, Alexander. 1962. *Economic Backwardness in Historical Perspective.* Cambridge, MA: Belknap Press.

Ghosh, Atish R., Mahvash S.Qureshi, Jun Il Kim, and Juan Zalduendo. 2014. Surges. *Journal of International Economics* 92 (2): 266–85.

Glagau, Otto. 1876. The Stock Market and Founding-Era Swindle in Berlin. German History in Documents and Images.

Global Financial Development Database (GFDD), The World Bank. Latest version: www.worldbank.org/en/publication/gfdr/data/global-financial-development-database.

Gommel, Rainer. 1992. Entstehung und Entwicklung der Effektenbörse im 19. Jahrhundert bis 1914. In *Deutsche Börsengeschichte*, edited by Hans Pohl, 135–207. Frankfurt: Fritz Knapp.

Gorton, Gary. 2009. Information, Liquidity, and the (Ongoing) Panic of 2007. *American Economic Review* 99 (2): 567–72.

Gorton, Gary B., and Ellis W. Tallman. 2018. *Fighting Financial Crises: Learning from the Past*. Chicago: University of Chicago Press.

Gourevitch, Peter A. 1996. The Macropolitics of Microinstitutional Differences in the Analysis of Comparative Capitalism. In *National Diversity and Global Capitalism*, edited by Suzanne Berger and Ronald Dore, 239–62. Ithaca, NY: Cornell University Press.

Grossman, Richard S. 2010. *Unsettled Account: The Evolution of Banking in the Industrialized World since 1800*. Princeton, NJ: Princeton University Press.

Grossman, Emiliano. 2006. Europeanization as an Interactive Process: German Public Banks Meet State Aid Policy. *Journal of Common Market Studies* 44 (2): 325–48.

Guiso, Luigi, Michael Haliassos, and Tullio Jappelli, eds. 2002. *Household Portfolios*. Cambridge, MA: MIT Press.

Hackethal, Andreas. 2003. German Banks and Banking Structure. Working Paper Series: Finance & Accounting No. 106, Frankfurt, Goethe University.

Hail, Luzi, and Christian Leuz. 2006. International Differences in the Cost of Equity Capital: Do Legal Institutions and Securities Regulation Matter? *Journal of Accounting Research* 44 (3): 485–531.

Hainmueller, Jens, Jonathan Mummolo, and Yiqing Xu. 2019. How Much Should We Trust Estimates from Multiplicative Interaction Models? Simple Tools to Improve Empirical Practice. *Political Analysis* 27 (2): 163–92.

Hall, Peter A., and David W. Soskice. 2001. *Varieties of Capitalism: The Institutional Foundations of Comparative Advantage*. Oxford: Oxford University Press.

Hammond, Bray. 1957. *Banks and Politics in America, from the Revolution to the Civil War*. Princeton, NJ: Princeton University Press.

Hardie, Iain, and David Howarth. 2013. *Market-Based Banking and the International Financial Crisis*. Oxford: Oxford University Press.

Hardie, Iain, David Howarth, Sylvia Maxfield, and Amy Verdun. 2013. Banks and the False Dichotomy in the Comparative Political Economy of Finance. *World Politics* 65 (4): 691–728.

Hardie, Iain, and Huw Macartney. 2016. EU Ring-Fencing and the Defence of Too-Big-to-Fail Banks. *West European Politics* 39 (3): 503–25.

Helleiner, Eric. 1994. *States and the Reemergence of Global Finance: From Bretton Woods to the 1990s*. Ithaca, NY: Cornell University Press.

2014. *The Status Quo Crisis: Global Financial Governance after the 2008 Meltdown*. Oxford: Oxford University Press.

Henderson, William Otto. 1975. *The Rise of German Industrial Power, 1834–1914*. Berkeley: University of California Press.

1939. *The Zollverein*. Cambridge, UK: Cambridge University Press.

Henning, F. W. 1992. Börsenkrisen und Börsengesetzgebung von 1914 bis 1945 in Deutschland. In *Deutsche Börsengeschichte*, edited by Hans Pohl, 209–90. Frankfurt: Fritz Knapp.

Hernández, Enrique, and Hanspeter Kriesi. 2016. The Electoral Consequences of the Financial and Economic Crisis in Europe. *European Journal of Political Research* 55 (2): 203–24.

Hilferding, Rudolf. 1910. *Das Finanzkapital. Eine Studie über die jüngste Entwicklung des Kapitalismus*. Vienna: Wiener Volksbuchhandlung.

Hobolt, Sara B., and Catherine E. de Vries. 2015. Issue Entrepreneurship and Multiparty Competition. *Comparative Political Studies* 48 (9): 1159–85.

2016. Turning against the Union? The Impact of the Crisis on the Eurosceptic Vote in the 2014 European Parliament Elections. *Electoral Studies* 44: 504–14.

Hobolt, Sara B., and Christopher E. Wratil. 2015. Public Opinion and the Crisis: The Dynamics of Support for the Euro. *Journal of European Public Policy* 22 (2): 238–56.

Hockin, Thomas A. 2009. Creating an Advantage in Global Capital Markets: Final Report and Recommendations. Report of the Expert Panel on Securities Regulation in Canada, Ottawa.

2003. Letter to the Wise Persons Committee to Review the Structure of Securities Regulation in Canada. Restructuring the Regulatory Framework of the Securities Industry in Canada. Letter to the Wise Persons Committee to Review the Structure of Securities Regulation in Canada.

Hof, Patrik. 2008. *Kurswechsel an der Börse: Kapitalmarktpolitik unter Hitler und Mussolini*. Munich: Mpress Meidenbauer.

Hollyer, James R., B. Peter Rosendorff, and James Raymond Vreeland. 2015. Transparency, Protest, and Autocratic Instability. *American Political Science Review* 109 (4): 764–84.

Holtfrerich, Carl-Ludwig. 1999. *Frankfurt as a Financial Centre: From Medieval Trade Fair to European Banking Centre*. Munich: C. H. Beck.

Howarth, David, and Lucia Quaglia. 2013. Banking on Stability: The Political Economy of New Capital Requirements in the European Union. *Journal of European Integration* 35 (3): 333–46.

2014. The Steep Road to European Banking Union: Constructing the Single Resolution Mechanism. *Journal of Common Market Studies* 52 (S1): 125–40.

International Monetary Fund. 2011. *Germany: Technical Note on Banking Sector Structure. IMF Country Report*. Washington, DC: International Monetary Fund.

2016. *Strengthening the International Monetary System: A Stocktaking*. IMF Policy Paper, Washington, DC: International Monetary Fund.

Iversen, Torben, and David Soskice. 2012. Modern Capitalism and the Advanced Nation State: Understanding the Causes of the Crisis. In *Coping with Crisis: Government Reactions to the Great Recession*, edited by Nancy Bermeo and Jonas Pontusson, 35–64. New York: Russell Sage Foundation.

Jacobs, Alan M., and Steven Teles. 2007. The Perils of Market Making: The Case of British Pension Reform. In *Creating Competitive Markets: The Politics of Regulatory Reform*, edited by Marc Karnis Landy, Martin A. Levin, and Martin M. Shapiro, 157–83. Washington, DC: Brookings Institution Press.

James, Harold. 1984. The Causes of the German Banking Crisis of 1931. *The Economic History Review* 37 (1): 68–87.

1986. *The German Slump: Politics and Economics 1924–1936*. New York: Oxford University Press.

Johns, Leslie, and Rachel L. Wellhausen. 2016. Under One Roof: Supply Chains and the Protection of Foreign Investment. *American Political Science Review* 110 (1): 31–51.

Johnson, Simon, and James Kwak. 2011. *13 Bankers: The Wall Street Takeover and the Next Financial Meltdown*. New York: Vintage.

Jones, Erik, R. Daniel Kelemen, and Sophie Meunier. 2016. Failing Forward? The Euro Crisis and the Incomplete Nature of European Integration. *Comparative Political Studies* 49 (7): 1010–34.

Jordà, Òscar, Moritz Schularick, and Alan M. Taylor. 2011. Financial Crises, Credit Booms, and External Imbalances: 140 Years of Lessons. *IMF Economic Review* 59 (2): 340–78.

Jordana, Jacint, and Guillermo Rosas. 2014. When Do Autonomous Banking Regulators Promote Stability? *European Journal of Political Research* 53 (4): 672–91.

Judt, Tony. 2006. *Postwar: A History of Europe since 1945*. New York: Penguin.

Kaltenborn, Rolf. 1964. The American Stock Exchange. In *The Principal Stock Exchanges of the World*, edited by David Eugene Spray, 21–32. Washington, DC: International Economic Publishers.

Kaminsky, Graciela L., and Carmen M. Reinhart. 1999. The Twin Crises: The Causes of Banking and Balance-of-Payments Problems. *American Economic Review* 89: 473–500.

Kapstein, Ethan B. 1994. *Governing the Global Economy: International Finance and the State*. Cambridge, MA: Harvard University Press.

Katsanidou, Alexia, and Simon Otjes. 2016. How the European Debt Crisis Reshaped National Political Space: The Case of Greece. *European Union Politics* 17 (2): 262–84.

Keller, Elisabeth. 1988. Introductory Comment: A Historical Introduction to the Securities Act of 1933 and the Securities Exchange Act of 1934. *Ohio State Law Journal* 49 (2): 329–52.

Kindleberger, Charles P. 1990. *Historical Economics: Art or Science?* New York: Harvester Wheatsheaf.

1973. *The World in Depression, 1929–1939*. Berkeley: University of California Press.

King, Michael R., and Dan Segal. 2008. Market Segmentation and Equity Valuation: Comparing Canada and the United States. *Journal of International Financial Markets, Institutions and Money* 18 (3): 245–58.

King, Michael R., and Timothy J. Sinclair. 2003. Private Actors and Public Policy: A Requiem for the New Basel Capital Accord. *International Political Science Review* 24 (3): 345–62.

Kitchen, Martin. 1978. *Political Economy of Germany, 1815–1914*. London: Croom Helm.

Kitching, Andrew. 2009. *Securities Regulation: Calls for a Single Regulator*. Report. Parliamentary Information and Research Service. Library of Parliament of Ottawa.

Konoe, Sara. 2010. Policy Shifts and the Changing Role of Banks: A Comparison between Japan and Germany. *Journal of Japanese Law* 15 (29): 81–102.

Konzelmann, Suzanne J., Marc Fovargue-Davies, and Olivier Butzbach. 2013. The "Not So Global" Crisis. In *Banking Systems in the Crisis: The Faces of Liberal Capitalism*, edited by Suzanne J. Konzelmann and Marc Fovargue-Davies, 1–31. London: Routledge.

Kose, M. Ayhan, Eswar Prasad, Kenneth S. Rogoff, and Shang-Jin Wei. 2006. *Financial Globalization: A Reappraisal.* Working Paper 12484, National Bureau of Economic Research.

Krippner, Greta R. 2011. *Capitalizing on Crisis: The Political Origins of the Rise of Finance.* Cambridge, MA: Harvard University Press.

Kroszner, Randall S., and Raghuram G. Rajan. 1994. Is the Glass-Steagall Act Justified? A Study of the U.S. Experience with Universal Banking before 1933. *The American Economic Review* 84 (4): 810–32.

Kroszner, Randall S., and Philip E. Strahan. 1999. What Drives Deregulation? Economics and Politics of the Relaxation of Bank Branching Restrictions. *The Quarterly Journal of Economics* 114 (4): 1437–67.

Laeven, Luc, and Fabian Valencia. 2008. Systemic Banking Crises: A New Database. IMF Working Paper 08/224.

Lavelle, Kathryn C. 2013. *Money and Banks American Political System.* New York: Cambridge University Press.

Leblang, David, and Shanker Satyanath. 2006. Institutions, Expectations, and Currency Crises. *International Organization* 60 (1): 245–62.

2008. Politically Generated Uncertainty and Currency Crises: Theory, Tests, and Forecasts. *Journal of International Money and Finance* 27 (3): 480–97.

Leblond, Patrick. 2013. Cool Canada: A Case of Low Market-Based Banking in the Anglo-Saxon World. In *Market-Based Banking and the International Financial Crisis*, edited by Iain Hardie and David Howarth, 201–17. Oxford: Oxford University Press.

Lehmann, Sibylle H. 2010. The German Elections in the 1870s: Why Germany Turned from Liberalism to Protectionism. *The Journal of Economic History* 70 (1): 146–78.

Levi, Margaret. 1997. A Model, a Method, and a Map: Rational Choice in Comparative and Historical Analysis. In *Comparative Politics: Rationality, Culture, and Structure*, edited by Mark I. Lichbach and Alan S. Zuckerman, 19–41. New York: Cambridge University Press.

Lewis, Michael. 2010. *The Big Short: Inside the Doomsday Machine.* New York: W. W. Norton.

Lowenstein, Roger. 2015. *America's Bank: The Epic Struggle to Create the Federal Reserve.* New York: Penguin.

Lowy, Martin E. 1991. *High Rollers: Inside the Savings and Loan Debacle.* New York: Praeger Publishers.

Lucas, Robert E., Jr. 1990. Why Doesn't Capital Flow from Rich to Poor Countries? *American Economic Review* 80 (2): 92–6.

Luther, Martin. 2015. *On Commerce and Usury (1524).* London: Anthem Press.

Lütz, Susanne. 2002. *Der Staat und die Globalisierung von Finanzmärkten: Regulative Politik in Deutschland, Grossbritannien und den Vereinigten Staaten.* Frankfurt: Campus Verlag.

Macey, Jonathan R., and Geoffrey P. Miller. 1991. Origin of the Blue Sky Laws. *Texas Law Review* 70 (2): 347–98.

MacIntosh, Jeffrey G. 1997. A National Securities Commission for Canada? In *Reforming the Canadian Financial Sector*, edited by Thomas J. Courchene and Edwin H. Neave, 185–242. Kingston, ON: John Deutsch Institute for the Study of Economic Policy, Queens University.

Mahoney, James. 2001. Path-Dependent Explanations of Regime Change: Central America in Comparative Perspective. *Studies in Comparative International Development* 36 (1): 111–41.

Manger, Mark, and Thomas Sattler. 2014. Mercantilism in a Liberal World Order: The Origin of Persistent Current Account Imbalances. Presented at the International Political Economy Annual Conference, Washington, DC.

Marx, Erich. 1913. *Die Entwicklung Der Deutschen Provinzbörsen: Eine volkswirtschaftl. Studie.* Berlin: Verlag f. Fachlit.

Matthijs, Matthias, and Mark Blyth, eds. 2015. *The Future of the Euro.* New York: Oxford University Press.

Matthijs, Matthias, and Kathleen McNamara. 2015. The Euro Crisis' Theory Effect: Northern Saints, Southern Sinners, and the Demise of the Eurobond. *Journal of European Integration* 37 (2): 229–45.

Mayer, Colin, and Ian Alexander. 1990. Banks and Securities Markets: Corporate Financing in Germany and the United Kingdom. *Journal of the Japanese and International Economies* 4 (4): 450–75.

Mayer, Jacob Peter. 1998. *Max Weber and German Politics.* New York: Psychology Press.

McDowell, Daniel. 2016. *Brother, Can You Spare a Billion? The United States, the IMF, and the International Lender of Last Resort.* New York: Oxford University Press.

McKay, Huntly W. F. 1964. The Stock Exchanges of Canada. In *The Principal Stock Exchanges of the World: Their Operation, Structure, and Development*, edited by David Eugene Spray, 33–66. Washington, DC: International Economic Publishers.

McKeagan, David. 2009. Development of a Mature Securities Market in Montreal from 1817 to 1874. *Business History* 51 (1): 59–76.

McKinsey Global Institute. 2017. *The New Global Dynamics of Financial Globalization.* Washington, DC: McKinsey & Co.

McNamara, Kathleen. 2002. Rational Fictions: Central Bank Independence and the Social Logic of Delegation. *West European Politics* 25 (1): 47–76.

Mendoza, Enrique G., and Marco E. Terrones. 2012. An Anatomy of Credit Booms and Their Demise. NBER Working Paper 18379.

Mertens, Bernd. 2007. Das Aktiengesetz von 1937 – unpolitischer Schlussstein oder ideologischer Neuanfang? *Zeitschrift für Neuere Rechtsgeschichte* 29 (2): 88–117.

Michie, Ranald C. 1988. The Canadian Securities Market, 1850–1914. *Business History Review* 62 (1): 35–73.

2006. *The Global Securities Market: A History.* Oxford: Oxford University Press.

Mody, Ashoka. 2018. *Eurotragedy: A Drama in Nine Acts.* London: Oxford University Press.

Monnet, Cyril, and Erwan Quintin. 2005. Why Do Financial Systems Differ? History Matters. ECB Working Paper No. 442, Frankfurt, European Central Bank.

Morck, Randall. 2010. Shareholder Democracy in Canada. NBER Working Paper 16558, Cambridge, MA.

Morck, Randall, and Bernard Yeung. 2009. Never Waste a Good Crisis: An Historical Perspective on Comparative Corporate Governance. *Annual Review of Financial Economics* 1 (1): 145–79.

Mosley, Layna, and David Andrew Singer. 2008. Taking Stock Seriously: Equity-Market Performance, Government Policy, and Financial Globalization. *International Studies Quarterly* 52 (2): 405–25.

2009. The Global Financial Crisis: Lessons and Opportunities for International Political Economy. *International Interactions* 35 (4): 420–9.

Mügge, Daniel. 2010. *Widen the Market, Narrow the Competition: Banker Interests and the Making of a European Capital Market.* Colchester, UK: ECPR Press.

Nathan, Otto. 1944. *Nazi War Finance and Banking.* Cambridge, MA: National Bureau of Economic Research.

Neely, Christopher J. 1999. An Introduction to Capital Controls. *Federal Reserve Bank of St. Louis Review* 81: 13–30.

Neufeld, Edward Peter. 1972. *The Financial System of Canada: Its Growth and Development.* New York: St. Martin's Press.

Newman, Abraham L., and Elliot Posner. 2018. *Voluntary Disruptions: International Soft Law, Finance, and Power.* Transformations in Governance. New York: Oxford University Press.

Nipperdey, Thomas. 1992. *Deutsche Geschichte 1866–1918.* Vol. 2 Machtstaat der Demokratie. Munich: Beck.

Oatley, Thomas, and Robert Nabors. 1998. Redistributive Cooperation: Market Failure, Wealth Transfers, and the Basle Accord. *International Organization* 52 (1): 35–54.

Obstfeld, Maurice. 2012. Does the Current Account Still Matter? *American Economic Review* 102 (3): 1–23.

Obstfeld, Maurice, and Kenneth S. Rogoff. 2009. Global Imbalances and the Financial Crisis: Products of Common Causes. CEPR Discussion Paper No. DP7606, London.

Pagliari, Stefano, and Kevin L. Young. 2014. Leveraged Interests: Financial Industry Power and the Role of Private Sector Coalitions. *Review of International Political Economy* 21 (3): 575–610.

2016. The Interest Ecology of Financial Regulation: Interest Group Plurality in the Design of Financial Regulatory Policies. *Socio-Economic Review* 14 (2): 309–37.

Pepinsky, Thomas B. 2009. *Economic Crises and the Breakdown of Authoritarian Regimes: Indonesia and Malaysia in Comparative Perspective.* New York: Cambridge University Press.

2012. The Global Economic Crisis and the Politics of Non-transitions. *Government and Opposition* 47 (2): 135–61.

Pflanze, Otto. 2014. *Bismarck and the Development of Germany, Volume II: The Period of Consolidation, 1871–1880*. Princeton, NJ: Princeton University Press.

Pierson, Paul. 2004. *Politics in Time: History, Institutions, and Social Analysis*. Princeton, NJ: Princeton University Press.

Plochmann, G. 1908. The German Bourse Law. *The North American Review* 187 (630): 742–8.

Porter, Tony. 1993. *States, Markets, and Regimes in Global Finance*. New York: St. Martin's Press.

Portes, Richard. 2009. Global Imbalances. In *Macroeconomic Stability and Financial Regulation: Key Issues for the G20*, edited by Mathias Dewatripont, Xavier Freixas, and Richard Portes, 19: Vol. 19. London: CEPR.

Posner, Elliot. 2009. *The Origins of Europe's New Stock Markets*. Cambridge, MA: Harvard University Press.

Prasad, Eswar, Raghuram G. Rajan, and Arvind Subramanian. 2007. The Paradox of Capital. *Finance & Development* 44 (1): 1–7.

Puri, Poonam. 2013. Canada: "Bank Bashing" Is a Popular Sport. In *Banking Systems in the Crisis: The Faces of Liberal Capitalism*, edited by Suzanne J. Konzelmann and Marc Fovargue-Davies, 155–85. London: Routledge.

2009. Legal Origins, Investor Protection, and Canada. *Brigham Young University Law Review* 2009 (6): 1671–700.

2010. The Capital Markets Perspective on a National Securities Regulator. *The Supreme Court Law Review: Osgoode's Annual Constitutional Cases Conference* 51 (1): 603–23.

Puri, Manju, Jörg Rocholl and Sascha Steffen. 2011. Global Retail Lending in the Aftermath of the US Financial Crisis: Distinguishing between Supply and Demand Effects. *Journal of Financial Economics* 100 (3): 556–78.

Quaglia, Lucia. 2010. *Governing Financial Services in the European Union: Banking, Securities and Post-Trading*. London: Routledge.

2012. The "Old" and "New" Politics of Financial Services Regulation in the European Union. *New Political Economy* 17 (4): 515–35.

Rajan, Raghuram G. 2005. *Has Financial Development Made the World Riskier?* Working Paper 11728, Cambridge, MA, National Bureau of Economic Research. Available at www.nber.org/papers/w11728. Accessed November 2, 2017.

1992. Insiders and Outsiders: The Choice between Informed and Arm's-Length Debt. *The Journal of Finance* 47 (4): 1367–400.

Reid, Margaret. 1988. *All-Change in the City: The Revolution in Britain's Financial Sector*. London: Macmillan Press.

Reinhart, Carmen M., and Vincent R. Reinhart. 2008. *Capital Flow Bonanzas: An Encompassing View of the Past and Present*. Working Paper 14321, National Bureau of Economic Research.

Reinhart, Carmen M., and Kenneth S. Rogoff. 2011. From Financial Crash to Debt Crisis. *The American Economic Review* 101 (5): 1676–706.

2009a. The Aftermath of Financial Crises. *American Economic Review* 99 (2): 466–72.

2009b. *This Time Is Different: Eight Centuries of Financial Folly*. Princeton, NJ: Princeton University Press.

Rethel, Lena, and Timothy J. Sinclair. 2012. *The Problem with Banks*. London: Zed Books.

Rey, Hélène. 2015. Dilemma Not Trilemma: The Global Financial Cycle and Monetary Policy Independence. Working Paper 21162, National Bureau of Economic Research.

Riesser, Jacob. 1911. *The German Great Banks and Their Concentration in Connection with the Economic Development of Germany*. Report of the National Monetary Commission, U.S. Senate. Washington, DC: Government Printing Office.

Ritschl, Albrecht. 2005. Der späte Fluch des Dritten Reichs: Pfadabhängigkeiten in der Entstehung der bundesdeutschen Wirtschaftsordnung. *Perspektiven der Wirtschaftspolitik* 6 (2): 151–70.

Roe, Mark J. 1994. *Strong Managers, Weak Owners: The Political Roots of American Corporate Finance*. Princeton, NJ: Princeton University Press.

Romer, Christina D., and David H. Romer. 2017. New Evidence on the Aftermath of Financial Crises in Advanced Countries. *American Economic Review* 107 (10): 3072–118.

Rosas, Guillermo. 2006. Bagehot or Bailout? An Analysis of Government Responses to Banking Crises. *American Journal of Political Science* 50 (1): 175–91.

2009. *Curbing Bailouts: Bank Crises and Democratic Accountability in Comparative Perspective*. Ann Arbor: University of Michigan Press.

Rosenbluth, Frances McCall. 1989. *Financial Politics in Contemporary Japan*. Ithaca, NY: Cornell University Press.

Schneider, Christina J. 2019. *The Responsive Union: National Elections and European Governance*. New York: Cambridge University Press.

Schonhardt-Bailey, Cheryl. 1998. Parties and Interests in the "Marriage of Iron and Rye". *British Journal of Political Science* 28 (2): 291–332.

Schularick, Moritz, and Alan M. Taylor. 2012. Credit Booms Gone Bust: Monetary Policy, Leverage Cycles, and Financial Crises, 1870–2008. *The American Economic Review* 102 (2): 1029–61.

Seligman, Joel. 1982. *The Transformation of Wall Street: A History of the Securities and Exchange Commission and Modern Corporate Finance*. Boston: Houghton Mifflin.

Simmons, Beth A. 1994. *Who Adjusts?: Domestic Sources of Foreign Economic Policy During the Interwar Years*. Princeton, NJ: Princeton University Press.

Singer, David Andrew. 2004. Capital Rules: The Domestic Politics of International Regulatory Harmonization. *International Organization* 58 (3): 531–65.

2007. *Regulating Capital: Setting Standards for the International Financial System*. Ithaca, NY: Cornell University Press.

Smith, Adam. 2003. *The Wealth of Nations*. New York: Bantam Dell.

Smith, Andrew. 2012. Continental Divide: The Canadian Banking and Currency Laws of 1871 in the Mirror of the United States. *Enterprise & Society* 13 (3): 455–503.

Smith, Philip. 1986. *Harvest from the Rock: A History of Mining in Ontario*. 1st ed. Toronto: Macmillan of Canada.

Sobel, Andrew C. 1994. *Domestic Choices, International Markets: Dismantling National Barriers and Liberalizing Securities Markets*. Ann Arbor: University of Michigan Press.

Sobel, Robert. 1965. *The Big Board: A History of the New York Stock Market*. New York: Free Press.

Sorkin, Andrew Ross. 2010. *Too Big to Fail: The Inside Story of How Wall Street and Washington Fought to Save the Financial System – and Themselves*. New York: Penguin.

Spoerer, Mark. 1996. *Von Scheingewinnen zum Rüstungsboom: Die Eigenkapitalrendite der deutschen Industrieaktiengesellschaften 1925–1941*. Stuttgart: Franz Steiner Verlag.

Sprague, Irvine H. 1986. *Bailout: An Insider's Account of Bank Failures and Rescues*. New York: Basic Books.

Steinberg, Jonathan. 2011. *Bismarck: A Life*. Oxford: Oxford University Press.

Stern, Gary H., and Ron J. Feldman. 2004. *Too Big to Fail: The Hazards of Bank Bailouts*. Washington, DC: Brookings Institution Press.

Stoetzler, Marcel. 2009. *The State, the Nation, and the Jews: Liberalism and the Antisemitism Dispute in Bismarck's Germany*. Lincoln: University of Nebraska Press.

Story, Jonathan, and Ingo Walter. 1997. *Political Economy of Financial Integration in Europe: The Battle of the Systems*. Cambridge, MA: MIT Press.

Streeck, Wolfgang. 1997. German Capitalism: Does It Exist? Can It Survive? *New Political Economy* 2 (2): 237–56.

Swank, Duane. 2002. *Global Capital, Political Institutions, and Policy Change in Developed Welfare States*. Cambridge, UK: Cambridge University Press.

Sylla, Richard, and George David Smith. 1995. Information and Capital Market Regulation in Anglo-American Finance. In *Anglo-American Financial Systems: Institutions and Markets in the Twentieth Century*, edited by Michael D. Bordo and Richard Sylla, 179–206. New York: Irwin Professional Publishing.

Temin, Peter. 2008. The German Crisis of 1931: Evidence and Tradition. *Cliometrica* 2 (1): 5–17.

Tett, Gillian. 2009. *Fool's Gold: The Inside Story of J. P. Morgan and How Wall St. Greed Corrupted Its Bold Dream and Created a Financial Catastrophe*. New York: Free Press.

Thelen, Kathleen. 2004. *How Institutions Evolve: The Political Economy of Skills in Germany, Britain, the United States, and Japan*. Cambridge Studies in Comparative Politics. New York: Cambridge University Press.

Tilly, Richard. 2009. Banking Crises in Three Countries, 1800–1933: An Historical and Comparative Perspective. Lecture Delivered at the Award of the Helmut Schmidt Prize in German-American Economic History, German Historical Institute, Washington, DC.

1996. Banks and Industry: Lessons from History. In *European Economic Integration as a Challenge to Industry and Government*, edited by Richard Tilly and Paul Welfens, 397–435. New York: Springer.

1986. German Banking, 1850–1914: Development Assistance for the Strong. *Journal of European Economic History* 15 (1): 113–52.

1997a. German Industrialisation and Gerschenkronian Backwardness. In *The Economic Development of Germany since 1870*, edited by Wolfram Fischer, 273–98. London: Edward Elgar.

1997b. On the Development of German Big Banks as Universal Banks in the 19th and 20th Centuries: Engines of Growth or Power Block? In *The Economic Development of Germany since 1870*, edited by Wolfram Fischer, 227–48. London: Edward Elgar.

Tomz, Michael, Jason Wittenberg, and Gary King. 2003. Clarify: Software for Interpreting and Presenting Statistical Results. *Journal of Statistical Software* 8 (1): 1–30.

Tooze, Adam. 2018. *Crashed: How a Decade of Financial Crises Changed the World*. New York: Viking.

Trebbi, Francesco, Atif Mian, and Amir Sufi. 2012. Political Constraints in the Aftermath of Financial Crises. *VoxEU*. Available at https://voxeu.org/article/political-constraints-aftermath-financial-crises. Accessed August 20, 2018.

Tsingou, Eleni. 2015. Club Governance and the Making of Global Financial Rules. *Review of International Political Economy* 22 (2): 225–56.

Tucker, Albert. 1978. *Steam into Wilderness*. Toronto: Fitzhenry & Whiteside.

Tucker, Paul. 2018. *Unelected Power: The Quest for Legitimacy in Central Banking and the Regulatory State*. Princeton, NJ: Princeton University Press.

United States Senate. 1914. *Regulation of the Stock Exchange: Hearings before the Committee on Banking and Currency*. Washington, DC: Government Printing Office.

Vogel, Steven K. 1998. *Freer Markets, More Rules: Regulatory Reform in Advanced Industrial Countries*. Ithaca, NY: Cornell University Press.

de Vries, Catherine E. 2018. *Euroscepticism and the Future of European Integration*. Oxford: Oxford University Press.

Waite, Peter B. 1971. *Canada 1874–1896: Arduous Destiny*. Toronto: McClelland and Stewart.

Wallich, Paul. 1905. *Die Konzentration im deutschen Bankwesen*. Stuttgart: Union deutsche Verlagsgesellschaft.

Walter, Stefanie. 2016. Crisis Politics in Europe: Why Austerity Is Easier to Implement in Some Countries Than in Others. *Comparative Political Studies* 49 (7): 841–73.

2013. *Financial Crises and the Politics of Macroeconomic Adjustments*. New York: Cambridge University Press.

Weber, Manfred. 2002. The German Banking Market: Structural Change. *Die Bank* 7: 6–11.

Weitz, Eric D. 2013. *Weimar Germany: Promise and Tragedy*. Princeton, NJ: Princeton University Press.

Whelan, Karl. 2010. *Global Imbalances and the Financial Crisis*. Briefing Papers for the European Parliament's Committee on Economic and Monetary Affairs. Brussels: European Parliament.

White, Eugene. 1983. *The Regulation and Reform of the American Banking System, 1900–1929*. Princeton, NJ: Princeton University Press.

Whiteside, John F. 1985. The Toronto Stock Exchange and the Development of the Share Market to 1885. *Journal of Canadian Studies* 20 (3): 64–81.

Wilf, Meredith. 2016. Credibility and Distributional Effects of International Banking Regulations: Evidence from US Bank Stock Returns. *International Organization* 70 (4): 763–96.

Winecoff, W. Kindred. 2014. Bank Regulation, Macroeconomic Management, and Monetary Incentives in OECD Economies. *International Studies Quarterly* 58 (3): 448–61.

Winkler, Heinrich August. 2006. *Germany: The Long Road West, 1789–1933*. Oxford: Oxford University Press.

Wistrich, Robert S. 1982. *Socialism and the Jews: The Dilemmas of Assimilation in Germany and Austria-Hungary*. Rutherford, NJ: Fairleigh Dickinson University Press.

Wolf, Martin. 2008. *Fixing Global Finance*. Baltimore: Johns Hopkins University Press.

Woll, Cornelia. 2014. *The Power of Inaction: Bank Bailouts in Comparison*. Cornell *Studies in Political Economy*. Ithaca, NY: Cornell University Press.

Wood, John H. 2005. *A History of Central Banking in Great Britain and the United States*. New York: Cambridge University Press.

Young, Kevin L., and Sung HoPark. 2013. Regulatory Opportunism: Cross-National Patterns in National Banking Regulatory Responses following the Global Financial Crisis. *Public Administration* 91 (3): 561–81.

Zucker, Stanley. 1975. *Ludwig Bamberger: German Liberal Politician and Social Critic, 1823–1899*. Pittsburgh, PA: University of Pittsburgh Press.

Zweig, Phillip L. 1985. *Belly Up: The Collapse of Penn Square Bank*. New York: Crown Books.

Index

POLITICAL ECONOMY OF INSTITUTIONS AND DECISIONS

Other Books in the Series *(Continued from page ii)*

Gary W. Cox, *Marketing Sovereign Promises: Monopoly Brokerage and the Growth of the English State*
Gary W. Cox and Jonathan N. Katz, *Elbridge Gerry's Salamander: The Electoral Consequences of the Reapportionment Revolution*
Tine De Moore, *The Dilemma of the Commoners: Understanding the Use of Common-Pool Resources in Long-Term Perspective*
Adam Dean, *From Conflict to Coalition: Profit-Sharing Institutions and the Political Economy of Trade*
Mark Dincecco, *Political Transformations and Public Finances: Europe, 1650–1913*
Mark Dincecco and Massimiliano Gaetano Onorato, *From Warfare to Wealth: The Military Origins of Urban Prosperity in Europe*
Raymond M. Duch and Randolph T. Stevenson, *The Economic Vote: How Political and Economic Institutions Condition Election Results*
Jean Ensminger, *Making a Market: The Institutional Transformation of an African Society*
David Epstein and Sharyn O'Halloran, *Delegating Powers: A Transaction Cost Politics Approach to Policy Making under Separate Powers*
Kathryn Firmin-Sellers, *The Transformation of Property Rights in the Gold Coast: An Empirical Study Applying Rational Choice Theory*
Clark C. Gibson, *Politicians and Poachers: The Political Economy of Wildlife Policy in Africa*
Daniel W. Gingerich, *Political Institutions and Party-Directed Corruption in South America*
Avner Greif, *Institutions and the Path to the Modern Economy: Lessons from Medieval Trade*
Jeffrey D. Grynaviski, *Partisan Bonds: Political Reputations and Legislative Accountability*
Stephen Haber, Armando Razo, and Noel Maurer, *The Politics of Property Rights: Political Instability, Credible Commitments, and Economic Growth in Mexico, 1876–1929*
Ron Harris, *Industrializing English Law: Entrepreneurship and Business Organization, 1720–1844*

Anna L. Harvey, *Votes without Leverage: Women in American Electoral Politics, 1920–1970*
Shigeo Hirano and James M. Snyder Jr., *Primary Elections in the United States*
Murray Horn, *The Political Economy of Public Administration: Institutional Choice in the Public Sector*
John D. Huber, *Rationalizing Parliament: Legislative Institutions and Party Politics in France*
Sean Ingham, *Rule of Multiple Majorities: A New Theory of Popular Control*
John E. Jackson, Jacek Klich, and Krystyna Poznanska, *The Political Economy of Poland's Transition: New Firms and Reform Governments*
Jack Knight, *Institutions and Social Conflict*
Michael Laver and Kenneth Shepsle, eds., *Cabinet Ministers and Parliamentary Government*
Michael Laver and Kenneth Shepsle, eds., *Making and Breaking Governments: Cabinets and Legislatures in Parliamentary Democracies*
Margaret Levi, *Consent, Dissent, and Patriotism*
Brian Levy and Pablo T. Spiller, eds., *Regulations, Institutions, and Commitment: Comparative Studies of Telecommunications*
Leif Lewin, *Ideology and Strategy: A Century of Swedish Politics (English edition)*
Gary Libecap, *Contracting for Property Rights*
John Londregan, *Legislative Institutions and Ideology in Chile*
Arthur Lupia and Mathew D. McCubbins, *The Democratic Dilemma: Can Citizens Learn What They Need to Know?*
C. Mantzavinos, *Individuals, Institutions, and Markets*
Mathew D. McCubbins and Terry Sullivan, eds., *Congress: Structure and Policy*
Gary J. Miller, *Above Politics: Bureaucratic Discretion and Credible Commitment*
Gary J. Miller, *Managerial Dilemmas: The Political Economy of Hierarchy*
Ilia Murtazashvili, *The Political Economy of the American Frontier*
Douglass C. North, *Institutions, Institutional Change, and Economic Performance*
Elinor Ostrom, *Governing the Commons: The Evolution of Institutions for Collective Action*
Sonal S. Pandya, *Trading Spaces: Foreign Direct Investment Regulation, 1970–2000*
John W. Patty and Elizabeth Maggie Penn, *Social Choice and Legitimacy*
Daniel N. Posner, *Institutions and Ethnic Politics in Africa*
J. Mark Ramseyer, *Odd Markets in Japanese History: Law and Economic Growth*

J. Mark Ramseyer and Frances Rosenbluth, *The Politics of Oligarchy: Institutional Choice in Imperial Japan*

Stephanie J. Rickard, *Spending to Win: Political Institutions, Economic Geography, and Government Subsidies*

Meredith Rolfe, *Voter Turnout: A Social Theory of Political Participation*

Jean-Laurent Rosenthal, *The Fruits of Revolution: Property Rights, Litigation, and French Agriculture, 1700–1860*

Michael L. Ross, *Timber Booms and Institutional Breakdown in Southeast Asia*

Shanker Satyanath, *Globalization, Politics, and Financial Turmoil: Asia's Banking Crisis*

Norman Schofield, *Architects of Political Change: Constitutional Quandaries and Social Choice Theory*

Norman Schofield and Itai Sened, *Multiparty Democracy: Elections and Legislative Politics*

Alberto Simpser, *Why Governments and Parties Manipulate Elections: Theory, Practice, and Implications*

Alastair Smith, *Election Timing*

Pablo T. Spiller and Mariano Tommasi, *The Institutional Foundations of Public Policy in Argentina: A Transactions Cost Approach*

David Stasavage, *Public Debt and the Birth of the Democratic State: France and Great Britain, 1688–1789*

Charles Stewart III, *Budget Reform Politics: The Design of the Appropriations Process in the House of Representatives, 1865–1921*

George Tsebelis and Jeannette Money, *Bicameralism*

Georg Vanberg, *The Politics of Constitutional Review in Germany*

Nicolas van de Walle, *African Economies and the Politics of Permanent Crisis, 1979–1999*

Stefanie Walter, *Financial Crises and the Politics of Macroeconomic Adjustments*

John Waterbury, *Exposed to Innumerable Delusions: Public Enterprise and State Power in Egypt, India, Mexico, and Turkey*

David L. Weimer, ed., *The Political Economy of Property Rights Institutional Change and Credibility in the Reform of Centrally Planned Economies*